I Dared to Call Him Father

I Dared to Call Him Father

Bilquis Sheikh
with Richard Schneider

Kingsway Publications
Eastbourne

First published by in the USA by Chosen Books 1978

First British edition 1979
This 2-in-1 edition 2008

In the interests of confidentiality the names of some individuals have been changed.

Cover design: PinnacleCreative.co.uk
Front cover photo C Paha_l | Dreamstime.com

ISBN 978 1 84291 401 4

KINGSWAY COMMUNICATIONS LTD
26–28 Lottbridge Drove, Eastbourne BN23 6NT, UK
www.kingsway.co.uk

Printed in Great Britain

To my grandson Mahmud, my little prayer partner,
who has been a source of joy and comfort
to me through many lonely hours

1

A Frightening Presence

The strange prickly feeling grew inside me as I walked slowly along the graveled paths of my garden. It was deep twilight. The scent of late narcissus hung heavy in the air. What was it, I wondered, that made me so uneasy?

I stopped my walk and looked around. Inside my home some distance across the broad lawn the servants were beginning to flick on lights in the dining area. Outside all seemed peaceful and quiet. I reached out to snip off some of the pungent white blossoms for my bedroom. As I leaned over to grasp the tall green stems, something brushed past my head.

I straightened in alarm. What was it? A mist-like cloud—a cold, damp unholy presence—had floated by. The garden suddenly seemed darker. A chilling breeze sprang up through the weeping willows and I shivered.

Get hold of yourself, Bilquis! I scolded. My imagination was playing tricks on me. Nevertheless, I gathered my flowers and headed quickly toward the house where windows glowed in warm reassurance. Its sturdy white stone walls and oaken doors offered protection. As I hurried along the crunchy gravel path I found myself glancing over my shoulder. I had always laughed at talk of the supernatural. Of course there wasn't anything out there. Was there?

As if in answer, I felt a firm, very real and uncanny tap on my right hand.

I screamed. I rushed into the house and slammed the door behind me. My servants ran to me, afraid to make any comment at all, for I must have looked like a ghost myself. It wasn't until bedtime that I finally found the courage to speak to my two handmaids about the cold presence. "Do you believe in spiritual things?" I asked, on concluding my story. Both Nur-jan and Raisham, one a Muslim, the other a Christian, avoided answering my question but Nur-jan, her hands fluttering nervously, asked me if she could call the village *mullah*, a priest from the mosque, who would bring some holy water to cleanse the garden. But my common sense had returned and I rebelled at submitting to the superstition of the ignorant. Besides, I didn't want any word of this to spread in the village. I tried to smile at her concern, and told her, a little too abruptly I'm afraid, that I didn't want any holy man on my grounds pretending to remove evil spirits. Nevertheless, after the maids left the room, I found myself picking up my copy of the Koran. But after struggling through a few pages of the Muslim Holy Book, I wearied of it, slipped it back within its blue silken case, and fell asleep.

I slowly awakened the next morning like a swimmer struggling to the surface, a thin high chant piercing my consciousness:

"Laa ilaaha illa Ilaah,
Muhammed resolu'lla!"

The sing-song words drifted through the filigree of my bedroom window:

"There is no God but Allah:
And Muhammed is his Prophet."

It was a comforting sound, this Muslim call to prayer because it seemed so utterly normal after the previous night. It was a call I had heard almost without exception every morning of my 46 years. I envisioned the source of the rolling chant.

Some moments before in the little nearby Pakistani village of Wah, our old muezzin had hurried through the door at the base of an ancient minaret. Inside its cool interior he had trudged up curving stone steps worn smooth by the sandals of generations of Muslim holy men. At the top of the prayer tower, I could imagine him hesitating at the carved teak door leading to the parapet to catch his breath. Then, stepping outside to the railing, he threw back his bearded head and in syllables fourteen hundred years old called the faithful to prayer.

"Come to prayer, come to salvation,
Prayer is better than sleep."

The haunting cry floated through the morning mist across cobblestone lanes in Wah still cold from the October night, drifted across my garden to curl along the house's old stone walls now ruddy in the light of the rising sun.

As the last wisps of the ancient chant hung above me, I remembered the eerie experience in the garden the night before, and quickly turned to morning routines that would be comforting just because they were so ordinary. I sat up and reached for the golden bell on my marble bedside table. At its musical tinkle, my maid Nur-jan hurried in out of breath as usual. Both of my handmaids slept in a room adjoining mine and I knew that they had already been up for an hour, waiting for my call. Morning tea in my bed was a *must*. Nur-jan began laying out my silver brushes and combs. She was a willing teen-aged girl, plump and giggly, but a bit clumsy. When she dropped a brush, I scolded her sharply.

Raisham, my other handmaid, older and quieter, a tall graceful woman, slid into the room bearing a large covered tea tray. She placed it on my bed table, drew back the white linen to expose the sterling service and poured me a cup of steaming tea.

Sipping the scalding ambrosia, I sighed in satisfaction; tea was better than prayer. My mother would have been shocked at my thought. How many times had I watched her place her prayer rug on the tiled bedroom floor, then, facing the holy city of Mecca, kneel and press her forehead to the rug in prayer. Thinking of my mother I looked over to the dressing case on my table. Fashioned centuries ago of sandalwood and covered with engraved sterling silver, it had belonged to Mother and her mother before her. Now it was my heirloom to treasure. After finishing two cups of tea I leaned forward, a sign for Raisham to begin brushing my graying waist-length hair while Nur-jan carefully worked on my nails.

As the two worked, they gossiped in easy familiarity about news from the village, Nur-jan chattering and Raisham making quiet thoughtful comments. They talked about a boy who was leaving home for the city and a girl soon to be married. And then they discussed the murder that happened in a nearby town where Raisham's aunt lived. I could sense Raisham shudder as the news came up. For the victim had been a Christian. She was a young girl who had been staying in a Christian missionary's home. Someone had stumbled across her body in one of the narrow lanes criss-crossing her village. There was supposed to have been an investigation by the constabulary.

"Any news about the girl?" I casually asked.

"No, Begum Sahib," said Raisham quietly, as she carefully began to work a braid in my hair. I could understand why Raisham, a Christian herself, didn't want to talk about the murder. She knew as well as I did who had killed that girl. After all, the girl had forsaken her Muslim faith to be baptized a Christian. So the brother, infuriated by the shame this sin had brought upon his family, had obeyed the ancient law of the faithful that those who fall away from their faith must be slain.

Even though Muslim edicts may be stern and harsh, their interpretations are sometimes tempered with mercy and compassion. But there are always the zealots who carry out the letter of the Koran law to the extreme.

Everyone knew who had killed the girl. But nothing would be done. It had always been this way. A year ago, the Christian servant of one of the missionaries ended up in a ditch, his throat cut, and nothing had been done there either. I put the sad little story out of my mind and made ready to get up. My maids hurried to the closet and returned with several silken saris for my selection. I pointed to a jewel-embroidered one and after they helped drape it about me, they quietly bowed themselves out of my chamber.

Sunlight now flooded my bedroom, giving its white walls and ivory-colored furnishings a saffron glow. The sunlight glinted from a gold-framed photograph on my dressing table and I stepped over and picked it up, angry, because I had put the picture face down the day before; one of the servants must have set it up again! The engraved frame enclosed a photograph of a sophisticated-looking couple smiling at me from a corner table in a luxurious London restaurant.

In spite of myself I looked at the picture again, as one does when he keeps pressing a hurting tooth. The dashing man with dark mustache and burning eyes had been my husband, General Khalid Sheikh. Why did I keep this picture! Hate surged within me as I looked at the man I once felt I could not live without. When the photo had been taken six years before, Khalid had been Pakistan's Minister of Interior.

The glamorous-looking woman next to him had been me. As daughter of a conservative Muslim family which for seven hundred years had been landed gentry in this cool-climated Northwest Frontier Province of what had once been northern India, I had been hostess to diplomats and industrialists from all over the world. I had been accustomed to sojourns in Paris and London where I spent my time shopping on the Rue de la Paix or in Harrods. The lithsome woman who smiled from the photo no longer existed, I thought as I looked in the mirror. The soft pale skin had bronzed, the lustrous black hair was now streaked with gray, and disillusionment had etched deep lines in her face.

The world of the photograph had crumbled into fragments five years before when Khalid left me. Suffering the shame of rejection, I had fled the sophisticated life of London, Paris and Rawalpindi to seek refuge here in the quiet peace of my family's ancestral estate nestled at the foot of the Himalayan

Mountains. The estate comprised the little hill country village of Wah where I had spent so many happy days as a child. Wah was surrounded by gardens and orchards which many generations of my family had planted. And the big stone palatial home with its towers, terraces and huge echoing chambers seemed as old as the snow-crowned Safed Koh mountains which loomed in the west. However, my aunt also lived in this house and desiring further seclusion, I moved to a smaller house the family had built on the outskirts of Wah. Inset like a jewel in twelve acres of gardens, this house, with bedrooms upstairs and living, dining and drawing rooms downstairs, promised the solace I needed.

It gave me more. For when I arrived, much of the extensive gardens had become overgrown. This was a blessing, for I buried much of my sorrow in the lush soil as I plunged into the restoration of the grounds. I made some of the twelve acres into formal gardens with walls and flower beds and left some of the area natural. Slowly the gardens, with their countless musical springs, became my world until by then, in the year 1966, I had the reputation of a recluse who secluded herself outside of town nestled amongst her flowers.

I looked away from the gold-framed photo in my hand, placed it face down again on the table and turned to my bedroom window looking toward the village. Wah ... the very name of the village was an exclamation of joy. Centuries before, when this was but a hamlet, the legendary Moghul emperor Akbar traveled through here and his caravan stopped to rest by a spring in what was now my surroundings. He gratefully sank down under a willow, and exclaimed in joy, "Wah!" thus naming the area forever.

But the memory of this scene gave me no release from the unsettled feeling which had been hovering over me ever since the strange experience of the evening before.

However, I tried to dispel it as I stood at my window. It was morning again, I told myself, the next day, a safe time with familiar routines and warm sunlight. The previous night's episode seemed as real, but as remote, as a bad dream. I drew the white drapes aside and breathed in deeply of the fresh morning air, listening to the hissing of the sweeper's broom on the patio. A fragrance of wood smoke from early morning cooking fires drifted up to me and the rhythmic thumping of water-mill wheels sounded in the distance. I sighed in satisfaction. This was Wah, this was my home, this was, after all, safety. This was where Nawab Muhammad Hayat Kahn, a prince and feudal landowner, had lived seven hundred years ago. We were his direct descendants and my family was known throughout India as the Hayats of Wah. Centuries ago the caravans of emperors would turn off the Grand Trunk Road to visit my ancestors. Even in my earlier days notables from all over Europe and Asia would take the same road, once an ancient caravan route across India, to see my family. But now, usually only members of my family would follow it to my gate. Of course this meant that I didn't see many people who were not part of my immediate household. I did not much care. My fourteen house servants were enough company. They and their ancestors had served my family for generations. Most important, I had Mahmud.

Mahmud was my four-year-old grandson. His mother, Tooni, was the youngest of my three children. A slim attractive woman, Tooni was a medical doctor at Holy Family Hospital in nearby Rawalpindi. Her former husband was a prominent landlord. However, they had an unhappy marriage and their relationship deteriorated a little each year. During their long bitter disagreements, Tooni would send Mahmud to visit me until she and her husband reached another uneasy truce. One day, Tooni and her husband came to see me. Could I keep one-year-old Mahmud for a while until they settled their differences?

"No," I said. "I do not want him to become a tennis ball. But I will be willing to adopt him and raise him as my own son." Sadly, Tooni and her husband never could settle their differences and they finally divorced. However, they did approve my adopting Mahmud, and it was working out quite well. Tooni came to see Mahmud often and the three of us were very close, particularly since my two other children lived far away.

Later that morning Mahmud pedaled his tricycle across the brick terrace shaded by almond trees. He had been with me for over three years and this lively cherubic child with deep brown eyes and button nose was the only joy of my life. His pealing laughter seemed to lift the spirit of this secluded old house. Even so I worried about how he would be affected by living with such a downcast person as me. I tried to compensate by making sure his every need was anticipated, and this included his own staff of three servants, in addition to my own eleven, to dress him, bring out his toys and pick them up when he was through playing with them.

But I was troubled about Mahmud. For several days he had refused to eat. This was particularly strange, for the boy was always visiting the bake kitchen to cajole my cooks into giving him sugar biscuits and snacks. Earlier that morning I had gone downstairs, walked through the terrazzo entranceway out to the terrace. After exchanging a warm hug with Mahmud, I asked his servant if the child had eaten.

"No, Begum Sahib, he refuses," the maid said in a near whisper. When I pressed Mahmud to take some food, he just answered that he was not hungry.

I was really disturbed when Nur-jan came to me alone and suggested timorously that Mahmud was being attacked by evil spirits. Startled, I looked at her sharply, remembering the disquieting experience of the night before. What did all this mean? Once again I asked Mahmud to eat, but to no avail. He wouldn't even touch his favorite Swiss chocolates which I had imported especially for him. His limpid eyes looked up to me when I offered him the package. "I'd love to eat them, Mum," he said, "but when I try to swallow it hurts." A cold chill ran through me as I looked at my little grandson, once so lively and now so listless.

I immediately summoned Manzur, my chauffeur, also a Christian, and ordered him to get the car out. Within an hour we were in Rawalpindi to visit Mahmud's doctor. The pediatrician examined Mahmud carefully and he reported that he could find nothing wrong.

Fear chilled me as we rode back to the estate. Looking at my little grandson sitting quietly beside me, I wondered. Could Nur-jan *possibly* be right? Was this something that went beyond the physical? Was it … something in the spirit world attacking him? I reached over and put my arm around the child, smiling at myself for entertaining such ideas. Once, I remembered, my father had told me about a legendary Muslim holy man who could perform miracles. I laughed aloud at the idea. My father was displeased, but that was the way I felt about any such claims. Still, today, holding Mahmud close as the car turned off the Grand Trunk Road onto our lane, I found myself toying with an unwelcome thought: Could Mahmud's problem be related to the mist in the garden?

When I shared my fears with Nur-jan, her henna-tipped fingers flew to her throat and she begged me to call the village *mullah* and ask him to pray for Mahmud and sprinkle holy water over the garden.

I debated her request. Even though I believed in basic Muslim teachings, for several years I had drifted away from the many rituals, the praying five times a day, the fasting, the complicated ceremonial washings. But my concern for Mahmud overcame my doubts and I told Nur-jan that she could call the holy man from the village mosque.

The next morning Mahmud and I sat at my window impatiently awaiting the *mullah*. When I finally saw him making his way up the steps of the veranda, his thin ragged coat flapping about him in the chilling fall wind, I was both sorry I had asked him and angry that he wasn't walking faster.

Nur-jan brought the bony old man to my quarters, then withdrew. Mahmud watched the man curiously as he opened his Koran. The *mullah*, whose skin matched the ancient leather of his holy book, looked at me through crinkled eyes, laid a gnarled brown hand on Mahmud's head and in a quavering voice began reciting the Kul. This is the prayer every Muslim recites when he is about to begin any important act, whether to pray for the sick or to enter a business agreement.

The *mullah* then started to read from the Koran in Arabic—the Koran is always read in Arabic since it would be wrong to translate the very words that God's angel had given the prophet Muhammad. I became impatient. I must have started to tap my foot.

"Begum Sahib?" the *mullah* said, holding the Koran out to me. "You, too, should read these verses." He referred to the Sura Falak and Sura Naz, verses to be repeated when one is troubled. "Why don't you repeat these verses as well?"

"No," I said, "I will not. God has forgotten about me and I have forgotten about God!" But at the hurt look on the old man's face I softened. After all, he had come here at my request and with Mahmud's welfare in mind. "All right," I said, taking the worn volume. I let it fall open, then read the first verse my eyes fell on:

> *Muhammad is the Messenger of God, and those who are with him are hard against the unbelievers. ...*

I thought of the Christian girl who had been murdered, and about the mist that appeared in my garden shortly after she was killed, and above all about Mahmud's mysterious ailment. Could they be related? Surely any angry spiritual power would never link me and Mahmud with a *Christian*. I shuddered.

But the holy man seemed satisfied. Despite my reservations he returned for three days in a row to recite verses over Mahmud.

And, just to complete the series of mysterious, unsettling events, Mahmud did get better.

How was I supposed to think about all these happenings?

I was soon to find out. For without knowing it, events had been set in motion which would shatter the world I'd known all my life.

2

The Strange Book

After these experiences I found myself drawn to the Koran. Perhaps it would help explain the events and at the same time fill the emptiness within me. Certainly its curved Arabic script held answers which had often sustained my family.

I had read the Koran before of course. I remembered exactly how old I was when I first started learning Arabic so that I could read our holy book: I was four years, four months and four days old. This was the day every Muslim child began to unravel the Arabic script. The moment was marked by a great family banquet, to which all my relatives came. It was then, in a special ceremony, that the wife of our village *mullah* began teaching me the alphabet.

I especially remember my Uncle Fateh (we children called him Grand Uncle Fateh; he wasn't really my uncle—all older kinsmen are called Uncle or Aunt in Pakistan). Grand Uncle Fateh was the relative closest to our family, and I remember clearly how he watched me at the ceremony, his sensitive aquiline face glowing with pleasure as I heard again the story of how the angel Gabriel began giving Muhammad the words of the Koran on that fateful "Night of Power" in the year 610 A.D. It took me seven years to read the holy book through for the first time but when I finally finished, there was cause for yet another family celebration.

Always before, I had read the Koran as an obligation. This time, I felt I should really search its pages. I took my copy, which had belonged to my mother, relaxed on the white eiderdown coverlet of my bed, and began to read. I started with the initial verse, the first message given to the young prophet Muhammad as he sat by himself in a cave on Mount Hira:

> *Recite: In the name of thy Lord who created,*
> *Created Man of a blood clot.*
> *Recite: And thy Lord is the Most Generous,*
> *Who taught by the Pen,*
> *Taught man that he knew not.*

At first I was lost in the beauty of the words. But later on in the book there were words that did not comfort me at all:

> *When ye have divorced women, and they have reached their term, then retain them in kindness or release them in kindness.*

My husband's eyes had been like black steel when he told me that he didn't love me any more. I shriveled inside as he spoke. What had happened to all our years together! Could they be dismissed just like that? Had I, as the Koran said, "reached my term"?

The next morning I picked up the Koran again, hoping to find in the curling script the assurance I needed so desperately. But the assurance never came. I found only directives for how to live and warnings against other beliefs. There were verses about the prophet Jesus whose message, the Koran said, was falsified by early Christians. Though Jesus was born of a virgin, he was not God's son. *So say not "Three,"* warned the Koran against the Christian concept of the Trinity. *Refrain; better is it for you. God is only One God.*

After several days of applying myself to the holy book, I put it down one afternoon with a sigh, got up and walked down to my garden where I hoped to find some peace in nature and in old memories. Even at this time of the year, the lush greenness persisted, brightened here and there by colorful alyssum which still blossomed. It was a warm day for fall and Mahmud skipped along the paths where I had walked as a child with my father. I could picture Father now, walking beside me here, wearing his white turban, impeccably dressed in his conservative British suit from Savile Row as befitted a government minister. Often he would call me by my full name, Bilquis Sultana, knowing how much I enjoyed hearing it. For Bilquis was the first name of the Queen of Sheba and everyone knew Sultana signified royalty.

We had many good conversations. And in later years we enjoyed talking about our new country, Pakistan. He was so proud of it. "The Islamic Republic of Pakistan was created especially as a homeland for South Asian Muslims," he said. "We're one of the largest countries under Islamic law in the world," he added, pointing out that 96% of our country's population was Muslim, with the rest made up mostly of scattered groups of Buddhists, Christians, and Hindus.

I sighed and looked up beyond my garden trees to the lavender hills in the distance. I could always find solace with my father. In his later years I had become a companion to him, often discussing our country's rapidly changing political situation with him and explaining my views. He was so gentle, so understanding. But now he was gone. I remembered standing by his open grave in the Muslim cemetery of Brookwood outside of London. He had travelled to London for surgery and had never recovered. Muslim custom requires that a body be buried within 24 hours of death and by the time I reached the cemetery his coffin was ready to be lowered into the grave. I couldn't believe I'd never see my father again. They unfastened the coffin lid so I could have one last look at him. But the cold gray clay in that box was not him; where had he gone? I stood there numbly wondering about it all as they refastened the coffin, each shrill squeal of the screws biting into the damp wood sending pain through me.

Mother, with whom I was also very close, died seven years later, leaving me completely alone.

There in my garden, shadows had lengthened and again I stood in twilight. No, the comfort I had sought in memories proved only to bring achings. Softly in the distance I could hear the muezzin's sunset prayer call; its haunting strains only deepened the loneliness within me.

"Where? Oh Allah," I whispered to the prayer rhythms, "*where* is the comfort You promise?"

Back in my bedroom that evening I again picked up my mother's copy of the Koran. And as I read I was again impressed by its many references to Jewish and Christian writings which preceded it. Perhaps, I wondered, I should continue my search among those earlier books?

But that would mean reading the Bible. How could the Bible help since, of course, as everyone knew, the early Christians had falsified so much of it. But the idea of reading the Bible became more and more insistent. What was the Bible's concept of God? What *did* it say about the prophet Jesus? Perhaps after all I should read it.

But then came the next problem: where would I get a Bible? No shops in our area would carry one.

Perhaps Raisham would have a copy. But I dismissed the thought. Even if she did, my request would frighten her. Pakistanis have been murdered for even appearing to persuade Muslims to turn traitor-Christian. I thought of my other Christian servants. My family warned that I should not employ Christian servants because of their notorious lack of loyalty and untrustworthiness. But I didn't let that bother me; as long as they could fulfill their duties, I was satisfied. Doubtless they weren't very sincere anyhow. After all, when the Christian missionaries came to India, they found it easy to make converts among the lower classes. Most of these were the sweepers, people so low in the social order that their work was limited to cleaning the streets, walks and gutters. We Muslims called these servile ones "rice Christians." Wasn't that the reason they accepted a false religion, mainly to get the food, clothes and schooling which the missionaries doled out?

We looked upon the missionaries themselves with amusement; they busied themselves so eagerly over these poor creatures. In fact, only a few months before, my chauffeur Manzur, a Christian, asked if he could show my garden to some local missionaries who had admired it through the fence.

"Of course," I said gratuitously, thinking of poor Manzur who evidently wanted so much to impress these people. A few days later from my drawing room window I watched the young American couple stroll through the garden. Manzur had referred to them as the Reverend and Mrs. David Mitchell. Both had pale brown hair, pale eyes and wore drab western clothes. What colorless creatures, I thought. Even so, I did pass word on to the gardener to give these missionaries some seeds if they wished them.

But thinking of them gave me my answer to getting a Bible. Manzur would get one for me. Tomorrow I would give him the assignment.

So I summoned him to my apartment the next morning. He stood at attention before me in his white pantaloons, the nervous twitch in his face making me uneasy, as it always did.

"Manzur, I want you to get me a Bible."

"A Bible?" his eyes widened.

"Of course!" I said, trying to be patient. Since Manzur didn't know how to read, I was sure he didn't own a Bible. But I felt he could get one for me. When he mumbled something I could not understand I repeated, simply but firmly, "Manzur, get me a Bible."

He nodded, bowed and left. I knew why he was resisting my request. Manzur was made of no firmer stuff than Raisham. They were both remembering that murdered girl. Giving a Bible to a sweeper was one thing; bringing a Bible to a person of the upper classes was quite something else. Word of this could get him into deep trouble indeed.

Two days later Manzur was driving me to Rawalpindi to see Tooni.

"Manzur, I do not have the Bible as yet."

I could see his knuckles whiten on the steering wheel.

"Begum, I will get you one."

Three days later I summoned him to the house.

"Manzur, I have asked you to bring me a Bible three times, and you have not." The twitch in his face became more noticeable. "I'll give you one more day. If I do not have one by tomorrow you will be fired."

His face turned ashen. He knew I meant it. He wheeled and left, his chauffeur boots clicking on the terrazzo floor.

The next day just before a visit from Tooni, a little Bible mysteriously appeared on my downstairs drawing room table. I picked it up, and examined it closely. Cheaply bound in a gray cloth cover, it was printed in Urdu, a local Indian dialect. It had been translated by an Englishman 180 years before and I found the old-fashioned phraseology difficult to follow. Manzur had evidently got it from a friend; it was almost new. I leafed through its thin pages, set it down and forgot about it.

A few minutes later Tooni arrived. Mahmud ran in just behind her, squealing, because he knew his mother would have brought him a toy. In a minute Mahmud raced through the French doors to the terrace with his new airplane, and Tooni and I settled down to our tea.

It was then that Tooni noticed the Bible resting on the table near me. "Oh, a Bible!" she said. "Do open it and see what it has to say." Our family views any religious book as significant. It was a common pastime to allow a holy book to fall open, point blindly at a passage to see what it said, almost like having it give a prophecy.

Lightheartedly, I opened the little Bible and looked down at the pages.

Then, a mysterious thing happened. It was as if my attention were being drawn to a verse on the lower right hand corner of the right page. I bent close to read it:

> *I will call that my people, which was not my people; and her beloved, which was not beloved. And it shall be, that in the place where it was said unto them, Ye are not my people, there shall they be called sons of the living God.*
>
> Romans 9:25–26

I caught my breath and a tremor passed through me. Why was this verse affecting me so! *I will call that my people, which was not my people. ... In the place where it was said unto them, Ye are not my people, there shall they be called sons of the living God.*

A silence hung over the room. I looked up to see Tooni poised expectantly, ready to hear what I had found. But I could not read the words out loud. Something in them was too profound for me to read as amusement.

"Well, what was it Mother?" asked Tooni, her alive eyes questioning me.

I closed the book, murmured something about this not being a game anymore, and turned the conversation to another subject.

But the words burned in my heart like glowing embers. And they turned out to be preparation for the most unusual dreams I have ever had.

3

The Dreams

It wasn't until the next day that I again picked up the little gray Bible. Neither Tooni nor I referred to the Bible again after I had switched the conversation to another subject. But throughout the long afternoon the words in that passage simmered just below the surface of my consciousness.

Early in the evening of the next day, I retired to my bed-chamber where I planned to rest and meditate. I took the Bible with me and settled among the soft white cushions of my divan. Once again I leafed through its pages and read another puzzling passage:

> *But Israel, following the Law of righteousness, failed to reach the goal of righteousness.*
>
> Romans 9:31

Ah, I thought. Just as the Koran said; the Jews *had* missed the mark. The writer of these passages might have been a Muslim,

I thought, for he continued to speak of the people of Israel as not knowing God's righteousness.

But the next passage made me catch my breath.

> *For Christ means the end of the struggle for righteousness-by-the-Law for everyone who believes in him.*
>
> Romans 10:4

I lowered the book down for a moment. Christ? *He* was the end of the struggle? I continued on.

> *For the secret is very near you, in your own heart, in your own mouth. ... If you openly admit by your own mouth that Jesus Christ is the Lord, and if you believe in your own heart that God raised him from the dead, you will be saved.*
>
> Romans 10:8–9

I put the book down again, shaking my head. This directly contradicted the Koran. Muslims knew the prophet Jesus was just human, that the man did not die on the cross but was whisked up to heaven by God and a look-alike put on the cross instead. Now sojourning in an inferior heaven, this Jesus will someday return to earth to reign for forty years, marry, have children, and then die. In fact, I heard that there is a special grave plot kept vacant for the man's remains in Medina, the city where Muhammad is also buried. At the Resurrection Day, Jesus will rise and stand with other men to be judged before God Almighty. But this Bible said Christ was raised from the dead. It was either blasphemy or…

My mind whirled. I knew that whoever called upon the name of Allah would be saved. But to believe that Jesus Christ *is* Allah? Even Muhammad, the final and greatest of the messengers of God, the *Seal of the Prophets*, was only a mortal.

I lay back on my bed, my hand over my eyes. If the Bible and Koran represent the same God, why is there so much confusion and contradiction? How could it be the same God if the God of the Koran is one of vengeance and punishment and the God of the Christian Bible is one of mercy and forgiveness? I don't know when I fell asleep. Normally I never dream, but this night I did. The dream was so lifelike, the events in it so real, that I found it difficult the next morning to believe they were only fantasy. Here is what I saw.

> *I found myself having supper with a man I knew to be Jesus. He had come to visit me in my home and stayed for two days. He sat across the table from me and in peace and joy we ate dinner together. Suddenly, the dream changed. Now I was on a mountain top with another man. He was clothed in a robe and shod with sandals. How was it that I mysteriously knew his name, too? John the Baptist. What a strange name. I found myself telling this John the Baptist about my recent visit with Jesus. "The Lord came and was my guest for two days," I said. "But now He is gone. Where is He? I must find Him! Perhaps you, John the Baptist, will lead me to Him?"*

That was the dream. When I woke up I was loudly calling the name, "John the Baptist! John the Baptist!" Nur-jan and Raisham rushed into my room. They seemed embarrassed at my shouting and began fussily to prepare my toilette. I tried to tell them about my dream as they worked.

"Oh, how nice," giggled Nur-jan as she presented my tray of perfumes. "Yes, it was a blessed dream," murmured Raisham as she brushed my hair. I was surprised that as a Christian, Raisham wouldn't be more excited. I started to ask her about John the Baptist but checked myself; after all, Raisham was just a simple village woman. But who *was* this John the Baptist? I had not come across the name in what I had read so far in the Bible.

For the next three days I continued reading both the Bible and the Koran side by side, turning from one to the other. I found myself picking up the Koran out of a sense of duty, and then eagerly turning to the Christian book, dipping into it here and there to look into this confusing new world I had discovered. Each time I opened the Bible a sense of guilt filled me. Perhaps this stemmed from my strict unbringing. Even after I had become a young woman, Father would have to approve any book I read. Once my brother and I smuggled a book into our room. Even though it was completely innocent, we were quite frightened, reading it.

Now as I opened the Bible, I found myself reacting in the same manner. One story riveted my attention. It told of the Jewish leaders bringing a woman caught in adultery to the prophet Jesus. I shivered, knowing what fate lay in store for this woman. The moral codes of the ancient east were not very different from ours in Pakistan. The men of the community are bound by tradition to punish the adulterous woman. As I read of the woman in the Bible standing before her accusers, I knew that her own brothers, uncles and cousins stood in the forefront, ready to stone her.

Then the Prophet said: *Let him who is without sin cast the first stone* (John 8:7).

I reeled as in my mind's eye I watched the men slink away. Instead of supervising her lawful death, Jesus had forced her accusers to recognize their own guilt. The book fell into my lap as I lay there deep in thought. There was something so logical, so right about this prophet's challenge. The man spoke truth.

Then three days later I had a second strange dream:

I was in the bedchamber when a maid announced that a perfume salesman was waiting to see me. I arose from my divan elated, for at this time there was a shortage of imported perfumes in Pakistan. I greatly feared running low on my favorite luxury. And so in my dream I happily asked my maid to show the perfume salesman in.

He was dressed in the manner of perfume salesmen in my mother's day when these merchants travelled from house to house selling their wares. He wore a black frock coat and carried his stock in a valise. Opening the valise, he took out a golden jar. Removing the cap, he handed it to me. As I looked at it I caught my breath; the perfume glimmered like liquid crystal. I was about to touch my finger to it when he held up his hand.

"No," he said. Taking the golden jar he walked over and placed it on my bedside table. "This will spread throughout the world," he said.

As I awakened in the morning, the dream was still vivid in my mind. The sun was streaming through the window, and I could still smell that beautiful perfume; its delightful fragrance filled the room. I raised up and looked at my bedside table, half expecting to see the golden jar there.

Instead, where the jar had been, now rested the Bible!

A tingle passed through me. I sat on the edge of the bed pondering my two dreams. What did they mean? Where I had not dreamed in years, now I had two vivid dreams in a row. Were they related to each other? And were they related to my recent brush with the realities of the supernatural world?

That afternoon I went for my usual stroll in the garden. I was still bemused by my dreams. But now something else was added. It was as if I felt a strange delight and joy, a peace beyond anything I had ever known before. It was as if I were close to the Presence of God. Suddenly, as I stepped out of a grove into a sun-flooded open area, the air around me seemed to be alive with another lovely fragrance. It wasn't the fragrance of flowers—it was too late for any of the garden to be in bloom—but a very real fragrance nonetheless.

In some agitation I returned to the house. Where did that fragrance come from? What was happening to me? Who could I talk to about what was happening to me? It would have to be someone with a knowledge of the Bible. I had already swept aside the thought of asking my Christian servants. In the first place it was unthinkable to ask information of them. They probably had never even read the Bible and wouldn't know what I was talking about. No, I had to talk to someone who was educated and who knew this book.

As I considered this question a shocking idea came to mind. I fought the thought. That would be the last place I should go for help.

But a name kept returning to me so compellingly that I finally rang for Manzur.

"I want you to get the car out for me." And then as an afterthought I added: "I'll be driving myself."

Manzur's eyes widened. "Yourself?"

"Yes, myself, if you please." He left, reluctantly. Rarely had I taken my car out that late in the evening. I had been an officer in the Royal Indian Army women's division in World War II and had driven ambulances and staff cars thousands of miles over all kinds of terrain. But wartime was one thing and even then I was in the company of someone. The daughter of Nawab nobility was not expected to drive her own car in normal life, especially not at night.

But I knew I couldn't risk Manzur knowing what I was about to do and resultant servants' gossip. I was convinced there was only one source where I could find the answer to my questions: Who was John the Baptist? What was this fragrance all about?

So it was with extreme reluctance that evening that I headed for the home of a couple I barely knew, the Reverend and Mrs. David Mitchell who had visited my garden that summer. As Christian missionaries, they were the last people with whom I'd want to be seen.

4

The Encounter

My black Mercedes idled in the driveway. Manzur stood at the driver's door which he kept closed until the last moment protecting the car's warmth against the chill of that autumn evening. His dark eyes were still questioning my decision, but without comment. I got into the warm car, settled behind the wheel and drove off into the twilight, the Bible on the seat beside me.

Everyone knew where everyone else lived in this village of Wah. The Mitchells' home stood near the entrance of the Wah cement works from which my family derived part of its income. It served as the center of a strange little community about five miles outside of town. The homes had been built as temporary quarters for British troops during World War II. I recalled from the few times I had ventured into the area that the drab, uniform houses had lost most of their whitewash; their tin roofs showed signs of much patchwork. A strange mixture of expectancy and fear filled me as I drove along. I had never been in a Christian missionary home before. I was hopeful of learning the identity of my mystery man, John the Baptist, and yet I feared a certain—what should I call it, "influence?"—from those who might answer my question.

What would my forebears think of this visit to a Christian missionary? I thought, for instance, of my great-grandfather who had accompanied the famed British General Nicholson through the Khyber Pass in one of the Afghanistan wars. What shame this visit would bring on my family. We had always associated the missionaries with the poor and social outcasts. I imagined a conversation with an uncle or aunt in which I defended myself by telling them of my strange dreams. "After all," I said in the scene I was playing out in my mind, "anyone would want to find out the meaning of such vivid dreams."

As I approached the Mitchells' area in the dim light of early evening, it was just as I remembered it, except that the look-alike bungalows seemed, if possible, even more drab. After searching up and down narrow lanes, I found the Mitchells' house near the cement works, just where I thought it would be, a small whitewashed bungalow, sitting in a grove of mulberry trees. As a precaution I started to park some distance away until I caught myself. I was being far too afraid of what my family thought. So I parked squarely in front of the Mitchells', picked up the Bible and moved quickly toward the house. The yard, I noticed, was neat and the screened veranda well maintained. At least these missionaries kept their place in good repair.

Suddenly, the house door opened and a group of chattering village women filed out, dressed in the typical *shalwar qamiz*, a loose pajama-like cotton outfit, with a *dupatta* (scarf). I stiff-ened. They would know me of course; nearly everyone in Wah recognized me. Now the story would be gossiped all over the area that Begum Sheikh had visited a Christian missionary!

And sure enough as soon as the women saw me in the light that came from the Mitchells' open front door, their chatter ceased abruptly. They hurried past me to the street, each touching hand to forehead in the traditional salute. There was nothing I could do but continue toward the door where Mrs. Mitchell stood staring out into the dusk. Up close she looked just as I remembered her, from seeing her at a distance about town, young, pale, almost fragile. Only now she was wearing a *shalwar qamiz* like the village women. As soon as she saw me her mouth fell open. "Why … why, Begum Sheikh!" she exclaimed, "What? … But. … Come in," she said. "Come in."

I was glad enough to step inside the house, away from the village women's eyes which I knew would be fixed on my back. We went into the living room, small and simply furnished. Mrs. Mitchell drew up what appeared to be the most comfortable chair for me near the open fire. She herself did not sit down, but stood folding and unfolding her hands. I glanced at a circle of chairs in the middle of the room. Mrs. Mitchell explained that she had just completed a Bible study with some local women. She gave a nervous cough. "Uh, will you have some tea?" she said, brushing back her hair.

"No thank you," I replied. "I have come to ask a question." I looked about. "Is the Reverend Mr. Mitchell here?"

"No. He is on a trip to Afghanistan."

I was sorry. The woman standing before me was so young! Would she be able to answer my questions?

"Mrs. Mitchell," I ventured, "do you know anything about God?"

She sank down into one of the wooden chairs and looked at me strangely; the only noise in the room was the low hiss from the flames in the fireplace. Then she said quietly, "I'm afraid I don't know too much *about* God, but I do *know* Him."

What an extraordinary statement! How could a person presume to know God! Just the same, the woman's odd confidence gave me confidence too. Before I quite knew what was happening, I found myself telling her about my dream of the prophet Jesus and the man named John the Baptist. Strangely, I had difficulty controlling my voice as I related the experience. Even as I told her, I felt the same excitement I felt on that mountain top. Then, after describing the dream, I leaned forward.

"Mrs. Mitchell, I've heard about Jesus, but *who* is John the Baptist?"

Mrs. Mitchell blinked at me and frowned. I felt she wanted to ask if I had really never heard of John the Baptist, but instead she settled back again in her chair. "Well, Begum Sheikh, John the Baptist was a prophet, a forerunner of Jesus Christ, who preached repentance and was sent to prepare the way for Him. He was the one who pointed to Jesus and said: 'Look, the Lamb of God who takes away the sins of the world.' He was the one who baptized Jesus."

Why did my heart skip at the word "baptized?" I knew little about these Christians, but all Muslims had heard of their strange ceremony of baptism. My mind flitted to the many people who were murdered after their baptisms. And this also happened under British rule when supposedly there was freedom of religion. Even as a child I had put the two facts together: a Muslim was baptized, a Muslim died.

"Begum Sheikh?"

I looked up. How long had we been sitting there silently? "Mrs. Mitchell," I said, my throat tight, "forget I am a Muslim. Just tell me: what did you mean when you said you know God?"

"I know Jesus," Mrs. Mitchell said and I knew she thought she was answering my question.

Then she told me what God had done for her and for the world by breaking the dreadful deadlock between sinful man and Himself by personally visiting this earth in the flesh, as Jesus, and dying for all of us on the cross.

The room was quiet again. I could hear trucks passing on the nearby highway. Mrs. Mitchell seemed in no hurry to speak. Finally, hardly believing my own ears, I took a breath and heard myself saying quite distinctly, "Mrs. Mitchell, some peculiar things have been happening at our house lately. Events of the spirit. Good and bad, both. I feel as if I were in the midst of an immense tug of war, and I need all the positive help I can get. Could you pray for me?"

The woman appeared startled at my request, then, collecting herself, she asked if I wanted to stand up, kneel or sit down as we prayed. I shrugged, suddenly horrified. All were equally unthinkable. But there was this slender, youthful woman kneeling on the floor of her bungalow. And I followed her!

"Oh Spirit of God," said Mrs. Mitchell in a soft voice, "I know that nothing I can say will convince Begum Sheikh who Jesus is. But I thank You that You take the veil off our eyes and reveal Jesus to our hearts. Oh, Holy Spirit, do this for Begum Sheikh. Amen."

We stayed on our knees for what seemed like forever. I was glad for the silence, for my heart was strangely warmed.

At last Mrs. Mitchell and I arose. "Is that a Bible, Madame Sheikh?" she asked, nodding toward the little gray volume which I clutched to my breast in one hand. I showed her the book. "How do you find it?" she asked. "Easy to understand?"

"Not really," I said. "It is an old translation and I'm not at home in it."

She stepped into an adjacent room and returned with another book.

"Here is a New Testament written in modern English," she said. "It's called the Phillips translation. I find it much easier to understand than others. Would you like it?"

"Yes," I said, not hesitating.

"Start with the Gospel of John," Mrs. Mitchell advised, opening the book and placing a bit of paper in it as a bookmark. "That's another John, but he makes the role of John the Baptist very clear."

"Thank you," I said, touched. "And now I think I've taken too much of your time."

As I prepared to leave, Mrs. Mitchell said: "You know, it's so interesting that a dream brought you here. God often speaks to His children in dreams and visions."

As she helped me on with my coat, I wondered if I should share something about my other dream with her. The one about the perfume salesman. It seemed so … bizarre. But as had happened several times already in this strange evening, I found myself filled with a boldness that seemed almost to come from outside of me. "Mrs. Mitchell, can you tell me if there is a connection between perfume and Jesus?"

She thought for a moment, her hand on the door. "No," she said, "I can't think of any. However, let me pray about it."

As I drove home, I experienced for the second time that same fragrant Presence I had sensed in my garden earlier that day!

When I got home that night I read a little out of the portion of the Bible called "The Gospel of John," where the writer talked about John the Baptist, this strange man clad in camel skin who came out of the wilderness, calling people to prepare for the coming of the Lord. And then, there in the safety of my own bedroom, seated on my divan, surrounded by memories and traditions that were seven centuries old, a thought slipped sideways into my mind, unbidden, unwanted, quickly rejected. If John the Baptist was a sign from God, a sign pointing toward Jesus, was this same man pointing *me* toward Jesus, too?

Of course the thought was untenable. I put it out of mind and went to sleep.

That night I did sleep soundly.

As the muezzin called me to prayer the next morning. I was relieved to find myself seeing things clearly again. What a bizarre series of thoughts I had toyed with in the night! But now as the muezzin reminded me where truth lay, I felt secure again, away from these disturbing Christian influences.

Raisham came in just then, not with tea but with a note which she said had just been delivered to the house.

It was from Mrs. Mitchell. All it said was: "Read Second Corinthians, Chapter 2, Verse 14."

I reached for the Bible she had given me and searched until I found the chapter and verse. Then, as I read, I caught my breath:

> *Thanks be to God who leads us, wherever we are, on Christ's triumphant way, and makes our knowledge of Him spread throughout the world like a lovely perfume!*

I sat there in bed, and re-read the passage, my composure of a minute ago shattered. The knowledge of Jesus spreads like a lovely perfume! In my dream, the salesman had put the golden dish of scent on my bedside table and said that the perfume "would spread throughout the world." The next morning I had found my Bible in the same spot where the perfume had been laid! It was all too clear. I didn't want to think about it any more. Ring for tea, that's what I must do. Ring for my tea and bring life back into its proper focus quickly before something else went awry.

Even though Mrs. Mitchell had invited me back, I felt it best not to return. It seemed a prudent logical decision that I must now investigate this Bible on my own. I did not want to be pushed by any outside influence. However, one afternoon Nur-jan rushed into my room with an odd look in her eyes. "The Reverend and Mrs. Mitchell are here to see you," she gasped.

My hand flew to my throat. Why would they come *here?* I wondered. However, quickly composing myself, I asked the maid to bring them into the drawing room.

Sandy-haired David Mitchell, a lanky man with crinkly eyes, radiated the same friendly warmth as his wife. The two seemed so happy to see me that I forgot my discomfort over them coming to my house.

Mrs. Mitchell started to shake hands, then at the last minute threw her arms around me instead. I was stunned. No one outside the family, not even our closest friends, had ever embraced me in this way before. I stiffened but Mrs. Mitchell appeared to take no notice of my reaction. I found—in retrospect, I have to admit—that this display pleased me. There could have been no sham in her greeting.

"I'm so happy to meet 'the Flower Lady'," David exclaimed in a jovial American accent.

I glanced at Mrs. Mitchell and she laughed. "I should explain. When you came to our house, I wanted to let David know right away by telegram for we had often talked about you since we visited your garden last spring. However, I didn't want to use your real name, to protect you. As I was wondering how to refer to you in the wire, I glanced out my window and saw the flowers that had grown from the seeds your gardener gave us. The name came to me: 'Flower Lady,' and that became our code name for you."

I laughed. "Well, from now on, you can call me Bilquis."

"And please," she said, "call me Synnove."

It was a strange visit. I suppose I was half expecting pressure from the Mitchells to accept their religion, but nothing of the sort occurred. We drank a cup of tea and chatted. I did question Jesus being called the "son of God," for to Muslims there is no greater sin than to make this claim. The Koran states again and again that God has no children. "And this 'trinity'?" I asked. "God is three?"

In answer, David compared God to the sun which manifests itself in the three creative energies of heat, light and radiation, a trinity relationship which together makes the sun, yet singly is not the sun. And then shortly they left.

Again for several days I found myself alone with two books—the Koran and the Bible. I continued to read them both, studying the Koran because of the loyalty of a lifetime, delving into the Bible because of a strange inner hunger.

Yet, sometimes I'd draw back from picking up the Bible. God couldn't be in both books, I knew, because their messages were so different. But when my hand hesitated at picking up the book Mrs. Mitchell gave me, I felt a strange letdown. For the past week I had been living in a world of beauty, not a visible garden created by me from seeds and water, but an inner garden created from a new spiritual awareness. I first entered this world of beauty by way of my two dreams; then I became aware of this world a second time on the night I met the indefinably glorious Presence in my garden; and I had known it once again when I obeyed the nudging that prompted me to visit the Mitchells.

Slowly, clearly, over the next few days I began to know that there was a way to return to my world of beauty. And reading this Christian book seemed, for reasons that I could not grasp, the key to my re-entering that world.

And then one day little Mahmud came up to me holding the side of his head and trying not to whimper. "My ear, Mum," he cried in a pain-filled voice. "It hurts."

I bent down and examined him carefully. His usual ruddy brown complexion had paled, and although Mahmud was not a child to complain, I could see the tear stains on his little round tan cheeks.

I put him right to bed and crooned softly to him, his black hair too stark against the pillow. And then, after his eyes closed, I went to the telephone and rang the Holy Family Hospital in Rawalpindi. Within a minute Tooni was on the phone. She agreed that we should check Mahmud into the hospital the next afternoon for a complete examination the following day. I would be able to stay in an adjoining room and a maid would be given a smaller room adjacent to that.

It was toward evening when we checked into the comfortable arrangement. Tooni had the evening free to spend with us. Soon, Mahmud and his mother were giggling over some pictures

Mahmud was coloring in a book she had brought him. I was propped up in bed reading my Bible. I had also brought the Koran with me, but by now I read the Koran out of a sense of duty, more than interest.

Suddenly, the room lights flickered, and then went out. The room was dark.

"Another power failure," I said, exasperated. "Did you see any candles?"

In a moment the door opened and a nun stepped inside with a flashlight. "I hope you don't mind the dark," she said cheerily. "We'll get some candles shortly." I recognized her as Dr. Pia Santiago, a slightly built, bespectacled Filipino who was in charge of the whole hospital. We had met briefly on a previous visit. Almost at once another nun came in with candles and in a moment warm light flooded the room. Mahmud and Tooni resumed their visit and I was left to make conversation with Dr. Santiago. I couldn't help notice her staring at my Bible.

"Do you mind if I sit with you for a while?" Dr. Santiago asked.

"It would be a pleasure," I said, assuming it was just a courtesy visit. She moved to a chair near my bed and with a rustling of her white habit sat down.

"Oh," she said, taking off her glasses and wiping her brow with a handkerchief, "has this ever been a busy night."

My heart warmed to her. Muslims always had respect for these holy women who give up the world to serve their God; their faith may be misplaced, but their sincerity was real. We chatted but as the conversation continued, I could tell that this woman had something on her mind. It was the Bible. I could see her glancing at it with mounting curiosity. Finally she leaned forward and in a confidential tone asked, "Madame Sheikh, what are you doing with a Bible?"

"I am earnestly in search of God," I answered. And then, while the candles burned lower, I told her, very cautiously at first, then with mounting boldness, about my dreams, my visit with Mrs. Mitchell, and my comparing the Bible and the Koran. "Whatever happens," I emphasized, "I must find God, but I'm confused about your faith," I said finally, realizing that even as I spoke I was putting my finger on something important. "You seem to make God so … I don't know … *personal!*"

The little nun's eyes filled with compassion and she leaned forward. "Madame Sheikh," she said, her voice full of emotion, "there is only one way to find out why we feel this way. And that is to find out for yourself, strange as that may seem. Why don't you pray *to* the God you are searching for? Ask Him to show you His way. Talk to Him as if He were your friend."

I smiled. She might as well suggest that I talk to the Taj Mahal. But then Dr. Santiago said something that shot through my being like electricity. She leaned closer and took my hand in hers, tears streaming down her cheeks. "Talk to Him," she said very quietly, "as if He were your father."

I sat back quickly. A dead silence filled the room. Even Mahmud and Tooni's conversation hung between thoughts. I stared at the nun with the candlelight glinting off her glasses.

Talk to God as if He were my father! The thought shook my soul in the peculiar way truth has of being at once startling and comforting.

Then as if on cue everyone started talking at once. Tooni and Mahmud laughed and decided that the parasol should be colored purple. Dr. Santiago smiled, rose, wished us all well, gathered her habit about her and left the room.

Nothing else was said about prayer or Christianity. Yet I moved through the rest of that night, and the next morning, stunned. What made the experience especially mysterious was that the doctors could find nothing wrong with Mahmud and Mahmud kept saying that his ear did not hurt him one bit. At first, I was irritated at all the time and trouble this had taken. Then the thought occurred to me that perhaps, just perhaps, in some mystic way God had taken advantage of this situation to bring me into contact with Dr. Santiago.

Later that morning Manzur drove us all back to Wah. As we turned off the Grand Trunk onto our lane, I could see the gray roof of my home through the trees. Usually, I looked forward to home as a retreat from the world. But today there seemed to be a difference about my house, as if something special would happen to me there.

We drove up the long driveway, Manzur sounding the horn. The servants ran out and surrounded the car. "Is the little one well?" they all asked at once.

Yes, I assured them, Mahmud was fine. But my mind was not on homecoming festivities. It was on this new way to find God. I went up to my bedroom to consider all that had been happening. No Muslim, I felt certain, ever thought of Allah as his father. Since childhood, I had been told that the surest way to know about Allah was to pray five times a day and study and think on the Koran. Yet Dr. Santiago's words came to me again. "Talk *to* God. Talk to Him as if He were your Father."

Alone in my room I got on my knees and tried to call Him "Father." But it was a useless effort and I straightened in dismay. It was ridiculous. Wouldn't it be sinful to try to bring the Great One down to our own level? I fell asleep that night more confused than ever.

Hours later I awoke. It was after midnight, my birthday, December 12th. I was 47 years old. I felt a momentary excitement, a carry-over from childhood when birthdays were festivals with string bands on the lawns, games, and relatives coming to the house all day. Now, there would be no celebration, perhaps a few phone calls, nothing more.

Oh, how I had missed those childhood days. I thought of my parents as I liked to remember them best. Mother, so loving, so regal and beautiful. And Father. I had been so proud of him, with his high posts in the Indian government. I could still see him, impeccably dressed, adjusting his turban at the mirror before leaving for his office. The friendly eyes under bushy brows, the gentle smile, the chiseled features and aquiline nose.

One of my cherished memories was seeing him at work in the study. Even in a society where sons were more highly regarded than daughters, Father prized his children equally. Often, as a little girl, I would have a question to ask him and I would peek at him from around the door of his office, hesitant to interrupt. Then his eye would catch mine. Putting down his pen, he would lean back in his chair and call out, "Keecha?" Slowly, I would walk into the study, my head down. He would smile and pat the chair next to his. "Come, my darling, sit here." Then, placing his arm around me, he would draw me to him. "Now, my little Keecha," he would ask gently, "What can I do for you?"

It was always the same with Father. He didn't mind if I bothered him. Whenever I had a question or problem, no matter how busy he was, he would put aside his work to devote his full attention just to me.

It was well past midnight as I lay in bed savoring this wonderful memory. "Oh thank you …" I murmured to God. Was I really talking *to* Him?

Suddenly, a breakthrough of hope flooded me. Suppose, just suppose God were like a father. If my earthly father would put aside everything to listen to me, wouldn't my heavenly Father …?

Shaking with excitement, I got out of bed, sank to my knees on the rug, looked up to heaven and in rich new understanding called God "My Father."

I was not prepared for what happened.

5

The Crossroads

"Oh Father, my Father … Father God."

Hesitantly, I spoke His name aloud. I tried different ways of speaking to Him. And then, as if something broke through for me I found myself trusting that He was indeed hearing me, just as my earthly father had always done.

"Father, oh my Father God," I cried, with growing confidence. My voice seemed unusually loud in the large bedroom as I knelt on the rug beside my bed. But suddenly that room wasn't empty any more. *He* was there! I could sense His Presence. I could feel His hand laid gently on my head. It was as if I could *see* His eyes, filled with love and compassion. He was so close that I found myself laying my head on His knees like a little girl sitting at her father's feet. For a long time I knelt there, sobbing quietly, floating in His love. I found myself talking with Him, apologizing for not having known Him before. And again, came His loving compassion, like a warm blanket settling around me.

Now I recognized this as the same loving Presence I had met that fragrance-filled afternoon in my garden. The same Presence I had sensed often as I read the Bible.

"I am confused, Father ..." I said. "I have to get one thing straight right away." I reached over to the bedside table where I kept the Bible and the Koran side by side. I picked up both books and lifted them, one in each hand. "Which, Father?" I said. "Which one is Your book?"

Then a remarkable thing happened. Nothing like it had ever occurred in my life in quite this way. For I heard a voice inside my being, a voice that spoke to me as clearly as if I were repeating words in my inner mind. They were fresh, full of kindness, yet at the same time full of authority.

"In which book do you meet Me as your Father?"

I found myself answering: "In the Bible." That's all it took. Now there was no question in my mind which one was His book. I looked at my watch and was astonished to discover that three hours had passed. Yet I was not tired. I wanted to go on praying, I wanted to read the Bible, for I knew now that my Father would speak through it. I went to bed only when I knew I must for the sake of my health. But the very next morning I told my maids to see that I was not disturbed, took my Bible again and reclined on my divan. Starting with Matthew, I began reading the New Testament word by word.

I was impressed that God spoke to His people in dreams, five times in the first part of Matthew, in fact! He spoke to Joseph on behalf of Mary. He warned the Wise Men about Herod, and three more times He addressed Joseph concerning the protection of the baby Jesus.

I couldn't find enough time for the Bible. Everything I read, it seemed, was directing me to take some kind of closer walk with God.

I found myself standing at a great crossroads. So far I had met, personally, the Father God. In my heart I knew I had to give myself totally to His Son Jesus or else to turn my back on Him completely.

And I knew for certain that everyone I loved would advise me to turn my back on Jesus. Into my mind crowded the memory of a special, precious day years before when my father took me to our family mosque, just the two of us. We stepped into the soaring vaulted chamber. Taking my hand, Father told me with great pride and with strong identification that twenty generations of our family had worshipped there. "What a privilege you have, my little Keecha, to be part of this ancient truth."

And I thought of Tooni. Surely this young woman had enough worries already. And there were my other children; although they lived far away, they too would be hurt if I "became a Christian." And then there was my Uncle Fateh, who had watched so proudly the day I was four years, four months, four days old and began learning to read the Koran. And there was beloved Aunt Amina and all my other relatives, some hundred "uncles," "aunts" and "cousins." In the east, the family becomes *biraderi*, one community, with each member responsible to the other. I could hurt the family in many ways, even interfere with the opportunities of my nieces getting married, as they would have to live in the shadow of my decision if I chose to join the "sweepers."

But most of all I worried about my little grandson, Mahmud; what would happen to him! My heart caught at the thought of Mahmud's father. He was a very volatile man, who might easily try to take the boy from me if I became a Christian, therefore clearly demonstrating that I was unstable.

That day as I sat reading and thinking in my quiet room, these thoughts seared my heart. Suddenly, the realization of the pain I might inflict on others became too much for me and I stood up, crying. I threw a wrap around me and walked into the cold, winter garden, my refuge where, it seemed, I could think best.

"Oh Lord," I cried, as I paced the graveled path, "could You really want me to leave my family? Can a God of love want me to inflict pain on others?" And in the darkness of my despair, all I could hear were His words, the words which I had just read in Matthew:

> *Anyone who puts his love for father or mother above his love for me does not deserve to be mine, and he who loves son or daughter more than me is not worthy of me. ...*
>
> Matthew 10:37–38

This Jesus did not compromise. He did not want any competition. His were hard, uncomfortable words, words I did not want to hear.

Enough! I couldn't take the pressure of the decision any longer. On impulse I ran back to the house, summoned Manzur and announced to the somewhat startled housekeeper that I was going to Rawalpindi. I would be gone for a few days. She could reach me at my daughter's if there were need. Manzur drove me into Rawalpindi where I did spend several days feverishly shopping, buying toys for Mahmud, perfumes and saris for myself. Not surprisingly, as I continued my spree, I found myself drifting away from the warmth of His Presence. Once when a shopkeeper spread out a piece of cloth and showed me the gems embroidered in a rich design, I suddenly saw the shape of the cross in the pattern. I snapped at the shopkeeper and fled. The next morning I went back to Wah neither determined to remain a Muslim nor determined to become a Christian.

Then one evening as I relaxed before the fire, I found myself picking up the Bible again. Mahmud was in bed. It was quiet in the living room. A wind in the garden rattled the windows, the fire snapped and hissed.

I had read straight through all the Gospels and the Book of Acts, and that night I had reached the last book in the Bible. I was fascinated by Revelation, even though I understood very little of it. I read as if directed, strangely confident. And then abruptly I came to a sentence that made the room spin. It was the 20th verse of the third chapter of Revelation:

> *See, I stand knocking at the door. If anyone listens to my voice and opens the door, I will go into his house and dine with him, and he with me.*

And dine with Him, and He with me!

I gasped, letting the book fall in my lap.

This was my dream, the dream where Jesus was having dinner with me! At the time I had had no knowledge of a book called Revelation. I closed my eyes and once again I could see Jesus sitting across the table from me. I could feel His warm smile, His acceptance. Why, the glory was there too! Just as it had been with the Father. It was the glory that belonged to His Presence!

Now I knew that my dream had come from God. The way was clear. I could accept Him, or reject Him. I could open the door, ask Him to come in permanently, or I could close the door. I would have to make my full decision *now*, one way or the other.

I made up my mind and knelt in front of the fire.

"Oh God, don't wait a moment. Please come into my life. Every bit of me is open to You." I did not have to struggle, or worry about what would happen. I had said Yes. Christ was in my life now, and I knew it.

How unbearably beautiful. Within a few days I had met God the Father and God the Son. I got up and started to prepare for bed, my mind whirling. Did I dare take one more step? I remembered that in the book of Acts, at Pentecost, Jesus had baptized His followers with the Holy Spirit. Was I supposed to follow this same pattern? "Lord," I said, as I laid my head back on my pillow, "I have no one to guide me except You Yourself. If You intend for me to receive this Baptism in the Holy Spirit then of course I want what You want. I am ready." Knowing I had placed myself completely in His hands, I drifted off to sleep.

It was still dark when I was awakened in a state of vibrant expectancy that morning of December 24, 1966. I looked at my luminescent clock and the hands pointed to 3:00 A.M. The room was bitterly cold but I was burning with excitement.

I crawled out of bed and sank to my knees on the cold rug. As I looked up, I seemed to be looking into a great light. Hot tears flowed down my face as I raised my hands to Him and cried out: "Oh Father God, baptize me with Your Holy Spirit!"

I took my Bible and opened it to where the Lord said:

> *John used to baptize with water, but before many days are passed you will be baptized with the Holy Spirit.*
>
> Acts 1:5

"Lord," I cried, "if these words of Yours are true, then give this baptism to me now." I crumpled face down on the chilled floor where I lay crying. "Lord," I sobbed, "I'll never want to get up from this place until You give me this baptism." Suddenly, I was filled with wonder and awe. For in that silent pre-dawn room I saw His face. Something surged through me, wave after wave of purifying ocean breakers, flooding me to the tips of my fingers and toes, washing my soul.

Then the powerful surges subsided, the heavenly ocean quieted. I was completely cleansed. Joy exploded within me and I cried out praising Him, thanking Him.

Hours later, I felt the Lord lift me to my feet. He wanted me to get up now. I looked out the filigreed windows and saw that it was nearly dawn.

"Oh, Lord," I said, as I lay back in my bed. "Could the heaven you speak of be any better than this? To know You is joy, to worship You is happiness, to be near You is peace. *This* is heaven!"

I doubt if I slept two hours that early dawn. In no time at all my maidservants came in to help me dress. For the first morning that I could remember, I did not say one cross word to them. Instead there was an air of calm and peace in the sun-flooded room. Raisham actually hummed a song as she brushed my hair, something she had never done before.

All that day I roamed through my house, silently praising God, hardly able to contain the joy within myself. At lunch, Mahmud looked up from his pancakes and said: "Mum, you look so smiley; what has happened to you?"

I reached over and tousled his shiny black hair. "Give him some *halwa*," I told the cook. This dish made from wheat, butter and sugar was his favorite sweet. I told Mahmud that we would be celebrating Christmas at the Mitchells' home.

"Christmas?" said Mahmud.

"It's a holiday," I said, "a little like Ramazan." That, Mahmud did understand. Ramazan was the month of the Muslim year when Muhammad received his first revelation. So for this month, each year, Muslims fast from sunrise to sunset each day until at last the drums thunder in the mosques and we load ourselves with delicacies, sweet and sour fruit, spinach leaves dipped in batter and fried, delicately cooked eggplant, succulent kabobs. Christmas I supposed would indeed be a little like Ramazan. And I was right. When David met us at the door of the Mitchells' house, the scent of delicious cooked foods floated around him, and laughter sounded from within the room.

"Come in! Come in!" he exclaimed, drawing us into the living room filled with a holiday spirit. A Christmas tree glowed in the corner and the laughter of the two Mitchell children, just a little older than Mahmud, rang out from another room. Mahmud happily joined them at their play.

I could not contain my joy any longer. "David!" I cried, using his first name without thinking, "I am a Christian now! I have been baptized in the Holy Spirit!"

He stared at me for a moment, then drew me into the house. "Who told you about the Holy Spirit Baptism?" he asked, his gray eyes wide. He began laughing joyously and praising God. Hearing his "Hallelujah!" Synnove rushed into the room from the kitchen and David again asked: "Who told you?"

"Jesus told me," I laughed. "I read it in the Bible's Book of Acts; I asked God for it and received it."

Both David and Synnove looked bewildered. But then suddenly they rushed to me. Synnove put her arms around me and broke into tears. David joined her. Then the three of us stood there, arms around each other, praising God for what He had done.

That night I began a diary into which I put all the wonderful things the Lord had been doing for me. If I should die—and I had no idea what might happen to me once word got out that I had become a Christian—at least I wanted this record of my experience to remain. As I sat at my desk writing my experiences, I did not realize that He was making preparations to begin my education.

6

Learning to Find His Presence

Several surprises were waiting for me over the next several days, following my threefold encounters.

For one thing, I found I was experiencing dreams or visions, but quite unlike the two dreams that had started this whole incredible adventure. In fact my first experience left me shaken. I was resting in bed one afternoon thinking of my Lord when suddenly I felt as if I were floating right out my window. I felt sure I was not asleep and found myself passing right through the window filigree, and I caught a glimpse of the earth below. I became so frightened that I cried out in fear, and suddenly I found myself back in bed. I lay there slightly dazed, breathing shallowly, feeling a tingling in my legs as if they had been asleep, and then the blood was rushing back.

"What was it, Lord?" I asked. And then I realized that He had given me a special experience. "I'm so sorry, Lord," I apologized, "but You have picked up a coward."

Late that night it happened again. Only this time I talked to God through the experience and told Him I wasn't afraid. As I slipped back through my window I could only think I had been "floating" in a spiritual way. "But what is Your reason, my Lord?" I asked.

Turning to the Bible I searched His Word for something of this, for I began to fear that it might be something not of the Lord.

I sighed in relief when I read in the Acts of the Apostles (8:39) where the Spirit of the Lord suddenly whisked Philip away to the distant city of Azotus after he had baptized the Ethiopian eunuch.

Then I was given further confirmation when I read Paul's second letter to the Christians at Corinth. In chapter 12, in speaking of visions and revelations from the Lord, he wrote of being "caught up into the third heaven." He felt that only God knew whether or not it was an actual physical experience, and I felt the same about mine. As Paul added: "This man heard words that cannot … be translated into human speech."

I heard words, too, that I cannot translate but I shall never forget the scenes. During one such experience I saw a steeple soaring into heaven; suddenly before me were hundreds of churches, new ones, old ones, churches with different architectural styles, and then a beautiful gold church. Again the scene shifted and I saw downtown areas of cities rolling before me, modern centers and old-fashioned village squares. It was all so clear; I could discern the skyscrapers, clock towers, and quaint ornate buildings.

Then my heart shook as I saw a man riding a red horse, his right hand wielding a sword; he galloped about the earth under cloud masses. Sometimes he rose until his head touched the clouds, and sometimes his steed's flashing hooves scraped the earth.

I couldn't get over the feeling that these must have been given to me for a particular, still unknown, reason.

I also found as I read the Scriptures that it was an experience completely unlike any other time I had spent with the Bible. Something happened to me as I went through the book; instead of reading the Bible, I found myself living it. It was as if I stepped through its pages into that ancient world of Palestine when Jesus Christ walked the stony roads of Galilee. I watched as He preached and taught, as He lived out His message in everyday situations, and as He displayed the power of the Spirit, and finally as He went to the cross and passed victoriously through the experience of death.

I also discovered to my surprise that the effect of Bible reading was beginning to be felt by others. This was brought home to me one morning when my maids were preparing my toilette. Nur-jan was arranging the silver combs and brushes on a tray when she accidently spilled the whole thing. There was a great clatter. She stiffened, her eyes wide; I knew she was expecting my usual onslaught. And indeed I was about to scold her when I caught myself. Instead, I found myself saying, "Don't worry, Nur-jan. They didn't break."

Then there was a peculiar boldness that began to take shape in my life. Up until then I had been afraid to let anyone know of my interest in Christ. For one thing, I dreaded the thought of people making jokes about the "sweeper Begum." Of more concern, I was afraid my family would ostracize me; Mahmud's father might even try to take him away. I was even fearful lest some fanatic take to heart the injunction: *he who falls away from his faith must die*.

So I was really not anxious to be seen at the Mitchells. The group of women who came out of David's and Synnove's house that first night still gave me concern. My own servants certainly knew that something unusual was happening to me. When I put all this together I was living in a state of constant uneasiness, not knowing when the pressure against me would begin.

But after my three encounters with God, I found myself making a surprising admission to myself one day. As far as I was concerned, my decision to become a Christian was now public information. As the Bible says, I was "confessing Jesus with my lips." "Well," I said to myself as I stood at my bedroom window one day, "we'll just let the results fall where they may."

I didn't expect results quite so quickly. Soon after Christmas, 1966, the downstairs maid came to me with her eyebrows arched, "Mrs. Mitchell is here to see you, Begum," she said.

"Oh?" I said, trying to sound casual, "show her in." My heart pounded as I walked to the door to meet my guest. "I am so honored to have you visit," I said, making sure that the maid, hovering in the background, heard me.

Synnove came to invite me to dinner. "There will be a few others there, people we are sure you would like to meet," she said.

Others? I felt the old wall rise within me. Synnove must have caught the hesitant look in my eyes for she sought to reassure me. "Most of them are Christians," she said. "Some are English, some Americans. Would you come?" her eyes pleaded hopefully.

And of course—with more enthusiasm than I felt—I said that I would be delighted.

I wondered why many Christians were so often shy! I had been in contact with Christians before, usually at state dinner parties I had hosted as wife of a government official. The dinners were formal events, served by uniformed servants, amidst Belgian lace, with centerpieces of fresh flowers; lengthy affairs, with numerous courses each served separately on its own Spode china. There were many Christians of different nationalities among the guests, but not one of them ever mentioned his faith, even when it would have been a natural part of the conversation. The people I'd meet at the Mitchell's, I felt, would not be so backward.

The next day I drove the now becoming familiar route to the Mitchell's house. David and Synnove greeted me warmly and introduced me to their friends. I wonder how I would have felt if I'd known at the time how large a role some of these people were going to play in my life.

The first couple were Ken and Marie Old. Ken was an Englishman whose blue eyes twinkled humorously behind thick glasses. He was a civil engineer who wore an air of informality as easily as he wore his rumpled clothes. His wife Marie was an American nurse with a practical air offset by a beautiful smile. The others were warm and friendly people, too.

And then to my horror I found myself the center of attention. Everyone was eager to hear about my experiences. What I expected to be a quiet dinner turned out to be a question and answer period. The dining room was still—even the several children sat quietly—as I told about my dreams, and about my separate meetings with the three personalities of God.

At the end of the dinner David complimented his wife on the meal but said he felt that the spiritual nourishment of my story was even richer.

"I agree," said Ken Old. "I've seen you before, you know. I used to live in Wah. I would pass your garden in the early morning and admire your flowers. Sometimes you were in the garden but I must say you don't look like the same woman." I felt sure I knew what he meant. The Bilquis Sheikh of a few months ago had been an unsmiling person. "You are like a child," Ken went on to say, "who has suddenly been given a gift. In your face I see an incredible wonder at that gift. You treasure it more than anything you have ever possessed."

I was going to like this man.

I had enjoyable conversations with the others, and I realized that I had been right. These Christians were very different from Christians I had met at other dinner parties. Before the evening was over, each person had told a little about what the Lord was doing in his life. David was right. The meal was excellent, but the true feeding came from the Presence in that little house. I had never known anything similar, and I found myself wishing I could get this same feeding regularly.

Which is why, as I was about to leave, the comment from Ken struck me with such impact. Ken and Marie came up and took my hand. "You'll need some regular Christian fellowship now, Bilquis," said Ken. "Will you come to our house on Sunday evenings."

"Could you?" asked Marie hopefully.

And that is how I began regular meetings with other Christians. Sunday evenings we met at the Olds' house, a brick dwelling whose living room could barely hold the dozen people who crowded in. Only two were Pakistanis, the rest were Americans and Englishmen. I met new people, too, such as Dr. and Mrs. Christy. This thin energetic-looking American doctor was an eye specialist and his wife a nurse. Both were on the local mission hospital staff. At the meetings we sang, read the Bible, and prayed for each other's needs. It quickly became the high point of my week.

Then one Sunday I didn't particularly feel like going. So I rang up the Olds and gave some excuse. It seemed a little thing, but almost instantly I began to feel uneasy. What was it! I walked through the house restlessly checking on the servants' work. Everything was in order, yet everything seemed out of order.

Then I went to my own room and knelt down to pray. After a while Mahmud crept in, so quietly that I didn't know he was there until I felt his little soft hand in mine. "Mum, are you all right?" he asked. "You look funny." I smiled and assured him that, yes, I was all right. "Well you keep walking around *looking*. As if you'd lost something."

Then he was gone, skipping out the door and down the hall. I looked as if I had lost something?! Mahmud was right. And I knew right then what it was I had lost. I'd lost the sense of God's glory. It was gone! Why? Did it have something to do with my not going to that meeting at the Olds'? With my not having fellowship when I needed it?

With a sense of urgency I phoned Ken and said that I'd be there after all.

What a difference. Immediately I felt, actually felt, the return of warmth to my soul. I did go to the meeting, as I promised. Nothing unusual took place there, yet again I knew I was walking in His glory. Ken had apparently been right. I *needed* fellowship. I had learned my lesson. I determined from then on to attend regularly unless Jesus Himself told me not to go.

As I drew a little closer to God, here a step, there a step, I found myself hungering even more for His word through the Bible. Everyday, as soon as I arose, I would begin reading it with a never-failing sense of *nowness*. The Bible became alive to me, illuminating my day, shedding its light on every step I would take. It was, in fact, my lovely perfume. But here too I found a strange thing. One day Mahmud and I were to go to see his mother for the day. I was late getting to bed the night before and really didn't feel like getting up at dawn to have an hour with the Bible, so I told Raisham to wake me with my tea just before we were supposed to set off.

I didn't sleep at all well that night. I tossed and twisted and had bad dreams. When Raisham came in, I was exhausted. And I noticed that the entire day didn't go right.

Strange! What was the Lord saying to me? That He expected me to read the Bible *every* day?

That was the second time when I seemed to be stepping out of the glory of the Lord's Presence.

But the experience, nonetheless, left me with a strange sense of excitement. For I had the feeling that I was sitting on an important truth without realizing it. There were times when I was in the Presence and experienced that deep sense of joy and peace, and there were times when I lost the sense of His Presence.

What was the key? What could I do to stay close to Him?

I thought back over the times when He had seemed unusually close, way back to my two dreams and to the afternoon when I sensed the exquisite fragrance in my winter garden. I thought about the first time when I had gone to the Mitchells' and about the later times when I had read my Bible regularly, and gone to the Sunday meetings at the Olds'. Almost always these were times when I knew the Lord was with me.

And I thought about opposite times too, moments when I knew that I had lost this sense of His nearness. How did the Bible put it? *And grieve not the Holy Spirit of God* (Ephesians 4:30, KJV). Is that what happened when I scolded the servants? Or when I failed to nourish my spirit with regular Bible reading? Or when I just didn't go to the Olds'?

Part of the key to staying in His company was obedience. When I obeyed, then I was allowed to remain in His Presence.

I got out my Bible and searched in John until I found the verse where Jesus says:

> *When a man loves me, he follows my teaching. Then my Father will love him, and we will come to that man and make our home within him.*
>
> John 14:23

That was the Bible's way of expressing what I was trying to say. To stay in the glory. *That* was what I was trying to do!

And the key was obedience. "Oh Father," I prayed, "I want to be Your servant, just as it says in the Bible. I *will* obey You. I've always thought it a sacrifice to give up my own will. But it's no sacrifice because it keeps me close to You. How could Your Presence be a sacrifice!"

I had never got used to those times when the Lord seemed to speak so directly to my mind, as I am convinced He did right then. Who else but the Lord would have asked me to forgive my husband! *Love your former husband, Bilquis. Forgive him.*

For a moment I sat in shock. Feeling His love for people in general was one thing, but to love this man who had hurt me so much?

"Father, I just can't do it. I don't want to bless Khalid or forgive him." I recalled how once I had childishly even asked the Lord not ever to convert my husband because then he would have the same joy that I had. And now God was asking me to *love* this same man? I could feel anger rising within me as I thought of Khalid, and quickly put him out of my mind. "Maybe I could just forget him, Lord. Wouldn't that be enough?"

Was it my imagination or did the glow of the Lord's Presence seem to cool? "I can't forgive my husband, Lord. I have no capacity to do so."

My yoke is easy and my burden is light (Matthew 11:30).

"Lord, I can't forgive him!" I cried. Then I listed all the terrible things he had done to me. As I did, other wounds surfaced, hurts that I had pushed into the back of my mind as too humiliating to think about. Hate welled within me and now I felt totally separated from God. Frightened, I cried out like a lost child.

And quickly, miraculously, He was there, with me in my room. Flinging myself at His feet, I confessed my hate and my inability to forgive.

My yoke is easy and my burden is light.

Slowly, deliberately, I swung my terrible burden over to Him. I let go of my resentment, my hurt, and the festering outrage, placing it all in His hands. Suddenly I sensed a light rising within me, like the glow of dawn. Breathing freely, I hurried to my dresser and took out the gold-framed picture and looked down at Khalid's face. I prayed: "Oh Father, take away my resentment and fill me with Your love for Khalid in the name of my Lord and Savior, Jesus Christ."

I stood there for a long time, looking at the picture. Slowly the negative feeling within me began to fade. In its place came an unexpected love, a sense of caring for the man in the photo. I couldn't believe it. I was actually wishing my former husband well.

"Oh bless him, Lord, give him joy, let him be happy in his new life."

As I willed this, a dark cloud lifted from me. A weight was removed from my soul. I felt peaceful, relaxed.

Once again I found myself living in His glory.

And once again I found myself wanting never to leave His company. As a reminder to myself of this desire, I went downstairs, late as it was, and found some henna dye. With it I drew a large cross on the back of both hands to remind me always.

Never, if I had anything to say about it, would I again deliberately step away from His company.

It would take me a long time, I was sure, to learn the skill of living in the glow of His Presence, but it was a training time I welcomed with immense excitement.

And then one night I had a terrifying experience. I did not know I would be hearing from another side.

7

The Baptism of Fire and Water

I had been sound asleep that night in January 1967 when I was startled awake by my bed shaking violently.

An earthquake? My heart was gripped by a nameless terror. And then I sensed a horrible malevolent presence in my room; one that was definitely evil.

Suddenly I was thrown out of my bed; whether I was in my physical body or spirit I do not know. But I was pushed and thrown about like a straw in a hurricane. The face of Mahmud flashed before me and my heart cried out for his protection.

This must be death coming for me, I thought, my soul quaking. The awful presence engulfed me like a black billowing cloud and instinctively I screamed out to the One Who now meant everything to me. "Oh Lord Jesus!" At this I was shaken mightily, as a dog ravages his prey.

"Am I wrong to call on Jesus?" I cried to God in my spirit. At this a great strength surged through me and I called out: "I *will* call on Him! Jesus! Jesus! Jesus!"

At this the powerful ravaging subsided. I lay there worshipping and praising the Lord. However, sometime around 3:00 in the morning, my eyelids became too heavy and I slipped to sleep.

I was awakened in the morning by Raisham bringing me my morning tea. I lay there for a moment feeling such a sense of relief. As I closed my eyes in prayer, I saw the Lord Jesus Christ standing before me. He wore a white robe and a purple cape. He gently smiled at me and said, "Don't worry; it won't happen again."

I felt then that my harrowing experience was Satanic, a test Jesus permitted for my own good. I recalled the cry that came from deep within my soul: "I *will* call on His Name, I *will* say Jesus Christ."

My Lord was still standing before me. *It is time for you to be baptized in water, Bilquis*, He said.

Water baptism! I had heard the words distinctly, and I didn't like what I heard.

As soon as I could I dressed and asked Nur-jan and Raisham to see that I wasn't disturbed until lunchtime. I stood at the window thinking. The morning air was cool; and pale steam drifted up from the garden springs. I knew that the significance of baptism is not lost on the Muslim world. A person can read the Bible without arousing too much hostility. But the sacrament of baptism is a different matter. To the Muslim this is the one unmistakable sign that a convert has renounced his Islamic faith to become a Christian. To the Muslim, baptism is apostasy.

So, here was a difficult testing point. The issue was clearly drawn. Would I yield to the fear of being treated as an outcast, or worse, as a traitor, or would I obey Jesus?

First of all I had to be certain that I was really obeying the Lord, and not some illusion. For I was far too new at being a Christian to trust "voices." How could I test my impression better than through the Bible. So I went back to my Bible and read how Jesus Himself had been baptized in the Jordan. And I looked again at Paul's letter to the Romans where he talked about the rite in terms of death and resurrection. The "old man" dies, and a new creature arises, leaving all his sins behind.

Well, that was that. If Jesus was baptized, and if the Bible called for baptism, then of course I would obey.

That very moment I rang for Raisham.

"Please ask Manzur to get the car ready," I said. "I'm going to visit the Olds after lunch."

Shortly I was once again seated in Marie and Ken's small living room when I burst forth in my usual way. "Ken," I said, facing him squarely, "I'm sure that the Lord has told me to be baptized."

He looked at me for a long moment, his brow furrowing, perhaps trying to fathom the depth of my intention. Then Ken leaned forward and said, very, very seriously: "Bilquis, are you prepared for what may happen?"

"Yes, but …" I started to answer. Ken interrupted, his voice low.

"Bilquis, a Pakistani I met the other day asked if I were a sweeper in my own country." He looked at me levelly. "Do you realize that from now on you would not be *the* Begum Sheikh, the respected landowner with generations of prestige? From now on you will be associated with the sweeper Christians here?"

"Yes," I answered. "I do know that."

His words became still firmer and I steeled myself to look directly at him.

"And do you know," he continued, "that Mahmud's father can easily take him away from you? He could label you an unfit guardian."

My heart was stung. I had worried about this, but hearing Ken say it aloud made the prospect sound all the more possible.

"Yes, I know, Ken," I said weakly. "I realize many people will think I am committing a crime. But I want to be baptized, I must obey God."

Our conversation was interrupted by the unexpected arrival of the Mitchells. Ken immediately told them we had something important to discuss. "Bilquis," he said, "wants to be baptized."

Silence. Synnove coughed.

"But we don't have a tank for it," said David.

"How about the church in Peshawar?" asked Marie. "Don't they have a tank?"

My heart sank. Peshawar is the capital of the North-West Frontier Province. In every sense of the word it is frontier territory, a provincial town populated by conservative Muslims noted for their quickness to take action. Well, I thought, there goes any secrecy I might want to keep. The whole town would know within an hour.

It was left that Ken would make arrangements for us to go to Peshawar. We should hear from the pastor there in a day or two.

That evening my phone rang. It was my Grand Uncle Fateh. I loved this elderly gentleman dearly. He was always so interested in my religious instruction.

"Bilquis?" My uncle's authoritative voice sounded upset.

"Yes, Uncle?"

"Is it true that you are reading a Bible?"

"Yes." I wondered how he knew. What else had he heard?

Uncle Fateh cleared his throat. "Bilquis, don't *ever* talk about the Bible with any of these Christians. You know how argumentative they are. Their arguments always lead to confusion."

I started to interrupt him but he rode over my words. "Don't invite anyone …," he emphasized "... *anyone* to your house without consulting me! If you do, you know that your family will not stand by you."

Uncle Fateh was quiet for a moment as he paused to catch his breath. I took advantage of the opening.

"Uncle, listen to me." There was a strained silence on the other end of the wire. I plunged ahead. "Uncle, as you'll remember, no one has ever entered my home without an invitation." My uncle would remember, all right; I was well known for ruthlessly refusing to see callers who had not arranged their visits beforehand.

"You know," I concluded, "that I will meet whomever I like. Goodbye, Uncle."

I hung up the phone. Was this an omen of things to come as far as the rest of my family was concerned? If Uncle Fateh reacted so strongly just hearing that I read the Bible, what would happen when he and the rest of my family learned about my baptism? I didn't like to think.

Which only added fuel to my drive to be baptized right away. I wasn't sure I *could* resist pressure from scores of people I loved.

No word came from Ken.

The next morning as I was reading the Bible, I again ran across the story of the Ethiopian eunuch to whom Philip had brought the message of God. The first thing the eunuch did, as soon as he saw water, was to jump down out of the carriage to be baptized. It was as if the Lord was telling me all over again, "Get your baptism and get it now!" I felt sure He meant that if I waited much longer, something or someone might prevent it.

I leaped from my bed, realizing with fresh power that huge forces were marshalling to block me from what the Lord wanted me to do. I put down the Bible, summoned my maids who quickly dressed me and shortly I was speeding to the Mitchells'.

"David," I said, while we were still standing in the doorway, "is there any answer from Peshawar?"

"No, not as yet."

My voice rose. "Can't you baptize me here? Today? Now?"

David frowned. He ushered me in out of the cold morning air. "Now, Bilquis, we can't be in too much of a hurry about such a big step."

"I must obey my Lord. He keeps telling me to press on." I told him about my morning Bible reading, and about the new insistence from the Lord that He wanted me baptized before anything happened to me.

David held out his hands in helplessness. "I must take Synnove up to Abbottabad this afternoon and there isn't anything I can do now, Bilquis."

He put his hand on my arm. "Be patient, Bilquis. I'm sure we'll hear from Peshawar tomorrow."

I drove over to the Olds'.

"Please," I cried as Ken and Marie greeted me, "is there any way for me to be baptized immediately?"

"We asked our pastor," Ken said, taking me by the arm and leading me into the living room. "He says the whole matter has to go through the Session."

"Session?" I echoed. "What is that?"

He explained that his pastor wanted to baptize me but he had to get approval from his church's governing board. "This could take up to several days," he added, "and meanwhile anything could happen."

"Yes," I sighed, "word *would* get out." My mind raced desperately over all the possible circumstances.

Then Ken told me an amazing thing. In the middle of the night he had heard a man's voice directing him to "*Turn to page 654 in your Bible*." What a strange way, he thought, of giving a Bible reference. It was Job 13 and 14, and the verses shone out from the page. He read the verses that had so blessed him and which seemed meant for me. They started: *Wherefore do I take my flesh in my teeth, and put my life in mine hand? Though he slay me, yet will I trust in him*.

Was I ready for even *this*, I wondered? Was my trust *that* strong? I stood up and took Ken's arm. "Give me my water baptism now. And then, though He kill me, I am ready. I'll be better off in Heaven with my Lord."

I slumped down into a chair and looked up at Ken, apologizing. "I'm sorry, Ken. I'm getting upset. But one thing I know: the Lord said I should be baptized now. I shall put it to you bluntly. Are you going to help me or not?"

Ken sat back in his chair, ran his hand through his sandy brown hair. "Of course," he said, looking at Marie. "Why don't we go to the Mitchells' and see if there isn't something we can do?"

We drove back across the winding streets of Wah. For a while we sat quietly with the Mitchells in their living room in prayer. Then Ken sighed deeply, leaned forward and spoke to all of us. "I'm sure we all agree God has been guiding Bilquis in a most unusual way up until now. And if she insists her urgency to be baptized is from God, then let us not be a hindrance to her." He turned to David. "You're going to Abbottabad. Why don't Marie and I take Bilquis up there today, meet you and Synnove, and arrange for Bilquis' baptism there this afternoon? We'll forget about Peshawar."

Suddenly, it seemed the right thing to do and we all started making preparations. I hurried home, had Raisham pack an extra set of clothes which the Olds said I would need. "Something water won't hurt," Ken said.

Yet in the midst of all this I still felt uneasy. I even sensed the waning of my closeness to the Lord. Hadn't He in so many ways given me a specific urgent instruction? Hadn't He directed me to have my water baptism *now*?

A thought flicked through my mind. I dispelled the idea. It was unthinkable.

But when the thought persisted I asked my Lord in prayer: "Would it be all right, Father God?"

And thus on January 24, 1967, began a most unusual baptism.

Raisham stood before me, in answer to my call.

"Yes, Raisham," I said again. "Please fill the tub."

She turned to her duty, a puzzled expression on her face; never had I taken a bath at this hour of the day.

Raisham announced that my tub was ready; I dismissed her. What I proceeded to do may have some theological problems. But I wasn't thinking in theological terms. I was simply trying to be obedient to a strong urge which was backed up by Scripture. I was supposed to be baptized *now*, and with the impediments that I felt marshalling themselves, I had doubts about waiting even until the afternoon.

So, because I wanted more than anything else in the world to stay in the Lord's Presence, and the way to do that was through obedience, I walked into the bathroom and stepped into the deep tub. As I sat down, water rose almost to my shoulder. I placed my hand on my own head and said loudly: "Bilquis, I baptize you in the name of the Father and of the Son and of the Holy Ghost." I pressed my head down into the water so that my whole body was totally immersed.

I arose from the water rejoicing, calling out, and praising God. "Oh Father, thank You. I'm so fortunate." I *knew* that my sins had been washed away and that I was acceptable in the sight of the Lord.

I did not try to explain to Raisham what I had done and in her usual reserved manner she pointedly did not ask. Within a few minutes I was dressed, waiting for the Olds to take me to my baptism in Abbottabad. Again I didn't know what the theology of the situation was. I did know my motives. These Christian friends had taken such care of me, helping me. They had gone through a lot for me and I didn't want to confuse matters further. I would go ahead with the baptism, although some untrained instinct told me I had already done what the Lord wanted of me. I tried to read the Bible but my Spirit rejoiced so that I was unable to concentrate. I was back in the Glory again, just as I always was when I obeyed Him explicitly, with the Bible as my only check.

"Begum Sahib, Begum Sahib?"

I looked up. It was Raisham. The Olds were downstairs, waiting.

I told Mahmud I would be away for the rest of the day. I felt it better if he were not too involved in an event that might have unpleasant consequences. Then I went down to join Ken and Marie.

It was a two-hour drive to Abbottabad, along a road that was lined with firs and pines. I didn't mention my tub baptism. Instead I told about the many times I had travelled this same road on family outings, followed by several autos piled high with luggage. Silently I wondered if I should feel disloyal to this old heritage.

We arrived at the mission to find the Mitchells waiting with a Canadian medical doctor and his wife, Bob and Madeline Blanchard, who were our hosts. Along with them stood a Pakistani man. "This gentleman," said Synnove, "is Padri Bahadur, the minister who will baptize you."

I looked around at the others, including an Anglican doctor and another Pakistani minister.

"Perhaps this is prophetic, Bilquis," said Synnove. "Perhaps through you many Christians will be drawn closer, for this may be the first time in Pakistan that Baptists and Presbyterians and Anglicans have all gotten together in a common baptism."

There was an air of excitement about the room. Doors were closed, shades were drawn and I imagined what it was like back in the first century when Christians had their baptisms in the catacombs under Rome.

As we prepared for the ceremony, I looked around and asked, "But where is the tank?"

It developed there was none. Ken said that I would have to be sprinkled.

"But Jesus was immersed in the Jordan," I said.

We had crossed a river just before arriving at the mission station. "Why not take me back to the river?" I asked; but then I remembered that it was bitterly cold and others would have to get into that water too and I didn't press the point. Especially since I was certain that I had already received the sacrament.

And so I was baptized again, this time by sprinkling. While I was being sprinkled, I thought how the Lord must be chuckling. After the ceremony, I looked up to see tears streaming down the faces of others in the room. "Well," I laughed, "all this crying certainly doesn't encourage me!"

"Oh Bilquis," sniffed Synnove, coming up to throw her arms around me. She couldn't go on.

"Congratulations," said each of the others. Synnove sang a hymn, Ken read from the Bible, and then it was time to head for home again.

It was a quiet drive. There was no anxiety amongst us; it felt good just to be with Christians. We all said goodbye again amid tears, and I went into my house.

The comfortable mood was shattered as soon as I stepped through the door. The housekeeper rushed up to me, eyes wide, anxiety in her voice.

"Oh Begum Sahib, your family has been here asking about you! They say they know that you are mixing with Christians and. . . ."

I put up my hand. "Now stop!" I commanded, silencing the chatter. "Tell me who came."

As the housekeeper recited the names of those who had come to my house that day, a new apprehension filled me. These were the senior members of my family, uncles, elderly cousins, aunts, people who would come to my house in this manner only on a vitally important concern.

My heart sank. That night I ate with Mahmud, trying not to show my own fears, but just as soon as he went to bed I retired to my own room. I looked out the filigreed window; the snow had stopped falling and under the winter moon I could make out the outlines of the garden I loved. All around me I sensed the comfort of the old house I loved so much, my sanctuary, my retreat.

And now? Would I even be able to keep my home? It was a strange thought, for I had always had the security of family, money and prestige. Yet I felt without doubt that it was also a prophetic thought. The forces which I knew to be marshalling against me had already begun to express themselves through my family. Much of my "power," much of my "security" lay in the family. What would happen if suddenly they all began, at once, to oppose me?

Surely this was the very reason the Lord insisted that I have my baptism quickly, immediately. He knew me. He knew where I was most vulnerable.

I stood there looking out the window. Shadows from swaying trees played through the filigree.

"Oh Lord," I prayed, "please don't let them descend on me all at once. Please let them come one at a time."

No sooner had I breathed these words when there was a knock at the door. The downstairs maid came in to hand me a package. "This was just delivered for you," she said. Impatiently I tore off the wrapping to find a Bible. Inscribed on the fly leaf was: *To our dear sister on her birthday*—It was signed: "Ken and Marie Old."

I held it to my breast, thanking God for such good friends. Then I opened it and my eye was attracted to a page on which these words seemed to stand out: *I will scatter them abroad.* ...

At the moment the meaning of these words was a mystery to me.

8

Was There Protection?

I awakened the next morning full of apprehension. Today the family would come again, either en masse or one at a time. Either way I dreaded the awful confrontation. I dreaded the accusations, the angry warnings, the lures and threats which I knew were coming. Above all, I hated hurting them.

Not quite believing that God would answer my request, I had Raisham bring out my finest saris, chose the most attractive, issued word to the gate servant that I would be happy to see all visitors today, and then went to the drawing room. There I sat on one of the white silk chairs and read while Mahmud played with his toy cars, weaving them in and out of the paisley design of the large Persian rug on the floor.

The giant carved clock in the hall struck ten o'clock, eleven, and finally noon. Well, I thought, it looks as if they plan an afternoon visit.

Lunch was served and then while Mahmud napped I continued waiting. At last at three o'clock I heard the sound of a car stopping outside. I was steeling myself for battle when the car drove away! What was happening? I asked the maid and she said it was just someone making a delivery.

Evening darkened the tall windows of the drawing room, and shadows gathered high on the ceiling. Then there was a phone call for me. I glanced at the clock; it was seven. Were they phoning instead of coming in person?

I picked up the phone to hear a soft voice I recognized very well—Marie Old. She sounded quite worried. Word of my conversion was certainly out already, as yesterday's invasion of relatives showed. So why the concern?

"Are you all right?" Marie said. "I've been anxious about you."

I assured her that I was fine. As soon as I hung up the phone, I called for my wraps and asked that the car be sent around. At this time of the year, my family did not normally visit after eight o'clock so I felt it was safe to leave. Odd, how not one relative had called or visited.

I wanted reassurance from one of my Christian family. The Olds? Why had Marie called so mysteriously? I drove to the Olds' house and was surprised to find it completely dark.

And then, quite unexpectedly, quite abruptly, I was alarmed. As I stood at the gate leading into their yard I could feel fear settle over me, touching me with clammy cold horror. Dark thoughts came at me from dark corners of the yard. Surely I had been foolish to come out alone at night! What was that back in the shadows? My heart raced.

I turned. I was about to run for the car.

And then I stopped. No! This was no way to be acting. If I were a part of the Kingdom, I had a right to the King's protection. Standing there in the awesome darkness, still very much afraid, I deliberately willed myself back into the King's hands. "Jesus. Jesus. Jesus." I said over and over again. Incredibly the fear lifted. As soon as it had come, it was gone. I was free!

Almost smiling now, I turned toward the Olds' house. After a few paces, I saw a crack of light coming between two drawn curtains in the living room. I knocked.

The door slowly opened. It was Marie. When she saw me she gave a sigh of relief and quickly drew me into the house and hugged me.

"Ken! Ken!" she called.

He was there in a moment. "Oh thank God!" he exclaimed. "We were quite worried about you." Ken told me that the Pakistani Padri at my baptism had become quite concerned for my safety and had told them that they had made a mistake in leaving me alone.

"So, that's why you were so concerned on the phone, Marie!" I suppressed a nervous laugh. "Well, I expect the whole country will soon know about my conversion, but thank you anyhow. So far, nothing has happened. Even my family didn't show up and you can't know how grateful I am for that answer to prayer."

"Let's thank the Lord," Ken said, and the three of us knelt together in their living room as Ken thanked God for my protection and asked Him to continue to watch over me.

So, I returned home, the richer for having called on God's help in the face of fear by taking advantage of the Name of

Jesus. My servants said there had not been a phone call all that evening. Well, I thought as I prepared for bed, watch out for tomorrow.

Again, I waited in the drawing room all day, praying, thinking, studying the white mosaic floor tiles and the paisley print of the Persian rugs. There was not a word from anyone.

What was going on? Was this some kind of a cat and mouse game?

And then I thought to check with the servants. In Pakistan if you want to know anything, ask a household servant. Through an uncanny grapevine, they know everything about everybody.

Finally, I pinned down my handmaid Nur-jan: "Tell me, what happened to my family?"

"Oh Begum Sahib," she answered, suppressing a nervous giggle, "the strangest thing happened. It was as if everybody was busy at once. Your brother had to go to the annual Winter Cricket Tournament." I smiled; to my brother, cricket was more important than a sister who was on her way to hell. "Your Uncle Fateh had to go out of the province on a court case; your Aunt Amina needed to go to Lahore; two of your cousins were called out of town on business, and …"

I stopped her; she need not go on any further. The Lord had said He would scatter them and scatter them He did. I could almost hear my Lord chuckle. It wasn't, I felt sure, that the concerned members of my family would leave me alone, but now they would come one by one.

And so it was. The first emissary was my Aunt Amina, a regal woman in her seventies whose eastern beauty somehow always looked out of place in my drawing room with its modern western furniture. For years we had a close relationship of love and trust. Now as she walked in, her magnolia complexion was paler than usual and her gray eyes were rimmed with sadness.

We chatted a bit. Finally I could tell she was coming to the real reason for her visit. Clearing her throat, she sat back and, trying to sound casual, asked: "Er … Bilquis … uh … I have heard … that you have become a Christian. Is it true?"

I only smiled at her.

She shifted uneasily in her chair and continued. "I thought people were spreading false rumors about you." She hesitated, her soft eyes imploring me to say that it wasn't true.

"It is no lie, Aunt Amina," I said. "I have made a complete commitment to Christ. I have been baptized. I am now a Christian."

She slapped her hands over her cheeks. "Oh, what a great mistake!" she cried. She sat very still for a moment, unable to add anything. Then, slowly gathering her shawl around her, she stood and with frozen dignity walked out of my house.

I was crushed, but I asked the Lord to protect her from the devastating hurt she was feeling. I knew I had to discover His own prayer for my family. Otherwise, I would leave a swath of damaged loved ones behind me. "Lord," I said, "the ideal thing of course would be to have every one of these people come to know You. But I know that if they aren't converted, I know You still love them, and right now I ask that You touch each of these dear ones of mine with Your special blessing, starting, if You will, with my Aunt Amina. Thank You, Lord!"

Next day I had to say the same prayer. This time it was for Aslam, a dear elderly male cousin who came to see me. A lawyer, he lived about 45 miles from Wah. As the son of my father's brother, he had inherited many of my father's characteristics, the same warm smile, the gentle sense of humor. I was fond of

Aslam. From his attitude, I was sure that he had not heard the full particulars of my problem. We exchanged a few pleasantries, and then Aslam said:

"When is the family meeting? I'll pick you up and we'll go together."

I chuckled. "I don't know when the family meeting will be, Aslam, but I do know that I'll not be invited because the meeting is about me."

He looked so confused I knew that I had to explain everything. "But please go to the meeting, Aslam," I said, when I had finished. "Maybe you can put in a good word for me."

I watched him sadly make his way out of the house; it was obvious, I thought, that a climax was approaching. I had better get to Rawalpindi and Lahore as soon as possible. I didn't want Tooni and my son Khalid to hear garbled stories about me. There was nothing I could do in person about my daughter Khalida, for she lived in Africa. But I could face Khalid and Tooni. The very next day I set off for Lahore. Khalid had done quite well in business, and his home reflected it. A lovely town bungalow, it was surrounded by wide verandas and an immaculately groomed lawn.

We drove through his gate, parked by the entrance and walked up onto the broad veranda. Khalid well alerted by family and by a long phone call from me, hurried out to greet me. "Mother! How glad I am to see you," he said, though I sensed he welcomed me with a little embarrassment. We talked all that afternoon about what I had done, but in the end I knew Khalid did not understand at all.

Next I had to see Tooni. I drove to Rawalpindi and went straight to the hospital. I asked that Tooni be paged, and as I waited I wondered how I should go about telling her. Doubtless she had been hearing stories already. She certainly was aware firsthand that I had been reading the Bible. She may even have overheard fragments of my conversation with the Catholic nun, Dr. Santiago, in this same hospital when Mahmud had been admitted. One thing she surely did *not* know: how life-changing that visit with Dr. Santiago had been, for it was this little nun who encouraged me to pray to God as my Father.

"Mother!" I looked up to see Tooni hurrying toward me, her chestnut hair in stark contrast to her white starched uniform, her face beaming, her arms outstretched.

I rose, my heart pounding. How was I going to break the news to her! I tried to think of gentle ways, but the fear of pressure from Tooni was too much. Without daring to be circumspect, I blurted it out. "Tooni," I said, "be prepared for a shock, dear. Two days ago I was … I was *baptized.*"

Tooni froze, her hand half extended, her sensitive eyes filling with tears. She slumped on the couch next to me. "I thought it would be coming to this," she said in a voice I could hardly hear.

I tried to comfort her, with no success. "There's no point in pretending to work," Tooni said. So she got permission to leave early and together we drove over to her apartment. Tooni's phone was ringing as she unlocked the door; she rushed in, picked the receiver up, and turned to me. "It's Nina." This was a niece who also lived in Rawalpindi. "She wants to know if it's true." She turned back to the phone as Nina had evidently started talking again; even from where I stood I could hear Nina's voice rising. Then Tooni said softly: "Yes, it's true Nina. She's done it." Nina must have slammed down the phone, because Tooni took the receiver from her ear, looked at it, shrugged, and slowly replaced it on its cradle. It would be best to give her time to collect her thoughts. So I collected my things.

"Come see me, darling," I said, "when you feel you can. We'll talk." Tooni made no objections at all, so within minutes I was on the Grand Trunk Road headed home. The minute I arrived home my servants clustered around me. Nur-jan was wringing her plump hands and even Raisham's face was paler than usual. The phone had been ringing all day, relatives had been at the gate since early morning asking for me. Even as the servants chattered, the phone rang again. It was my sister's husband, Jamil, who worked with a British oil firm. I had always thought of Jamil as a man of the world, but now his voice didn't sound very self-assured.

"Bilquis, I have heard the strangest thing and cannot believe it," he said bluntly. "A business friend told me that he heard you had become a Christian. Of course, I laughed at him and assured him that could never happen."

Word really was spreading rapidly. I said nothing.

"Bilquis!" Jamil's voice was insistent. "Did you *hear* me?"

"Yes."

"That story isn't true is it?"

"Yes."

There was another silence. Then: "Well, that's nice," Jamil snapped. "You've just lost more than you can know. And for what? For just another religious viewpoint. That's what." He hung up.

In ten minutes Tooni was on the phone sobbing. "Mama, Uncle Nawaz just called to say that now Mahmud's father will be able to get him back. Nawaz says no court will allow you to keep him!"

I tried to comfort her but she hung up sobbing.

Late that evening while Mahmud and I were dining in my bedroom, Tooni and two of my nieces came to the house. I was startled by their ashen faces.

"Please sit down and join me," I said. "I'll have the servants bring your meal up."

Tooni and my nieces just picked at their food. I was happy to see the two young girls, but it was clear they weren't happy to see me. The conversation was trite and all three women kept glancing at Mahmud and making oblique suggestions that he go away to play. It was only after he finally did leave that one of the nieces leaned forward anxiously.

"Auntie, do you realize what this means for *other* people?" She broke into tears. "Have you thought of anybody else?" Her question was echoed in the brown eyes of my other niece who sat silently across from me.

I reached across the table and took the girl's slim hand. "My dear," I said sorrowfully. "There is nothing I can do but to be obedient."

Tooni now looked at me through tearful eyes and, as if she had not heard a word I said, begged me. "Mother, pack up and leave. Leave while there's something … or some-*one* … to leave with."

Her voice rose. "Do you know what people are saying? You'll be attacked. Your own brother may be compelled to take action against you!" And then she broke down sobbing. "My friends say you'll be murdered, Mommy!"

"I'm sorry, Tooni, but I'm not going to run away," I answered gently. "If I leave now I'll be running for the rest of my life." Determination rose within me as I spoke. "If He wishes, God can easily take care of me in my own house. And no one, *no one*," I said, "is going to push me out." I sat up in my chair, suddenly feeling very dramatic. "Let them come and attack!"

And then, as I sat there feeling so fiercely sure of myself, something happened. The warm personal Presence of God was gone. I sat, almost in panic, oblivious to the voices rising around me. But just as suddenly I realized what had happened. The old me, full of pride and stubbornness, had taken over. *I* was deciding what would happen, that no one would push me out of my home.

I sank back in my chair, barely aware that Tooni was speaking to me.

"… all right, then, Mommy," Tooni cried. "So you've become a Christian. Must you become a Christian martyr also?" She knelt by my chair and laid her head on my shoulder. "Don't you realize that we love you?"

"Of course, dear, of course," I murmured, stroking her hair. Silently I asked His forgiveness for being so headstrong. Wherever He wanted me to go was fine, even if it meant leaving my house. As I said this in my heart I once again felt the Presence of the Father. The whole exchange had taken but a few minutes, but even as the three women sitting in front of me continued talking, I was aware that life was going on at another level too. The Lord was right then, at that moment, working with me, teaching me. He was in the very process of showing me how to stay in His Presence.

"… so we will, then? All right?" It was Tooni's voice and I had no idea what she was asking me to agree to. Fortunately she went on. "If Mahmud's father comes after him, you can let me take him. I haven't become a Christian," she added pointedly.

Eventually the three girls quieted down. I asked them if they wouldn't like to spend the night and they agreed. As I bid Tooni and my nieces goodnight, I thought how our roles had changed. Once I was so protective and worried over them; now we were equally worried for each other. That night I prayed: "Lord, it's so difficult to talk to a person who doesn't have faith in You. Please help my family. I'm so worried for the welfare of my loved ones."

As I drifted off to sleep, I again seemed to have left my body as if floating. I found myself standing on a grassy slope surrounded by pine trees. A spring bubbled near me. All about me were angels, so many that they seemed to form a hazy mist. I kept hearing one name, "Saint Michael!". The angels gave me courage. And then I was back in bed. I got up and, still sensing this spiritual strength, went to Mahmud's room. I pointed to him in his bed and then went to my daughter's and nieces' rooms and did the same. I went back to my bedroom and got down on my knees. "Lord," I prayed, "You have shown me so many answers, now show me, I pray, what You are going to do with Mahmud. I would like to give Tooni some assurance."

I felt urged to open my Bible and this passage leaped up from the page: Genesis 22:12—"Lay not thine hand upon the lad, neither do thou anything unto him. …"

"Oh, thank You Father," I sighed.

At breakfast I was able to assure Tooni. "Darling, nothing is going to happen to your son; you never need worry." I showed her the Scripture given to me. Whether my faith was contagious or Tooni was touched by the Holy Spirit, I don't know. But her face did relax and she smiled for the first time in two days.

My daughter and nieces left my house on a somewhat less somber note that day. But the flow of other relatives and friends continued.

A few days later Raisham announced that there were *seven* people, all very dear concerned friends downstairs wanting to see me. I didn't want to face them without Mahmud. The boy should know everything that was going on. So I found him and together we went downstairs to the drawing room. There they sat in straight-backed formality far forward on their chairs. After the tea and cakes and small talk, one of those present cleared his throat. I steeled myself for what I knew was coming.

"Bilquis," said a friend I'd known since childhood, "we love you and we have been thinking over this thing you have done and we have a suggestion which we think will be of help to you."

"Yes?"

He leaned forward and smiled.

"Don't declare your Christianity publicly."

"You mean keep my faith a secret?"

"Well …"

"I can't," I said. "I can't play games with God. If I must die, I die."

All seven of them seemed to edge closer to me. An old friend of my father glared at me. I was about to glare back but caught myself. They thought they had my welfare at heart.

"I'm sorry," I said, "I just can't do what you ask." I explained that my faith had quickly, in little more than a month, become the most important thing in my life. "I cannot keep quiet about it," I said. I quoted them the Scripture where the Lord says: "Every man who publicly acknowledges me I shall acknowledge in the presence of my Father in Heaven, but the man who disowns me before men I shall disown before my Father in Heaven" (Matthew 10:32, 33).

"But," said another elderly gentleman, "you are in a very peculiar situation. I'm sure your God wouldn't mind if you kept quiet. He knows you believe in Him. That's enough." He quoted the Koran law on apostasy. "We're afraid," he said, "that someone will kill you."

I smiled but no one else was smiling. It was a pointless discussion, as they saw. When they rose to go I was given my ultimatum.

"Remember, Bilquis, if you get into trouble, none of your friends or family can stand by you. The ones who care the most will have to turn their backs on you."

I nodded. I well understood their words. I wished now that I had sent Mahmud out to play in the garden so that he would have heard none of this. When I looked at him, though, sitting on his little chair beside me, he just smiled. "It's all right," he seemed to be saying.

There were near tears as the group prepared to leave. A close friend of my mother kissed me. "Goodbye," she said. She repeated the word with a strange emphasis. Then she broke into tears, pulled herself away and hurried out the door.

The house seemed like a tomb after they left. Even Mahmud's usual noisy play was subdued.

Three weeks passed when the only sound in my house was the hushed voices of servants. If it weren't for the Mitchells and the Olds and for our regular Sunday evening meetings, I wonder if the freeze-out might not have worked.

Each day the family battle line was seen more clearly. I saw it in the anger on the face of a cousin I met in the bazaar. I felt it in the scornful glance of a nephew I passed on the street in Rawalpindi. It was there in the cold voice of an aunt who called to say that she wouldn't keep a luncheon appointment. The boycott had begun. My phone remained silent, and no one pulled the bell cord at my gate. Not one member of the family came to call, even to scold. I could not help but recall a verse from the Koran (Sura 74–20): *If you renounced the faith, you would surely do evil in the land and violate the ties of blood. Such are those on whom Allah has laid His curse leaving them bereft of sight and hearing.*

In a very real way this was happening. I had violated the ties of blood and I undoubtedly would not see or hear from my family anymore.

The normal chatter and laughter of the servants had quieted as they slipped in and out of my rooms. I could hardly get them to talk to me beyond the usual, "Yes, Begum Sahib."

And then one morning the boycott took a strange turn. There was a soft click of my door and I turned to see Nurjan quietly enter to minister my toilette. It was so unlike her usual exuberance. Raisham stepped in even more solemn than usual. As they proceeded to their tasks, they did not speak and I was bothered by the haunted look on both of their faces.

I waited for some word but Nur-jan continued her tasks silently, without the usual gossip or chatter. Raisham's face was graven. Finally, with a little of the old fire in my voice, I said:

"All right, I can tell something is wrong. Tell me about it."

The brushing halted as I heard the news. Except for Raisham, standing before me now, all of my Christian servants, including Manzur, had fled my house in the middle of the night.

9

The Boycott

What did it mean, this defection? Four servants quitting! In a town like Wah where any job was hard to come by, their decisions were hard to understand.

It was fear of course. Manzur was afraid because I asked him to get me a Bible and had him drive me to the home of missionaries. The other three Christian servants must have picked up his concern. They must have heard the rumblings of a volcano which would soon erupt and didn't want to be caught in the overflow.

But what about Raisham, this Christian servant who now began to brush my hair again? I could feel her graceful hands tremble as she started her work.

"And you?" I asked.

She bit her lip as she continued her brushing. "I probably shouldn't stay," she said softly. "It's going to be …"

"Very lonely," I concluded her statement.

"Yes," she said, swallowing, "and …"

"And you're afraid. Well, if you left, Raisham, I wouldn't blame you. You have to make up your own mind, just as I did. If you do stay though, remember that Jesus *told* us we would be persecuted for His sake."

Raisham nodded, her dark eyes moist. She took a hairpin out of her mouth and proceeded to do up my hair. "I know," she said sadly.

Raisham was quiet the rest of the day. Her concern affected Nur-jan who was approaching quiet hysteria. The next morning when I awakened I could hardly bring myself to ring the little bell. Who would be with me now? My bedroom door opened slowly and Nur-jan came in. Then, in the near darkness of winter's early hours another form followed. It was Raisham!

Later, I told her how much I appreciated her staying. She blushed. "Begum Sahib Gi," she answered softly, adding the affectionate third salutation which means, May you have long life, "as you serve the Lord, so I will serve you."

With the rest of my Christian servants gone, my house became even quieter, partly because I did not replace them all. My needs were simpler now that no family came by. I decided not to rehire Christians for a while. I found a new chauffeur, a Muslim named Fazad and a new Muslim cook's assistant, but I hired no one else. I was especially glad for Mahmud who continued to play happily in the house or garden. I encouraged him to invite friends over from the village, which suggestion Mahmud accepted quickly. Most of the children were slightly older, five or six, while Mahmud was still only five. But Mahmud nevertheless was their natural leader; I didn't think it was simply that he was their host, rather that seven hundred years of leadership was in the child's genes and could no more be denied than could his limpid brown eyes.

How much of this heritage was I putting in jeopardy? How much of the boy's rightful family ties was I threatening? Just yesterday he had asked again when his cousin Karim was going to take him fishing. Karim had promised to teach Mahmud the mysteries of catching the trout that slipped among the mossy rocks of our garden stream which joined the Tahmra River.

"Mum!" Mahmud had asked. "When is Karim going to come?"

I looked down at the boy whose eyes were shining, and I just didn't have the heart to tell him that his fishing party would never take place. Mahmud could not have been very drawn to Christianity so far. I read him Bible stories which he loved so much that I moved his bedtime from 8:00 to 7:30 so we could have plenty of time for them. But what were a few stories compared with a fishing trip. And friends. For bit by bit Mahmud's friends began to stop coming over. Mahmud couldn't understand this, and when I tried to explain it to him he looked at me in puzzlement.

"Mum," he said, "who do you love better, me or Jesus?"

What should I say! Especially right now when he was lonely. "God has to come first, Mahmud." I said, paraphrasing the Lord's warning that unless we put family after Him, we are not truly His own. "We have to put God first," I said, "even before the people we love most in the world."

Mahmud *seemed* to accept this. He *seemed* to be listening when I read him the Bible. Once, after I had read to him, "Come unto me all ye who are heavy laden and I will give you rest," I heard his nap-time pleas: "Jesus, I love You and I will come unto You, but … please don't give me rest. I don't like resting." He would even fold his hands and pray, but I knew that it was hard on him being alone and seeing me alone. Not one relative, friend or acquaintance turned off of the Grand Trunk Road any more toward my house; never did the phone ring.

Then at 3:00 one morning my white bedside phone did clamor. I reached toward the instrument, my heart pounding. No one would call at this hour unless there had been a death in the family. I picked up the phone and at first heard only heavy breathing. Then three words were thrown at me like stones:

"Infidel. Infidel. Infidel."

The phone went dead. I lay back on my bed. Who was it? One of the fanatics my uncles constantly warned me about? What might they do?

"Oh Lord, You know that I don't mind dying. But I'm an awful coward. I cannot stand pain. You know how I faint when the doctor gives me a needle. Oh, I pray that I will be able to bear pain if it comes." Tears filled my eyes. "I guess I'm not made of the stuff of martyrs, Lord. I'm sorry. Just let me walk with You through whatever comes next."

What did come next was a threatening, anonymous letter. "Let's be clear. There is only one word to describe you. Traitor." Then there was another letter and shortly still another. They all contained warnings. I was a turncoat and I would be treated as such.

Late one afternoon in the early summer of 1967, about six months after my conversion, I stood in my garden with the crumpled remains of one such letter in my fist. It was particularly vitriolic, calling me worse than an infidel, a seducer of the faithful. True believers, the letter said, had to burn me out like gangrene was burned out of a healthy limb.

Burn me out? Was this more than just a figure? I walked further into the garden, around which glowed beds of tulips, hyacinth and alyssum. Spring had blossomed into summer. Quinces flourished in the garden, and the last of the white petals were falling from the pear trees. I turned and looked back at my house. "They wouldn't touch my house!" I exclaimed inwardly. They wouldn't burn out a Begum! But, as if to confirm that I could no longer count on the protection of position and wealth, a caller came to pay me a visit. He was announced by a servant.

"General Amar is waiting to see you, Begum," she said.

My heart jumped. I looked through the garden gate and sure enough, there stood a familiar olive drab command car. General Amar was a dear old friend from my Army days. During World War II, I had been associated with him and now he was a top general in the Pakistani Army. We had kept in touch with each other through the years, particularly when my husband was Minister of the Interior and worked closely with him. Was he, too, coming to condemn me?

Soon I could hear his footsteps crunching on the pathway of the garden as he strode to meet me, all spit and polish in a natty khaki uniform, jodhpurs and leather boots. He took my hand, leaned over and kissed it. My apprehension lessened; evidently he was not on a mission of battle.

He looked at me, his dark eyes glinting humorously. As always the General came right to the point. "Is it true what people are saying?"

"Yes," I said.

"What made you do this?" he exclaimed. "You've put yourself in a very dangerous situation! I've heard rumors that some people want to kill you!"

I looked at him silently.

"All right," he added as he sat down on a garden bench, his leather belt creaking. "You know I'm like a brother to you?"

"I hope so."

"And, as a brother, I feel fondly protective toward you?"

"I hope so."

"Then, remember that my home is always open to you."

"I smiled. This was the first kind thing anyone had said to me."

"*But*," the general went on to say, "there is something you should know. That offer is a personal one." He reached over to a blossom, pulled it to him and sniffed it, then turned back to me, adding, "Officially, there wouldn't be much I could do, Bilquis."

"I know." I took the General's hand, we got up together, strolled onto the terrace and inside the house. As we walked I told him things had not been easy.

"And they won't get easier, my dear," my friend said in his matter of fact way. Later, after I had ordered tea in the drawing room, he asked with a quizzical smile: "Tell me, Bilquis, why did you do it?"

I explained what had happened and found that General Amar was listening carefully. How extraordinary! Here I was, without realizing it, doing what the missionaries called *witnessing*. I was speaking about Christ to a Muslim, and a high official at that. And he was listening! I doubt that I really reached General Amar that afternoon but he was in a reflective mood half an hour later when he bid me goodbye in the summer twilight, again pressing his lips to my hand.

"Remember, Bilquis," he said huskily, "anytime you need my help … anything I can do as a friend …"

"Thank you, Amar," I said.

He turned, his boot heels clicked down the hallway tiles and out into the early evening darkness to his waiting command car. And our solitary, strangely sad, visit was over. "I wonder if I'll ever see him again," I thought.

For the first time during this boycott, during the anonymous letters and phone calls, during the warnings of old friends, I was learning what it was to live from hour to hour. It was the opposite of worrying. It was waiting to see *what He was going to allow*. For I was convinced that nothing occurred without His permission. I knew, for instance, that pressure against me must become more intense. If that did happen, then He would have allowed it and I must learn to search for His Presence in the midst of seeming disaster. I would just live hour to hour, staying near Him. Yes, that was my key. Learn to keep His company, so that whatever happened, whenever it happened, I would still be in His glory.

With the increasing family pressure, I thought I knew how King David felt when, fleeing from his son, Absalom, he picked up his lyre and sang: "*But thou, O Lord, art a shield for me; my glory ...*" (Psalms 3:3). The glory which, I understand, he considered the unspeakable blessedness, joy, and felicity of the saints in heaven.

For the moment the pressure from my family was, still, the boycott. Not one member of the family came to call, even to scold. With rare exceptions none of my old friends called either. The sneers in the marketplace continued. So did the calculated exclusion from great moments in the family: births, deaths, weddings. Whenever I allowed myself to dwell on the loneliness this caused, I'd feel the glory begin to fade, and immediately I'd turn my thoughts by a sheer act of will to the times Jesus too had felt lonely.

It helped. But I found, a little to my surprise, that I desperately needed simple companionship. I who had been so aloof was now in need of closeness. Not even the Olds and the Mitchells came to the house anymore. For their own protection I advised them not to visit me.

One gray afternoon I retreated to my bedroom to read the Bible. It was unusually cold for early summer. A sharp wind rattled my windows. As I started to read, I felt a warmth on my hand and looked down to see a patch of sunlight resting on my arm. I glanced out of the window just in time to see the sun disappear again behind the clouds. For just one minute, it seemed He had reached down and touched my hand for comfort.

I looked up, "Oh my Lord," I said. "I am so lonely; even my cheeks feel dried up from lack of talking. Please send someone to talk to today."

Feeling somewhat foolish for asking for such a childlike thing, I returned to my Bible. After all, I had His company and that should be enough. But in a little while I was startled to hear an odd sound in the house, odd since it had been absent so long. There were voices downstairs.

I threw on my robe and flew out into the hall to meet Nur-jan running toward my room out of breath. "Oh, Begum Sahib," she squealed, "the Olds are here."

"Praise God," I exclaimed and hurried to meet them. Of course I saw Ken and Marie at our Sunday services in their house, but this was different, a midweek call. Marie rushed to me, taking my hand. "We just had to see you, Bilquis," she said, her blue eyes sparkling. "For no reason at all except we love being with you."

What a visit that was. I realized as we talked that I had been making a mistake not asking people over to visit me. Pride had kept me from admitting the need. Suddenly I had an inspiration. Why not invite people to my house on Sunday for the meetings? But wouldn't this be heaping gunpowder on the flames? I tried to quench the thought but it would not go away. Just as my friends were about to leave I said, quickly:

"Would you like to come here this Sunday night?"

The Olds looked at me a bit shocked.

"I mean it," I said, extending my hands sideways. "This old house needs some life."

And so it was decided.

That evening as I prepared to retire, I thought how wonderfully the Lord provides for us. When my family and friends were taken from me, He replaced them with His own family and friends. I slept peacefully and awakened to the feel of a warm sun streaming through my window. I got up and opened the window, reveling in the soft breeze that drifted in. In its earthy garden aroma I could smell the warm breath of the full summer now upon us.

I couldn't wait for Sunday evening to come. By Saturday afternoon that old house was filled with flowers; every floor, every window was scrubbed until it shone. I hinted to Raisham that she might like to join us but she became a bit flustered; she was not ready for such a bold step yet and I didn't press.

Sunday crept by while I kept Mahmud out of the drawing room, straightened the Persian carpet, constantly rearranged the flowers, and found a speck of dust here and there to wipe away. But at last I heard the gate open and cars crunch up the drive.

The evening was everything I had hoped for, with song and prayer and telling each other what the Lord was doing. Just twelve of us, plus Mahmud, sitting around comfortably in the drawing room, but I'd have sworn there were a thousand other guests too, unseen, welcome.

The evening had another peculiar purpose too, one I had not foreseen. It turned out that my Christian friends were still quite worried for me.

"Are you being extra careful?" It was Marie talking.

"Well," I laughed, "there is not much I can do. If someone wants to harm me, I'm sure he'll find a way."

Ken looked around the drawing room and out the large glass doors into the garden. "You really *don't* have much protection here," he said. "I hadn't quite realized how vulnerable you are."

"How about your bedroom?" asked Synnove. Everyone felt it wise to look over my room, so we all trooped up. Ken was particularly concerned by the windows, looking out on the garden; they were protected only by a glass pane and filigree screen.

He shook his head. "It really isn't safe, you know. You should do something about it, Bilquis; have some kind of heavy metal grill installed. Anyone could get through this."

I said I would see to it the next day.

Was it my imagination or did His glory fade just a little as I made the promise?

Eventually we said goodbye and I retired happier than I had been in a long time. The next day, however, as I was about to send for the ironworker in the village, I was once again aware of the quickly receding glory of the Lord. Why? Was it because I was about to take an action that was based on fear? It certainly did seem that every time I started to call the ironworker my action was stopped.

And then I realized why. When word got around the village that I was having my window barred, everyone would realize that I was fearful. I could just hear the gossip. "Ha! What kind of religion is Christianity, anyway. When you become a Christian you become fearful?" No. I decided, I would not have the window barred.

That night I went to bed confident that I had made the right decision. I fell asleep at once but suddenly I was awakened by a sound. I sat up, startled, but without fear. Before me appeared a breathtaking sight.

Through the walls of my room, in a supernatural way, I could see my whole garden. It was flooded with a heavenly white light. I could see every rose petal, every tree leaf, every blade of grass, every thorn. And over the garden hung a calm serenity. In my heart I heard my Father saying, "You did the right thing, Bilquis. I am with you."

Slowly the light faded and the room was dark again. I switched on my bedside lamp, lifted my arms and praised God. "Oh Father, how can I thank You enough? You have so much concern for each of us."

The next morning I called all of my servants together and told them that they could sleep in their own homes from now on if they chose to do so. Only Mahmud and I would sleep in the big house. The servants exchanged glances, some in surprise, some in joy, one or two in alarm. But I knew one thing at least had been accomplished. The decision put an end to any thought of protecting myself. And with the decision the glory came back and stayed for a longer time than usual. Perhaps this was necessary for the next turn of events.

One morning when Raisham was brushing my hair she remarked casually: "I hear that your Aunt's son, Karim, has died."

I shot out of my chair and looked at her incredulously. "No," I gasped. Not Karim, who was supposed to take Mahmud fishing! He was one of my favorites! What had happened? Why did I have to find out about even Karim's death through the servants! With steely willpower I got control of myself and forced my body back down into the chair so that Raisham could go on with her work. But my mind raced on. This could be just a rumor, I thought. Raisham could have mistaken the name. My heart rose a little. Later, I asked an elderly member of the staff to find out for me what had really happened. She went into the village and in an hour returned, downcast.

"I am sorry, Begum Sahib," she said. "But it is true. He died last night from a heart attack and the funeral is today."

Then, this servant who had a facility for learning everything, gave me news that hurt even more. My aunt, the servant told me, knowing how much I loved her son, had specifically asked my family to "be sure and tell Bilquis that my boy has died." No one followed her wishes.

Later I sat at my window pondering it all. I had been excluded from family events for six months, but never had the boycott hurt as it did now.

As I sat rocking softly I began to pray for His help and, as always, the help came. This time it was as if a warm cloak were placed gently on my shoulders. And with that sensation came an unusual plan of action. The very idea shocked me. It was so bold I knew it must be of the Lord.

10

Learning to Live in the Glory

As I sat at the window overlooking my garden, where Karim and I had played as children, a strong monsoon wind blowing up from India bent the tops of the trees. In it I seemed to be catching an extraordinary message which I could not believe I was correctly hearing.

"You can't really be telling me that Lord," I said smiling. "I'm just hearing voices! You don't want me to go to *Karim's funeral*. It would be unseemly. It would be in poor taste. I would end up offending people who are in mourning."

Even as I objected, I recognized once again the sense of His Presence beginning to fade. Immediately, with this sign, I began to wonder if perhaps I really were being told to do this extraordinary thing, to go straight into the face of the hostilities of the boycott.

Finally, breathing a deep sigh, I got up from my place at the window, shrugged and said aloud, "I'm beginning to learn,

Lord. My sense of the right thing to do is nothing compared with Yours! I'll go, since You are telling me to go."

And, of course, the sense of His Presence returned.

What an extraordinary series of experiences I was having with this coming and going of His glory. Still, I had the feeling that I was just on the verge of understanding what this was all about. How would I be able to learn to stay in His Presence for an ever increasing percentage of time? I did not realize that over the next two months I was to have a series of experiences which would take me a step further in this learning process.

I stood in the cobblestone lane in front of Karim's house, hesitating. In spite of my promise to obey, I felt as if I were a lonesome dove being thrown to a thousand cobras. Taking a deep breath I headed toward the stone house which stood among others like it. I walked into the courtyard and stepped onto the veranda, subject to the stares of the village people who were sitting around quietly. I went inside the old-fashioned house with its carved ceilings and white plastered walls where Karim and I had so often laughed, played and romped together.

There was no laughter now. On top of the gloom of the family in mourning was added the chill of a score of contemptuous glances directed my way. I looked toward a cousin with whom I had been very close. Our eyes met for a minute; my cousin quickly turned her head and began talking with a neighbor.

Now squaring my shoulders I stepped into the living room of Karim's house, then sat down on one of the thick cotton mattresses which had been placed on the floor surrounded by bolsters and cushions to lean on. I smoothed the sari around my legs. Suddenly people seemed to wake up, realizing who I was. The quiet soothing conversation that had filled the room suddenly halted. Even the women saying their beads, each bead signifying a prayer to Allah, ceased and looked up. The room, which had been hot with the early summer heat and with the scores of bodies packed shoulder to shoulder, suddenly seemed chilled.

I said nothing, made no attempt to be sociable, simply lowered my own eyes and said my own prayers. "Lord Jesus," I whispered to my heart, "do be with me as I represent You to this group of dear friends and relatives who are so saddened by Karim's death."

After fifteen minutes the quiet flow of conversation began again. It was time to pay my respects to Karim's wife. Holding my head high, I arose from the mattress and stepped into the adjoining room where Karim's body lay in its tall, deep coffin, structured according to the Muslim belief that a dead person must be able to sit up when the angels came to question him before he enters heaven. I gave my condolences to Karim's wife, then looked at the quiet face of my dear cousin shrouded in the new white cotton burial cloth and whispered to myself a prayer to Jesus for this man's spirit. Oh, how I wished I had been able to talk to him before he died.

A low humming filled the room as close family members prayed for Karim. The ladies stood and read verses from the Koran. It was all part of the life and death rhythm which I knew so well. I was turning my back on it all. Before sunset today, there would be a procession to the cemetery with all of the family following the bier. At the grave side the pallbearers would place the coffin on the ground and the priest would call out, *God is most great. Lord, this is Thy servant, the son of Thy servant. He used to testify that there is no God but Thee, and that Muhammad is Thy servant and Thy messenger. …*

As I stood listening to the soft moaning in the room, I saw Karim's mother kneeling at the bier. She looked so forlorn, I suddenly felt an overwhelming urge to go to her side. Did I dare? Would it be an affront? Should I say anything to her about Jesus? Probably not. Just my being there as a Christian was bringing Jesus to her side in a caring way.

So I stepped over to Karim's mother and put my arms around her, telling her in a soft crooning voice how sorry I was. "Karim and I were so close. May God bless you and comfort you." Karim's mother turned her face to me. Her dark tear-filled eyes thanked me and I knew that Jesus was even then comforting her sorrow-filled heart.

But Karim's mother was the only one in the room who seemed to accept what I was doing. As I left her and returned to sit down among the mourners, one male cousin—a close one too—made quite a show of rising to his feet and shuffling out of the room. Another cousin followed. And then another.

I sat there struggling with the emotions of my own sorrow for Karim and his family on the one hand and with this deep embarrassment on the other. My heart pounded. The hostility was reaching through my protection. It was all I could do to keep seated for the appropriate amount of time until I could stand, make my goodbyes and walk out of the room. Finally when I did leave I felt every eye in the household staring at me.

In my car I sat for a moment at the wheel, trying to collect myself. I had obeyed, but the cost was high. Certainly I would prefer to have remained at home rather than walk right straight into the maw of this open anger.

If I thought I would have to walk through this valley only once I was wrong. A few weeks later, just as midsummer's heat was beginning to settle over our district, another cousin died. Again, I heard of his death through my household. Again, obeying the Lord's direction, I found myself reluctantly walking into a room full of mourners, to the chilly discord of hate. As an act of will I focused my concern away from myself and toward the one person there who was really bereaved, my cousin's widow. She had a child just going on five, the same age as Mahmud. She looked so forlorn standing by herself at the coffin that I wept for her and for her husband.

And then just as I had done at Karim's funeral, I found myself being propelled toward this desperate woman. As I approached our eyes met, and I saw hesitation cross her tear-stained face. Then, with a look of sudden determination, knowingly going against the will of her family, she extended her hand to me. As I held her brown and shaking hand in my own I wept in silence. We exchanged only one or two words, but my heart was praying fervently that the Holy Spirit would reach into her bereavement and keep His promise, even to this Muslim dear one, "Blessed are they who mourn."

"Thank you, Bilquis, thank you," the widow said in a whisper as at last she released my hand. I embraced her and walked out of the room.

Oddly, there were two more funerals in quick succession. This was quite unusual even for a family of our size. But in each case I was told very clearly, very distinctly, by the Lord to get out of my safe little house and go into the place where I was needed. I was not to do too much talking. I was to let my caring presence be its own witness.

And all the while the Lord was working with me. He had so much to teach me, and He was using these funerals as His classroom.

It was during one of these visits to a family funeral that I discovered the next great secret of staying in His Presence.

At a Muslim funeral no one cooks or eats until the body is buried. This usually amounts to a day's fasting and is really not an ordeal. However, that day, as I sat isolated in the crowded room, I suddenly found that I wanted my usual afternoon tea. It was something, I said to myself, which I simply could not do without.

Finally, unable to control my desire, I stood and mumbled an excuse. I had to wash my hands, I said. I slipped out of the house and down the street to a small cafe. There I had my precious tea and returned to the mourners.

Immediately I felt a strange aloneness, as if a friend had left my side. Of course I knew what it was. The comforting Presence of His Spirit had left me.

"Lord," I said to myself, "what have I done?"

And then I knew. I had told a lie when I was excusing myself.

"But it was only a white lie, Lord," I said. I sensed no comforting from the Spirit. Just a deadness.

"But Lord," I pressed, "I don't have to follow those Muslim mourning practices any more. And besides, I just can't do without my tea. You know that."

No sense of His Spirit.

"But Father," I pressed on, "I couldn't tell them that I went out for tea and cake. That would have hurt them."

No Spirit.

"All right, Father," I said. "I understand. It was wrong for me to lie. I realize that I was seeking the approval of men and that I must live only for Your approval. I am truly sorry, Lord. I hurt You. With Your help I will not do that again."

And with those words His comforting Presence flooded me again, like rain falling on a parched lake bed. I was relaxed. I knew that He was with me.

And that was how I learned to move back into His Presence quickly. Whenever I did not feel His nearness, I knew that I had grieved Him. I would search backwards until I spotted the time *when I last knew His Presence*. Then I would review every act, every word or thought until I discovered where I had gone astray. At that point I would confess my sin and ask His forgiveness.

I learned to do this with increasing boldness. Through these exercises in obedience I learned the beautiful secret of repentance. Repentance, I discoverd, was not tearful remorse so much as admitting where I had gone wrong and avowing with His help never to make that mistake in the future. As I realized my own weakness, I could call upon His strength.

It was during this time that I discovered there was no such thing as an innocent white lie. A lie is a lie and is always of Satan, the father of lies. He uses "harmless" white lies to get us started in this insidious habit. Lies pave the way for greater temptations to come. Satan whispers that a white lie is "consideration" for other people. We bend ourselves to the world instead of to Jesus who is the Truth.

Though I learned this lesson at the funeral of a relative, it was the beginning of a new kind of life for me, one where I attempted to weed out all lying. From that day on I would try and catch myself every time I was about to commit a white lie. Once a missionary friend invited me to a gathering which I did not want to attend. I was all set to make the excuse that I had another engagement. A warning signal sounded within me and I stopped myself just in time. Instead, I found that I could be truthful and still not hurt anyone's feeling by simply saying, "I'm very sorry, but I won't be able to be there."

Or, there was the day when I sat down to write a letter to a friend in London and almost automatically began writing that I had been out of town for some time and had not been able to answer his last letter. I stopped, pen poised in midair.

Out of town? I had been here all the time. I crumpled the paper, dropped it into the wastebasket and started again. "Dear Friend: Please forgive me for not answering your wonderful letter sooner. ..."

Little things, certainly. But I was learning that to be careful in small things made it much easier to handle the larger temptations as they came. Besides, life was so much easier when I didn't have to spend a lot of time contriving.

Slowly, surely, it began to dawn on me that I was trying to live with Christ as my constant companion! Of course, it just wasn't possible to do this. So often I caught myself falling into my old ways! But I kept trying.

And in the process I discovered the practical side of the promise, "But seek ye first the kingdom of God, and his righteousness; and all these things shall be added unto you" (Matthew 6:33, KJV). For, as I made the attempt to put God first, some of my other heartfelt needs were given back to me.

One afternoon Raisham came to my room with a startled expression on her face.

"There's a lady in the drawing room waiting to see you," she said.

"Who is it?" I asked.

"Well, Begum Sahib, if I'm not mistaken it's the mother of Karim."

Surely she must be mistaken! Karim's mother would not be coming here!

I walked downstairs wondering who then it could be. But, as I turned the corner into the drawing room, sure enough there stood the mother of my dead cousin. Hearing my steps she looked up, came over and threw her arms around me.

"Bilquis," Karim's mother said, tears forming in her eyes, "I just had to come personally to tell you something. At first, at the funeral, I didn't see you among all the people. But I need to tell you how much comfort you were. It's … I don't know … something new. Something warm and special."

And at last I saw why I had not been allowed to speak of Jesus directly to Karim's mother during the time of her crushing bereavement. For that would have been to take advantage of her. Now however the situation was quite different. Gently and softly there in my drawing room I spoke to her about how much Jesus meant to me and how He was slowly and inexorably changing so many of my old imperious ways, replacing them with His warm human personality.

"It's true," Karim's mother said. "You did care. You really wanted to share my sorrow."

It was a short visit but a wonderful one. Encouraging in two directions: First, that another human being had actually noticed a change in me; and second, I hoped that this was the beginning of a break in the family boycott.

It didn't happen quickly though. Every time the phone rang it was one of my missionary friends. So one morning just before Mahmud's sixth birthday, when the phone rang I expected to hear Marie. Instead I heard the friendly voice of the mother of the second cousin who had died.

"Bilquis?"

"Yes."

"Bilquis, I just wanted to say how much I appreciate the help you gave my son's wife. She told me you really spoke to her heart."

How interesting. For I had said little. It was Christ who had done the consoling.

We exchanged a few pleasant words and then hung up.

Once again I could not help but be amazed at how Jesus had done the work through me when I said little or nothing about Him directly. It was my being there, representing His Spirit in this time of need that had been the helper.

Over the weeks a few other family members came for short visits. They'd drop by to see Mahmud on his birthday, bringing him sweets and toys. Ostensibly the reason for their visit was to see the boy. Actually, I knew, it was just a good excuse. They really had come to soften some of the hurt of the boycott. The visits were always strained and short. But they were bright, welcome chinks in the terrible wall that had been raised around me.

Almost a year had passed since I had made the decision to accept Christ's call. How the time was flying! Soon my birthday would be here again. One year since I had given myself to the

Lord. And now I was looking forward to my first real celebration of Christmas. I had of course seen Christmas celebrations when I was in Europe. But never had I known what Christmas was like viewed from the heart. I borrowed a creche from the Mitchells. When they came to the house with the little manger scene they also brought a small fir tree, and we all sang, "O Christmas Tree … O Christmas Tree …," while Mahmud squealed with delight. The servants put the tree in the drawing room and we all decorated it with paper ribbons.

There was something wrong, however.

Much as I enjoyed these festivities, there wasn't much real meaning in them. I began to wonder if I could celebrate Christmas in a way that expressed the change that had come into my life.

And then an idea came to mind. Why not throw a party for everyone—missionaries, and people from the village, even the sweepers. Immediately I heard the warning voice of my family cautioning me not to make a display of my faith; and I also heard the General's voice warning me that he could no longer give me official protection if I got in trouble. I knew the idea of such a Christmas party would be a threat to many. Yet, after much prayer it seemed to me my Presence was strongest when I began to make plans for the unusual gathering.

So I went ahead on Christmas Day and threw the party which caused such a stir in Wah. The village people arrived early and congregated around the tree in the drawing room. Then the missionaries came. Synnove led everyone in song. And then to my astonishment one of the servants announced that an aunt and some cousins from Rawalpindi had arrived on a drop-in visit!

My heart leaped. How would they react! I need not have worried—they reacted in typical upper class-fashion, I'm afraid. First their jaws dropped, then they quietly retired to another room where they sat alone in strained silence.

I did not want to ignore either group so I spent my time going from room to room. It was like running back and forth from a hot shower to a cold shower.

Finally, perhaps because of my own persistence, a few members of my family began to relax. Some even went into the drawing room and joined the festivities around the tree. By the end of the party they were passing small talk with the Olds and the Mitchells, if not with the sweepers.

The party heralded, I hoped, the start of a different kind of year. Not an easier one, just a different one. Because immediately in front of me lay many confusing crossroads which could lead me into trouble if I took a wrong turn. For along with the smattering of relatives and friends who were now returning, came a different kind of visitor. They were people who were determined to convert me back to the Muslim faith. I had a feeling that there were interested onlookers, anxious to see how I would react to these voices beckoning me back home. Should I keep a discreet silence, or should I really speak my mind?

The answer came to me, again, in terms of my Presence. For whenever I tried to be devious I felt uncomfortable and alone. But whenever I answered the loaded questions forthrightly and in love, then I felt that the Lord Himself was right with me.

One afternoon, for instance, there was a soft knock on my door. I was surprised, for it was two o'clock in the afternoon.

"Yes?" The door opened. It was Raisham. "Begum Sahib, you have a visitor."

There was a hesitancy in her soft voice. I had told Raisham that I preferred not to be bothered between noon and three in the afternoon. It was not an order however. A year ago I would have ordered Raisham sharply not to bother me for any reason between noon and three. Now I explained to her that I no longer considered time as something I owned; it belonged to the Lord. If something came up which she herself thought I should see to, then of course she was to come to my room no matter what the hour.

"Begum Sahib, the man is an Englishman." There was a glint of amusement in her brown eyes. "He says he wants to talk about God."

"All right," I said, wondering. "I'll be right down."

Waiting for me in the drawing room was a pale, sandy-haired Englishman. I was interested in noting that he wore typical Pakistani clothes, a white shirt and baggy trousers. With his pale face and white clothes he almost blended into the white walls of my drawing room. After apologizing for dropping in without an appointment, he came to the point. He said that he had travelled all the way from Karachi to see me; since he had converted from Christianity to Islam, members of my family thought we had interests in common. "Ah," I said to myself, "now I understand. Knowing how much I like the British, they think I will be impressed by an Englishman who has left his Christianity for Islam."

My visitor hemmed and hawed and launched into the purpose of his visit.

"Begum," the man said, "one thing really disturbs me about Muslims who convert to Christianity. It is the Bible. We all know that the Christian New Testament has been changed from what God gave."

He was expressing Islam's main charge against the Bible, that it had been so altered that today's version is untrustworthy. The original, Muslims claim, had agreed with the Koran.

"I hope you won't think I'm being facetious," I said. "I really do want to know something. I've heard often that the Bible was changed but I've never been able to learn who changed it. When were the changes made and what passages were corrupted?"

My visitor leaned back and looked up to the carved ceiling beams, his fingers drumming the arm of his chair. He did not answer. It was unfair of me I guess. As far as I knew there were no answers to these questions.

"You see," I went on, drawing on research I had made, "in the British Museum there are ancient versions of the Bible which were published nearly three hundred years before Muhammad was born. On every issue between Christianity and Islam these old manuscripts are identical with today's Bible. The experts say that in every basic essential today's Bible has not been changed from the original. This is important for me personally. For, to me the Bible has become an alive Word. It speaks to my soul and feeds me. It helps guide me. ..."

My visitor got to his feet in the middle of my sentence.

"... and so," I went on, "I find it quite important to know if there really are places where I'm fooling myself. Can you tell me?"

"You talk about the 'Word' almost as if it were living," my visitor said.

"I believe that Christ is living, if that's what you mean," I said. "The Koran itself says that Christ was the Word of God. I would love to talk with you about it sometime."

"I must be going."

And that was that. I saw my visitor to the door and invited him back. He never did return but others came, some well primed for battle and with such misconceptions! I'll never forget the man who accused Christians of worshipping three separate Gods.

"Your so-called Trinity consists of God, Mary, and Jesus!" he said. "You Christians say that God took a wife who was Mary and from their union Jesus was born. Allah can't have a wife!" he laughed.

I prayed quickly. And a clear line of thought came to mind.

"Do you read the Koran?" I asked.

"Of course."

"Well then, do you remember how the Koran says that Christ was given the Spirit of God?" I had often wondered how the Koran could have such marvelous truths as this. "You perhaps have heard of Sadhu Sundar Singh, the devout Sikh to whom Jesus appeared in a vision. This is how Jesus explained the Trinity to him: 'Just as in the sun there are both heat and light, but the light is not heat and the heat is not light, but both are one, though in their manifestation they have different forms, so I and the Holy Spirit, proceeding from the Father, bring light and heat to the world. … Yet We are not three but One, just as the sun is but one.'"

It was quiet in the room when I finished. My guest was deep in thought. Finally he arose, thanked me for giving him time and silently left the house.

As I watched his forlorn figure walk down the graveled driveway it occurred to me to wonder whether my little visits with people like the Englishman and this zealot were really being used by the Lord. I had no way of knowing, for I never heard from either of them again. It didn't matter. I perhaps should not even wonder about results. The only thing that did matter to me was obedience. If the Lord asked me to talk to these people, then that is what I should do.

As the winter rolled into spring, the Lord seemed to give me other ways of speaking too. I went to Lahore and—after a good but strangely uncommunicating visit with my son Khalid—I purchased a hundred copies of the Bible to give away to anyone who was interested. I also bought a quantity of Christian tracts. I gave them away at every opportunity, even leaving them in public restrooms. I'm not at all sure this did any good. Once, when I went back to the restroom, I found my little stack had dwindled but then I looked in the wastebasket. There, crumpled up, were the copies of my tracts.

"It seems so pointless, Lord," I said. "Am I doing what You want? Why is it, Lord," I said raising my hands to my waist in supplication, "that not one single time have I been able to see the results of talking about You?" There was the English convert to Islam, and the General, and all the servants who had fled, and the hundreds of times I had talked with members of my family and with friends—not one of these times bore visible fruit. "It's so puzzling, Lord! I just don't understand why You aren't using me."

As I prayed the sensation of Christ's Presence grew ever stronger in that room. He seemed to fill the atmosphere with strength and comfort. I heard in my heart the distinct suggestion, "Bilquis, I have only one question to ask you. Think back over those times when you have talked with your friends, and with your family. Think back over the times you have accepted people who have come to argue. Have you felt My Presence during those visits?"

"Yes Lord. Yes indeed I have."

"My glory was there?"

"Yes Lord."

"Then that's all you need. It is so often this way with friends. And family. The results are not your problem. All you have to worry about is obedience. Seek My Presence, not results."

So I continued on my course. The odd thing is that it became an increasingly stimulating and invigorating time. Once the Lord had taken my eyes off the "results" and turned them to His Presence, I could enjoy meeting friend after friend, relative after relative without the slightest feeling of frustration. I learned to take advantage of opportunities. Whether the conversation was on politics or clothes, I would ask God to prompt a question which would give me an opening. For example, once when I was talking to a niece, the conversation drifted to my former husband, who was now Pakistan's ambassador to Japan.

"What if Khalid came to your house?" she smiled, lifting an eyebrow.

I looked at her directly. "I would welcome him. I would serve him tea." My niece looked at me incredulously. "I have forgiven him," I continued. "And I hope that he has forgiven *me* for all that I did which hurt him."

"How can you forgive that way!" My niece knew that the breakup had been most difficult.

I explained that I certainly could not forgive in my own strength. I had asked Jesus to help me. "You know," I said, "Jesus invited us all to come to Him with our burdens. Jesus took my burden of hate from me."

My niece sat quietly for a while. "Well," she said, "that is a Christianity I have not heard about. If you're going to talk like that I'll be one of the first to come and learn about your Jesus."

Even here I was disappointed. I had high hopes. I believed that indeed my niece might return to the subject but she never did.

I did have times when the glory left me during this period. It always occurred in the same fashion. I would slip into Satan's trap of convincing me that I sounded pretty good! My arguments were really quite profound!

One day for instance a friend asked me, "Why do you have to be so exclusive? You'll have to admit that we all worship the same God, whether Christian, Muslim, Hindu, Buddhist or Jew. We may call Him by different names and approach Him from different directions, but in the end it's the same God."

"You mean He is like a mountain top to which different paths lead?"

He settled back balancing his cup of tea and nodded. And then I flew to the attack.

"Well," I said, "He may be a mountain top but there is only one path to Him, through Jesus Christ. The Lord said: 'I am the way, the truth and the life.' Not just *a* way," I added sharply, "but *the* way."

My friend put down his cup of tea, grimaced and shook his head. "Bilquis," he said, "did anyone ever tell you that you still come across as haughty?"

And instantly I knew that the man sitting in front of me was speaking for God. My arguments were right. They were Biblical and sound. But the Spirit had left. *Bilquis* was right. *Bilquis* was stating truth. Quickly I said a prayer of repentance and asked the Lord to take over.

"I'm sorry," I laughed. "If I come across as smug because I'm a Christian, then I'm not acting as Christ would want. The more I learn about Christ the more I need correcting. The Lord has so much to teach me and I know He is speaking right now through you."

My visitor left, perhaps closer to the Lord, perhaps not. I doubt that I shall ever know. But I do know that I was, step by painful step, learning to listen and to obey.

And then one night I had another one of those frightening experiences which came only after I had become a Christian. I was in my room preparing for bed when I suddenly felt a powerful presence of evil at my bedroom window. Instantly my mind turned to my Protector and I was warned from going near the window. I dropped to the floor in prayer, asking my Lord to cover me as a mother hen covers her chicks and I felt the strong cloak of His protection. When I arose, the presence at the window was gone.

The next morning, I drove over to the Mitchells. The sun shone brightly on their street but I was still shaking inside. Yet, as I walked up to their door, I felt hesitant about mentioning what happened to me for fear they wouldn't understand.

At the door, Synnove hugged me, then stepped back, her blue eyes questioning me.

"What's wrong, Bilquis?" she asked.

"Well," I ventured, "why do frightening things keep happening after one becomes a Christian?"

She ushered me into the living room where we sat down.

"I don't really know what you mean," she said puzzled. "Has someone threatened you?"

"Not someone," I answered, "*something*."

"Oh?" she said, and arose and got her Bible. "Here," she said, sitting down and flipping through its pages, "in Ephesians 6 it speaks about that kind of thing." She read: "*We are up against the unseen power that controls this dark world, and spiritual agents from the very headquarters of evil.*"

She looked up at me.

"That must be it," I said telling her something about what happened that night.

She listened thoughtfully, and then said, "Why don't you talk to the Olds about it?"

"Well," I said, giving a nervous laugh, "I don't know if I want to even *talk* about it any more."

And that's how I felt at the beginning of our get-together with the Olds that evening. I decided not to bring it up. I'd simply make a fool of myself, I thought. It was probably just my imagination.

However, as I sat talking with Marie Old on a sofa before the fire, I couldn't help mentioning it. I tried to sound light-hearted.

"The strangest thing happened to me last night, Marie," I said. "I had the most frightening experience and I can't explain it."

Her husband, Ken, in his usual relaxed manner, had been sitting in a window seat behind us reading a book. Hearing me, he laid his book down, looked up and sensing my reluctance to talk about it, he, in his own quiet way, gently drew me into explaining the whole episode.

When I finished, I tried to laugh. "And then again," I said lightly, "I may have had too much curry at dinner last evening!"

"Don't minimize the things the Lord will bring you through," he said quietly. "Supernatural things *do* happen." He walked around the sofa and sat in a chair facing us. His face was serious.

He explained the supernatural presence of evil and how God can allow it to come upon a person as a test. As an example, Ken pointed out in the Old Testament how God permitted Satan to attack Job and how He allowed the Evil One to tempt Christ in the wilderness. Both of these, Ken pointed out, were tests. And in each case, he added, Satan's intended victim emerged victorious because of his outspoken faith in God. I couldn't help remembering the attack I suffered the second night before my baptism.

Slowly, the learning continued. But what I did not know as I gratefully considered Ken's comforting teaching, was that the Lord had already started a process which was to leave me more and more alone, yet not lonely; more and more cut off from my family, yet part of a great, supportive family; more and more cut off from the roots which meant so much to me in Wah, yet with deepening roots in a new City.

It was because of these upcoming tests of endurance that He had been placing me, time after time, in situations where I had to depend solely on Him.

11

Winds of Change

The weaning process began one Sunday a few weeks later, during our regular prayer meeting. I thought that both the Olds and the Mitchells seemed unusually somber that evening.

"What's wrong?" I asked as we walked into the Olds' drawing room. Ken leaned his head back and stared at the ceiling.

"Marie and I are leaving on a year's furlough," he said abruptly.

My first reaction was panic at the thought of abandonment. What would I ever do without the Olds! Of course I would still have the Mitchells, but I depended on both families, together, to be my support. The Mitchells had brought me into my first contact with the church; the Olds had walked closely with me. Was this just a beginning? How long before I lost both families?

Marie must have read my heart. For she stepped over and took my hand. Tears filled her eyes as she spoke.

"My dear," Marie said, "you must realize that it will always be this way. Those we love will always be leaving. Only Jesus stays with you forever."

Ken now joined his wife at my side.

"There's another thing, Bilquis," Ken said. "You can be sure the Lord never leads you out of a safe situation unless He has a purpose. Because of that, you can start rejoicing now, even in the midst of the hurt."

We had only a few weeks more together, the Olds, the Mitchells and I. The departure date grew closer, carrying with it a sense of doom. We all tried to be faith-filled about the vacuum that would be created by Ken's and Marie's leaving but it was play-acting, not at all real.

It was a sad day when the Mitchells and I and others in our small Christian group went to the Olds' house for a goodbye send-off. We did our best even at this last moment to make it a celebration, but our hearts were heavy. We tried to see the moment as a chance not to "let them go" but to "send them out."

It was a brave show. But in our hearts, as we saw the Olds' heavily-loaded automobile lumber off toward the Grand Trunk Road, it seemed to us all that life could never again be as rich.

As I drove back to my own home that day I had a strange sensation of being on my own, now, alone in a hostile community. How ridiculous. The Mitchells were still in Wah, after all!

The weaning process took a new and unexpected turn late one morning, some months after the Olds left, when Dr. Daniel Baksh phoned me. He said he and Dr. Stanley Mooneyham, representing a group called World Vision, headquartered in

California, U.S.A., would like to visit me. I had never heard of his organization but my doors were open to anyone, even people who were curious to see what a Muslim-turned-Christian looked like.

Both arrived a few days later. When we finished dinner, Dr. Mooneyham began to speak and it was clear that he was no curiosity-seeker. He was interested in my conversion, all right, but I sensed that he would have been equally interested in the conversion of my gardener. As we sipped tea, he came to the point.

"Will you come to Singapore, Madame Sheikh," Dr. Mooneyham asked, "to testify for the Lord?"

"Singapore?"

"Billy Graham is arranging a large conference there called *Christ Seeks Asia*. It will be for Asiatic Christians of all kinds—Indonesians, Japanese, Indians, Koreans, Chinese, Pakistanis. Your testimony will be an inspiration to us."

It didn't sound right. I had enough to do right there in Wah without taking off for other parts of the world.

"Well," I said, "I'll pray about it."

"Please do!" Dr. Mooneyham said and then shortly he bid me goodbye.

Long after Dr. Mooneyham left, I sat on the veranda thinking and praying, as I had promised, about the invitation. One side of me said that I should take advantage of the opportunity. Another side of me said I should not even think of it.

And then an idea occurred to me.

My passport. Of course. It was just about to expire. It would have to be renewed if I were to go to Singapore. At that time in Pakistan there was much red tape involving passports. The situation was *impossible*. Some people sent their passports in for renewal and *never* got them back.

Why not let this situation act as a voice for the Lord? If He wanted me to go, He would take care of this passport detail.

That very afternoon I filled out the necessary information and posted the passport to the proper officials. As I slipped it in the mail box I had very little doubt that this would be my "No" to the Singapore trip.

A week later an official-looking government envelope came in the mail.

"Hmm," I smiled, "this will be the first step in getting my renewal, some more forms to fill out. And so it will go on for months."

I opened the envelope.

There, all renewed and officially stamped, was my passport.

So it was, a few months later, that I said goodbye to six-year-old Mahmud and drove down to Lahore. There I had a short visit with my son, Khalid, before going on to Karachi where I would board the jet for Singapore. Although it was now 1968 and a year and a half had passed since the Lord met me, Khalid was much like the rest of my family, now showing little interest in my discovery. I suspected that he considered me, at 48, embarked on a strange kind of trip. But I was to be respected as his mother, and we had an enjoyable visit.

Later as I boarded the jet in Karachi and considered the project I was just now undertaking, I had the impression that Khalid was right. What in the world was I doing on this airplane headed for Singapore! There were a lot of Christians aboard and I wasn't too sure I liked what I saw. I shrank from their exuberance. They were singing Gospel songs, shouting back and forth to each other across the aisles, sometimes raising their hands and crying, "Praise the Lord!" I was embarrassed. There was an artificial quality about the joy, not unlike the forced gaiety I had occasionally seen among conventioneers on the streets of London. I found myself muttering that if this was what it meant to travel in Christian circles, I wasn't interested.

What made the moment worse was that, for reasons which I could not define, I felt this trip held a personal significance beyond my safari to Singapore. It was as if the trip were prophetic, foretelling the type of life I would be called upon to lead.

"Oh no, Lord," I said to myself. "You must be playing with me!" Prophetic in what sense? That I was going to have to spend a lot of time among extroverts, traveling in jet airplanes? Back in Wah I was just getting comfortable in my role as a Christian, but that was in a provincial village. There I was in control, at least. Christianity to me was a very private joy, to be shared on my own terms. I definitely did not like the idea of parading myself before hundreds, perhaps thousands of strangers.

As the plane took off I stared out of the window, watching Pakistan fall away below me into the mist. Even though I knew that I would be coming back within just a few days, something warned me that in a very real shense this was a beginning. Although I would return to my home in the physical sense, in another sense I would never come back. This—this group of Christians on an airplane—was my home now.

What could I possibly mean by that! The idea appalled me.

From the Singapore airport we went straight to the conference hall where the meetings were already in progress.

And suddenly, quite to my surprise, I found that I was having a very different reaction to this group of assembled Christians.

There were thousands of men and women in the conference hall, the largest number of people I had ever seen gathered in one place. As I walked into the hall, everyone was singing "How Great Thou Art." I felt the familiar Presence of God's Spirit and had never known it to be so palpitating. Almost instantly I wanted to cry, not out of sadness but out of joy. Never before had I seen such a large crowd of people praising the Lord. I could hardly grasp it. So many people, from so many countries! Different races, different dress! Galleries of praising Christians seeming to rise forever.

Now this was different! Not at all like the group of people on the airplane. I then realized what I had been experiencing on the plane. Everything was suddenly very clear. Those people on the jetliner had been shy, nervous, perhaps even afraid. Afraid of the newness, afraid of flying. They were bluffing and posturing, not in the Spirit in spite of the language. They were no more moving in the Spirit than I was when I scolded one of the servants or reacted violently to an uncle when he tried to pressure me back into Islam. The problem had been their language. Christian talk fooled me. I should have recognized their Christianese as such, covering up a hurting.

But here in this conference center it was different. Socializing was over, worship had begun. If the prophecy I had felt meant being with groups like this, *that* I could appreciate and accept.

One thing still bothered me. Was I really supposed to stand up in front of these thousands of people to talk? It was one thing to speak about my experiences to people I knew personally in

Wah. But here? With all these strange-looking people from so many different continents? I did not feel at all safe.

I hurried over to my hotel where I tried to settle down. I looked out the window at teeming Singapore. How different Singapore was from London and Paris. People jostled each other on the streets, hawkers sang their wares and automobiles threaded through the melee, constantly sounding horns. The very press of people seemed to menace me here just as it did in the conference hall. I shuddered, thrust the curtain closed and retreated to the other end of the room where I sat down and tried to calm myself.

"Oh Lord," I cried, "where is Your comforting Spirit?"

And suddenly I recalled a childhood experience of walking with my father through the marketplace in Wah. Father cautioned me to stay by his side but, always active, I wanted to run off. One day I did. A flower display caught my attention and I ran over to it. Suddenly I realized that my father was not at my side. Panic filled me and I burst into tears. "Oh Father," I said, "come find me and I won't ever run away from you again!" Even as I spoke, there he was, his tall slender figure coming quickly toward me through the crowd. I was with him again! All I wanted now was to stay by his side.

As I sat in the hotel room, I realized that in fact I had left my heavenly Father again. By allowing myself to become anxious, I had run off from His comforting Presence. When would I learn that I cannot worry and trust God at the same time! I relaxed in my chair and felt at peace again.

"Oh thank You, Father," I said weeping in relief. "Please forgive me for stepping away from You. You are here, You are in that hall. I'll be safe."

A few minutes later in the hotel lobby, I felt a hand on my arm and heard a familiar voice. I looked around to see Dr. Mooneyham.

"Madame Sheikh, so good to have you here!" Dr. Mooneyham seemed happy enough to see me. "Are you still willing to speak?" It was as if he had been reading my mind.

"Don't worry about me," I said, smiling. "I'll be fine. The Lord is here."

Dr. Mooneyham just stood there, studying my face, as if making a decision about how to interpret my words. After all, I had been using Christianese too, and he wasn't going to take it at face value, possibly let it fool him as it had fooled me on the airplane. Dr. Mooneyham's eyes were reading my very soul. Then suddenly he seemed satisfied.

"Good," he said abruptly. "You're slated for tomorrow morning." He looked at his watch. "You'll have lots of prayer support."

Dr. Mooneyham had understood me correctly. The sense of security lasted through the next morning too, when indeed I did get up in front of those thousands of people gathered in the auditorium to speak of the way the Lord had found me in such a strange way. It was not at all difficult speaking. He was with me as I stumbled and fumbled my way through the talk, embracing me and encouraging me, assuring me that *He* was doing the communicating and not I. And as people surrounded me in loving fellowship after my talk, it was as if I had taken the first step in a new kind of work for the Lord.

The Lord also arranged my meeting a man who would become very important in my life, though I didn't realize it at the time. I was introduced to Dr. Christy Wilson, a kind gentleman who was pastor of a church in Kabul, Afghanistan, which ministered to foreign nationals. We found a rapport in the Lord's Spirit as we discussed his work.

Then, the meetings were over and I was on my way back to Wah. Once again I sensed that the whole trip had a strangely foretelling character, as if God had asked me to come with Him to Singapore so that I could learn more about a type of work He wanted me to do.

Well, I said to myself, at least I'll be headquartered in Wah. Perhaps I wouldn't mind *too* much, going out on an occasional trip from my comfortable and secure ancestral home.

But as the car turned off the Grand Trunk Road toward our house in the trees, I had no way of knowing that the weaning process was going to shatter more of that security.

12

A Time for Sowing

The next separation step came in the sad news that the Mitchells were leaving on furlough. It would be some time before they would return to Pakistan.

It was more than a year after Singapore. I was sitting in the Mitchells' living room with our small band of Christian professional men and women from the area. It was a sad occasion, the final get-together before David and Synnove left. I could not help thinking of the first time I had come to this same low-verandaed house as a hesitant seeker. So much had happened since then. I looked at the faces of these two who had been so close to me in my introduction to Christ: tall David, his hair graying, and earnest Synnove who had prayed for me so consistently.

"I'm going to miss you terribly, you know that," I said as we all stood on the small lawn in front of the Mitchells' house. "How will I ever get along without your fellowship!"

"Maybe the Lord is teaching you to get along without it," said Synnove. "He's always stretching us, you know, Bilquis, until we don't have a safe handhold left except Him."

It sounded good, but I still didn't like being stretched and told Synnove as much. She just laughed. "Of course you don't, dear Bilquis. Who ever wants to leave the safety of a womb. But adventure lies ahead!"

Synnove got into their old car and closed the door. One more embrace through the window and suddenly the Mitchells' car was rolling dustily away, away from the forlorn whitewashed buildings that had been officers' quarters during the war. Their car disappeared around the corner. Adventure, indeed! Here I was a lonesome Christian in a Muslim town. Would I be able to make it alone?

Several weeks passed, during which time, frankly, it was hard for me to sense the adventure Synnove promised, or the direction and purpose that Ken Old had foretold when he and Marie left what seemed such a long time ago. The Sunday evening meeting of Christians continued, first in one home then in another of the five of us who were left, but without the leadership of the Olds and Mitchells the meetings seemed to flounder.

Then one night after a listless meeting an idea struck me. Were we making a mistake trying to do things exactly as the Mitchells and the Olds had done? Our little group was surely going to atrophy if we didn't get some new blood in our midst. What would happen—and I felt my pulse quicken just at the thought—what would happen if we asked people to join the fellowship who were not professionals—not doctors and engineers and missionaries? Suppose we asked Christians and non-Christians alike, the sweepers, the lower classes, to join in fellowship. Perhaps in my own home since it was large and convenient. When I suggested the idea to our fellowship there was some initial resistance, then skeptical agreement. We decided to go ahead. Through direct invitations and through the grapevine also, I passed word along that a Christian evening would be held at my house Sunday night.

I was surprised at how many people turned up. Most were from Rawalpindi where word had travelled. And, just as I hoped, not all were Christians either. Many were simply hungry to find out more about the Christian God. With those of us from the original group as leaders, we sang and prayed and tried to do what we could to minister to the individual needs of the maids and day laborers and school teachers and business people who also came to the house.

Soon there was a fresh feeling to the Sunday fellowship. The responsibility was awesome. I and the others who were leaders in this small group spent hours on our knees, hours close to the Lord and the Word, trying to be sure that in no smallest way did we diverge from the direction. He wished us to take. All of a sudden the "resultless" period I had been experiencing was reversed. I was able to see actual conversions. The first to come to the Lord was a young widow. She cried her hurt and lonesomeness out and then asked the Lord in. It was extraordinary to see the transformation in her personality, from a gloomy, defenseless creature to a hope-filled child of God. Shortly a mechanic from a nearby garage came into the Lord's Kingdom, then a file clerk, then a sweeper.

And all in my own home. I felt honored indeed, although I kept wondering when I would start to hear from the family about this smudge on our reputation. But no one complained.

Not yet, anyhow. It was as if the family didn't want to admit what was happening. One day I tripped on a tile in my terrace, fell and suffered a slight bone fracture. My family didn't come; they telephoned instead. But at least they were telephoning!

If opposition to my slowly evolving Christian life was lessening from my family, it was still coming from within me at times. I was yet a very private person, possessive, counting my land and garden my own.

Across the lawn from my house is a road leading to the servants' quarters. Growing next to this road is a tree called the ber, which has a red fruit similar to the cherry. That summer after the Mitchells left, children from the village (perhaps encouraged by reports of a change in my personality) began coming right onto my property to climb the ber and help themselves to its fruit. The intrusion was bad enough, but when their shouts and squeals interrupted my rest time, I leaned out of my window and ordered the gardener to chase the children away. That very day I had the gardener cut the tree down. That would solve the problem permanently!

As soon as the tree was destroyed I realized what I had done. With the tree gone, so was the joy and peace of the Lord's Presence. For a long time I stood in my window staring at the empty place where it had been. How I wished now that the tree were still there so that I could hear the joyful shouts of the children. I realized what the true Bilquis Sheikh was like. All over again I knew that in my own natural self I would never be different. It was only through the Lord, through His grace, that any change could ever take place.

"Oh Lord," I said, "let me come back into Your Presence again please!" There was only one thing to do. Scattered throughout my garden were large trees heavy with summer fruit. The very next day I issued an open invitation to the village children to come and enjoy! And they did too. Even though I'm sure they tried to be careful, branches were broken, flowers trod upon.

"I think I see what You're doing, Lord," I said one afternoon after the children had gone home, and I was surveying the damage. "You found the garden itself to be a place that stood between us. You are weaning me even from the garden! You've taken it away to give to others. But look how they were enjoying it! It's Your garden. I give it up to them with great pleasure. Thank You for using this to bring me back into Your comforting Self."

He did return too. Until, that is, I once again needed a pruning. This time it wasn't the garden, it was my precious rest.

One cold November afternoon I was resting when Mahmud slipped into my room. He was becoming a youth now and his good-humored features foretold a handsome young-man-to-be. But now his face was concerned.

"Mum, there's a woman outside who wants to see you. She's got a baby in her arms."

I lifted my head. "Mahmud," I said, forgetting my own instructions to Nur-jan and Raisham, "You're eight years old now! You *know* that I don't want to see anyone at this time of day."

Mahmud had hardly left the room before the thought struck me: what would the Lord have done? And, of course, I knew what He would have done. He would have gone to the woman immediately, even if it were the middle of the night.

I called to Mahmud, who had not gone far enough down the hall to miss hearing me. Once again he stuck his brown face through the door.

"Mahmud," I said, "what does the woman want?"

"I think her baby is sick," Mahmud said, coming now into the room. I could see the concern in his eyes.

"Well bring her to the reception room then," I directed as I prepared to go downstairs.

In a moment I joined Mahmud, the woman and her child. The woman was dressed in the coarse, baggy clothes of a peasant. She might have been the baby's grandmother. She had a wizened face, shrunken shoulders and her pantaloons bagged around a thin frame. Only when she lifted her face and stared at me with deep brown eyes could I see that she herself was little more than a child.

"What can I do for you?" I asked, my heart melting.

"I heard about you in my village, and I walked here."

The place she mentioned was twelve miles away. No wonder the poor thing looked so tired. I sent servants for tea and sandwiches. I wondered if she were still nursing the baby; in some villages mothers nurse their children up to three years of age. The baby's eyes stared listlessly at the crystal chandelier, its tiny mouth still. I laid hands on the child's forehead to pray for him; it was hot and dry. As I laid hands on the mother's head, I could feel generations of my family wincing. In the old days, I would have been horrified if even this peasant's shadow had fallen on me.

My heart went out to these little ones, the mother and the child, as I asked God for healing in the name of Jesus. When the maid came I told her also to bring some vitamins for the mother. We visited for half an hour, the mother telling me of her life with a husband who had been crippled in an accident, the new baby, not enough food. And indeed she was nursing the baby—it was the cheapest way to feed him. When the mother finally rose to go, I restrained her with a gesture.

"No," I whispered. "Not yet. We must find some way to see to it that you and the baby are taken care of." Immediately as I said this, the old Bilquis Sheikh began to grow nervous. What if word got out to other needy people in Wah that the Begum Sahib in the big garden provided a soft touch? Wouldn't we be swamped with lines of other skinny, emaciated, sickly, desperate people?

But even as my heart whispered this question, I knew that I had no choice. Either I had meant it or I had not meant it when I gave myself *and all that I possessed* to the Lord.

"… and, of course, your husband needs attention too. Let's get you all to the hospital. And let's get some decent food into your bodies. Then, if your husband still can't find work, let me know."

That's all there was to the visit. I made arrangements for the hospital to bill me and waited. But the woman never returned. I was a little surprised. When I asked the servants if they knew what had happened to her, they—as usual—had the answer. She and the baby and her husband had indeed gone to the hospital, and now they were all better. The husband had work. My ego bridled at first at the ungratefulness of this woman for not returning to give thanks, but the Lord checked me. "Is that why you helped her? So that you could be thanked? I thought thanksgiving was supposed to go to Me!"

And of course He was right. I went back in my mind to the place where I first felt that *I* had taken care of this woman. Then I asked the Lord to forgive me, and never to allow me to fall into that trap again. "Lord," I sighed, "Your arm must be tired from picking me up so often."

It seemed through those days that I would have little moments of success in the job of living close to the Lord, only to be brought back to earth quickly with resounding failure. I wondered if this were the pattern usually followed in the Christian life. Since I had no one to talk to then, I had to carry these questions secretly.

One morning while Nur-jan was administering my toilette a redbird fluttered to the window sill.

"Oh!" I exclaimed, "look at what the Lord has sent us this morning!"

There was silence as Nur-jan quietly went on brushing my hair. I was a bit surprised; Nur-jan was normally so talkative. Then she observed shyly, "Begum Sheikh, do you know that when you start talking of the Lord your whole appearance changes?"

That afternoon I placed an order for several more Bibles at the mission shop in Islamabad. They were a special kind of Bible, designed for children. I had discovered the usefulness of these Bibles with Mahmud. I discovered also that the servants around the house were picking up the brightly illustrated little book. When the Bibles arrived, I made a special point of giving one to Nur-jan. Imagine my joy when one day she came to speak to me privately.

"Begum Sahib," Nur-jan said, her plump face full of emotion, "I have something to tell you. Do you remember how you have so often told us that if we want to know this Jesus, all we have to do is ask Him to come into our heart?" At this she broke into tears. "Well I did, Begum Sahib. And He did come in. I have never felt such love, ever, in my whole life!"

I couldn't believe my ears. I threw my arms about the girl and embraced her. We danced a little crying waltz around the bedroom.

"What an incredible piece of news, Nur-jan. Now we are three Christians—you and Raisham and I. We must celebrate!"

So Raisham and Nur-jan and I all had tea together. It wasn't the first time I had drunk tea with people of the serving class. But it still gave me a slight shock. As the three of us Christians daintily sipped our drinks and nibbled at our cake together, chatting like old friends, I found my mind wandering. What had happened to the woman who had retreated to this same estate, to hide from wealthy society? Here she was, sitting with the maids. How my family and friends would be scandalized. How my old friends and family would wonder! I thought back to the way I used to vent my frustrations in sharp orders and outbursts of temper. If I noticed dust on a chair rung, if the servants chatted too loudly in the kitchen, if my lunch were delayed a moment, the whole household could depend on an outburst. The Lord had really been working with me, and I felt His company with great satisfaction.

It was not that I wanted to become a saint. But I was beginning to learn that my responsibility of being a representative of Jesus Christ would not allow me to do anything that would dishonor His Name. And He was also teaching me that one's actions spoke louder than words when it came to witnessing for Christ.

But then I noticed a strange thing at our evening meetings. Nur-jan was not among the dozen villagers who were now joining us in my drawing room. How odd! One day after she had done my hair I asked her to stay behind for a moment. Wouldn't she like, I said, to join us this Sunday?

"But Begum," Nur-jan said, startled, her face whitening, "I just cannot talk about what happened to me, or go to a meeting. My husband is a devout Muslim. We have four children. If I say that I have become a Christian he will just turn me out,"

"But you *have* to declare your faith," I insisted. "There is no other way."

Nur-jan stared at me unhappily, then left the room, shaking her head and mumbling. I could just barely make out the words, "But it can't be done."

A few days later I was visiting the Reverend Mother Ruth whom I had also come to know at the Holy Family Hospital. I always enjoyed talking to her. The Reverend Mother mentioned how many people in Pakistan are secret believers.

"Secret believers!" I exclaimed. "I do not see how that is possible. If you are a Christian why aren't you shouting the news!"

"Well," said Mother Ruth, "look at Nicodemus."

"Nicodemus?"

"He was a secret believer. Check chapter three of the Gospel of John."

I opened my Bible then and there and began to read how this Pharisee came to Jesus late one night to find out more about His kingdom. I had often read this stirring chapter but not until then did I realize that of course Nicodemus was a secret believer.

"Perhaps at a later date Nicodemus expressed his belief openly," the Sister said. "But as far as the Scriptures show, he was careful not to let his fellow Pharisees know."

The next day I called Nur-jan into my room and read the verses about Nicodemus to her. "I'm sorry I made you uncomfortable," I said. "In time the Lord may show you how to declare your faith. In the meanwhile, just listen carefully to His leading."

Her face brightened. Later I watched her humming happily at her work. "I hope I did the right thing, Lord," I said. "What I have to watch is that I not set myself up in judgment against anyone."

Just a few days later I discovered for myself, with new intensity, how difficult it was to become a Christian in this part of the world.

One afternoon the phone rang. It was one of my uncles, a relative who had been particularly sharp with me. Even as the family boycott began to thaw slightly, this uncle had never been in touch, never spoken. His voice on the phone was sharp.

"Bilquis?!"

"Yes."

"I hear that you are leading others astray. You are taking them from the true faith."

"Well, dear Uncle, that's a matter of opinion."

I could imagine the man's face getting flushed with the anger that showed in his voice. "It's one thing for you to make these decisions yourself. Quite another for others to follow. You must stop this, Bilquis."

"Uncle, I appreciate your concern but I must remind you that you are to run your life and I will run my own."

The very next day when my new chauffeur was driving me home from a visit with Tooni, a man stood in the road and tried to stop the car. My chauffeur knew that I often stopped for hitchhikers. But he did not want to stop this time.

"Please don't ask me to stop, Begum," he said in a determined voice. He swerved around the man, his tires squealing on the edge of the highway.

"What do you mean?" I leaned forward in the seat. "You don't think that man was trying to …?"

"Begum …"

"Yes?"

"Begum, it's just that …" the man lapsed into silence and all my questioning could not drag any further information out of him.

But it was just a week later that another one of my servants slipped into my room minutes after I had retired for my afternoon rest.

She closed the door behind her.

"I hope you will not mind," she said in a low whisper. "But I simply must warn you. My brother was in the mosque in Rawalpindi yesterday. A group of young men began talking about the damage you are doing. They kept saying something would have to be done. Soon. To shut you up."

The girl's voice was shaking.

"Oh Begum Sahib," she said, "must you be so open? We are afraid for you and for the boy."

My heart skipped. Now it was my turn to wonder whether it had not been best to remain a secret believer in this land, and yes, even in this family where Jesus was anathema.

13

Storm Warnings

Two months passed after the report of threats against me. Nothing occurred more threatening than hostile glances from a few young men, and I began to wonder if the alarms were groundless.

Now it was Christmas time again, a few years after I had found the Babe of Bethlehem. Even though some family members had been visiting me, the warning phone call from my uncle reminded me that relationships within my family were still strained and I felt it would be a good idea to have a dinner party for my relatives and friends, to see if now we could do something further to heal the breach.

So I spent considerable time making up a guest list. Then one evening, before going to bed, I slipped that list into my Bible for safekeeping, intending to have the invitations sent out the next morning.

But that was never to take place.

For when I opened the Bible the next morning to take out the list my eyes fell on a passage. Incredibly, it read:

> *When you give a luncheon or a dinner party, don't invite your friends or your brothers or relations or wealthy neighbors, for the chances are they will invite you back, and you will be fully repaid. No, when you give a party, invite the poor, the lame, the crippled and the blind. That way lies real happiness for you. They have no means of repaying you, but you will be repaid when good men are rewarded—at the resurrection.*
>
> Luke 14:12

"Lord, is that Your word for me?" I wondered, holding the Bible in one hand and the guest list in the other. Sure enough, most of my relatives and neighbors and friends were well-to-do. I had told myself this was an opportunity to get Muslim and Christian together, but actually I saw that pride had been showing through. I wanted to demonstrate to my family that I still had friends among the wealthy class.

I crumpled up the list.

Instead, I did exactly what the Bible said. I made up a list of widows, orphans, unemployed and poor people of the village and then invited all of them to attend Christmas dinner. This included everyone, even all the beggars. I made some of the invitations myself, others I passed along through my own staff. News like this travels fast and soon my servants were bringing back word that the whole village was planning to come. For a moment I had misgivings. All those *people*. I thought of the pair of silk handmade Persian rugs I had recently ordered for the living room. Oh well, I thought, I could put the good things up out of the way during that time.

So we started preparations. Mahmud's eight-year-old enthusiasm was infectious as he helped me gather presents for the people who would come. We found woolen shirts for the boys, brightly colored garments for the young girls, rolls of red, pink and purple cloth for the women, warm pantaloons for the men, wraps and shoes for the children. The servants and I spent hours wrapping the gifts, tying the packages with silver ribbons.

One day there was a knock on the door. A group of womenfolk from Wah were standing outside. They wanted to help. "Not for pay, Begum," their spokesman explained. "We just want to help you put on the dinner."

Suddenly the whole celebration had become a community affair. For decoration, I asked a family of potters in the village to make lamps, the small oil pottery lamps still commonly used in that part of Pakistan. I ordered 500 of them. I had the village women come to the house, where we made wicks by twisting cotton into strands. As we worked, natural opportunities arose to talk about Christ. As we placed the lamps around the house, for instance, I told the story about the wise and foolish virgins.

The food was another exciting project. Again the village women helped me prepare typical Pakistani sweets and sliced almonds and the delicious legus nuts. They pounded silver paper into strips so thin we could stick them on the sweetmeats as a colorful foil.

The village people began to arrive at the house on December the 24th and continued coming for what turned out to be a week's festival. How beautiful all the lamps were decorating every cranny, sitting cheerily along rails and sills. Mahmud had a wonderful time playing with the village children. I had never seen these children's eyes sparkle so, nor, for that matter,

Mahmud's. Squealing and laughing filled the house. From time to time Mahmud would come to me with requests.

"Mum," he would say, "there are five more boys standing outside; can they come in?"

"Of course," I laughed, patting him on the back and feeling sure that there were more children in our house right now than lived in all of Wah. When I talked with the villagers about how Christ had instructed us to treat each other in this way their response was, "Did He *really* walk with people like us?"

"Yes," I said, "and today what we do for others, we do for Him."

Finally, after the festivities were over and I was able to slump down in a chair without worrying about sitting on a sleeping child, I sighed in contentment to God. "Is this what You wanted me to do?" And I seemed to hear the soft response: "Yes." And then I noticed: I had forgotten to put up the new Persian rugs. Yet they seemed none the worse for wear.

Many of the poor never forgot that party. About a month later, I heard through one of the servants about a funeral in Wah. The wife of the local *mullah* complained loudly that I had made a mistake losing my faith. Someone else, however, replied: "Have you seen the Begum Sahib lately? Have you done any of the things she has done since she became a Christian? If you want to learn anything about God, why don't you go see her?"

But there was another side to this experience too. For I learned that there were forces in Wah which did not take kindly to the party.

"Begum Sahib," an old retainer who worked in our garden stopped me one day. He touched his forehead. "A minute please?"

"Of course."

"Begum Sahib Gi, there is talk in the town that you should know about. One speaks about how the Begum has become a problem. There are those in the village who say they will have to do something about you."

"*About* me?" I said. "I don't understand."

"Neither do I, Begum Sahib. But I just feel you should know. ..."

Warnings like this, sometimes coming close together, sometimes spread months apart, began to occur with increasing regularity over the next year. It was almost as if the Father were trying to prepare me for a difficult time to come.

One day, for instance, three small boys came to our house from the village. Later I wondered if they were God's messengers, arriving in these little forms. For Mahmud came to me with news from the boys. He was shivering and his eyes were wide with fear.

"Mum, do you know what my friends said? They said that in the village people were planning to kill you. They will do it after Friday prayers." He began sobbing. "If you die, I will kill myself!"

What was I to do! I gathered Mahmud's eight-year-old form in my arms, stroked his tousled black hair and tried to comfort him. "My dear child," I said, "let me tell you a story." And I recounted to him the tale of Jesus' first sermon in Nazareth, when the crowd became so angry and determined to stone Him. "Mahmud," I said, "Jesus passed through the midst of them. There wasn't a thing anyone could do to Jesus until and unless the Father allowed it to happen. The same is true with you and me. We have His perfect protection. Do you believe that?"

"Do you mean we will never be hurt or harmed?"

"No, I don't mean that. Jesus was hurt. But only when His time had come to suffer. We do not need to live a life of constant fear that something terrible will happen to us. For it cannot happen to us until our moment has come. And maybe that will never happen. We will simply have to wait and see. But in the meantime we can live in great confidence. Do you understand?"

Mahmud looked at me and his brown eyes softened. Suddenly he smiled, wheeled on the spot and ran off to play, shouting happily. It was the best answer to my question he could possibly have given.

I wish I could say that I myself felt as confident. Not that I disbelieved what I had said to Mahmud. It was that my faith was not yet childlike. I rose and carried my Bible out into the garden. My heart was not exactly light. How dare they try to force me from my land!

The fall weather was crisp and dry; as I slowly walked along the graveled path, I could hear a fish splash in my little stream and the far-off call of a bird. Chrysanthemums and other summer leftovers cheered the path. I breathed the pleasant sparkling air. This was my land, and my people. This was my country. My family had served it well for seven hundred years. This was my home, and I could not, *would not* leave it!

Yet events were taking place which were totally out of my control, and which did not bode well for my stubborn determination to stay in my home.

In December of 1970, four years after my conversion, Pakistan had its first national one-man-one-vote election. It looked as if the People's Party would carry the day. And that was not exactly good news for me. For none of my highly placed friends were also friends of this party. "Islam our Faith, Democracy our Policy, Socialism our Economy" was the new party's slogan. It was a slogan designed to appeal to the man on the street. I know that the common ordinary Pakistani felt a new sense of power. Was this good for me? Probably it was good for the new Bilquis, but there was an inherent danger too. For nothing fires the zeal of a fanatic more than the belief that his government will back him in his exploits. My old reputation was certainly not that of a democrat; socialism did not fit the age-old traditions of our family; and Islam?—well, now I was a traitor.

I followed the events somewhat from a distance. One day, however, an old government friend of my father's from Sardar arrived. Despite his despair over my new faith, he had tried to stay close to me. From time to time he would call or visit just to make sure that everything was all right.

Now he sat with me on the white silk-covered divan in our drawing room, sipping tea.

"Bilquis," he said, his voice low, "are you aware of what is happening and how it can affect you?"

"Do you mean with the Pakistan People's Party?"

"They won the election of course. How much do you know about Zulfikar Ali Bhutto."

"I knew him well," I said.

"Don't you read the paper? Listen to the radio?"

"No, you know I don't take time for that."

"Well, I advise that you do take time. The government situation has changed. I doubt if you can count on him as you did on previous presidents," he added. "You have, my dear, lost what influence you may have had in high circles. That era is over."

Half an hour later as I waved my old friend out of the driveway and returned to call the maid to clean up, I realized that a strange thing had happened with my old friend's visit. It was as if he had spoken for the Lord, preparing me for the fact that my protective, influential friends were gone, bringing me one more step toward total dependence on the Lord.

It wasn't too long before I began sensing a growing hostility. I saw it in the eyes of men as I walked in Wah. I'll never forget the change in the attitude of a minor official with whom I discussed taxes on my property. In the past he had been a servile man, bowing and touching his forehead. Now the little fellow was openly hostile. It was evident in his clipped remarks and the contemptuous way he slapped the forms down in front of me.

And later as I was strolling along the road outside my house, I glimpsed a man who usually went out of his way to speak to me. Now I noticed something quite different. He caught sight of me, quickly turned his head and began to study the horizon as I passed. Inwardly, I chuckled. "Lord, don't we all behave like children!"

Interestingly, the new government seemed to have little effect upon my household staff. Except for Nur-jan, who was still quietly enjoying her new walk with Jesus, and Raisham, my other Christian servant, my entire staff were faithful followers of Muhammad. Yet a real affection existed between us. More than once my Muslim servants slipped into the bedroom to plead with me. "Please, Begum Sahib Gi," they said in low voices, "if you should have to leave … or if you should decide to leave … don't worry about us. We'll find work."

What a different relationship I had with my staff now than a short four years before.

Dreams, too, played a remarkable role during that time. Dreams had always been a part of my Christian experience, ever since the day I first met Jesus, who came in a dream to feast at the table with me. Now these strange and mystic experiences, such as Paul said he experienced, became even more active.

One night I found myself taken out in spirit and crossing the ocean at a terrific momentum. Like the speed of light I came to what I felt was New England, though I had never been to America. I came before a house, or was it a nursing home? I floated into a room with twin beds. In one lay a middle-aged woman with a round face, clear blue eyes and a mixture of gray and white short hair. A white embossed cotton spread in a triangular pattern covered the bed. She was obviously very ill; I sensed she had cancer. A nurse sat in a chair reading. And then I saw my Lord in the corner of the room. I kneeled down before Him and asked what I should do.

"Pray for her," He said. So I went to the woman's bed and prayed fervently for her healing.

In the morning I sat at my window still awed by what had happened in that room across the sea. Why did Jesus ask me to pray for the woman? He was right there. Yet He had asked me to pray for her. I was beginning to get a glimmer of a tremendous revelation. Our prayers are vital to our Lord. He works through them. I was led to the fifth chapter of James: *Believing prayer will save the sick man; the Lord will restore him and any sins that he has committed will be forgiven. ... Tremendous power is made available through a good man's earnest prayer. ...*

Thus our prayer releases this power into the person for whom we plead.

Another time I envisioned walking up a gangplank as if boarding a ship. The gangplank led into a room. Christ was standing in the room. He seemed to be giving me instructions. Then I walked back down the gangplank. At the end of it a lady was waiting, dressed in western clothes, a skirt and jacket. She appeared to have been waiting for me. She came up to me, linked her arm in mine and started to take me away.

"Where are we going, Lord?" I asked over my shoulder. But He would not tell me.

The dream seemed to be saying that I would be going on another trip. Although this time I would be going to an unknown destination, Jesus would be watching over the journey. The dream left me in a state of preparedness so that I was not startled by the news an old friend brought me.

In March 1971, just a few months after Bhutto had taken office, I had a visit from Yaqub, an old government friend. He had been close to our family for years. In fact, when my husband was Minister, there was a time when Pakistan was in an economic decline with a serious trade imbalance. Yaqub and I had helped inaugurate a self-help program which came to be called the *Simple Living Plan*. The basic idea was to encourage Pakistan industries to produce our own goods, lessening the need for imports.

We had followed each other around the country helping small factories and cottage industries get started. We had encouraged local people to weave fabric and then start production of clothing. We, ourselves, had voluntarily entered an austerity program, wearing homespun garments. It was all to the good, for the *Simple*

Living Plan was a success. As local factories began to thrive, the economic condition of Pakistan improved. Through the years since, Yaqub would occasionally visit me to discuss politics and world affairs. He knew a good deal about our family holdings, for he had visited the many estates we had throughout Pakistan, and he knew that most of our funds were tied up in real estate.

"Bilquis," he said, in a tone that was apologetic, "some friends and I have been talking and … er, the subject of your financial health has come up. Have you considered selling some of your land? I'm not sure how safe it is for you to have all of your funds tied up in real estate, with Bhutto promising land reform."

What a thoughtful thing for Yaqub to do. And not without risk either. With the growing hostility toward the ruling class of yesterday, his government staff car outside my house could easily serve to bring criticism on his own shoulders.

"Thank you, Yaqub," I said, trying to control my voice. "But as things stand now I am determined. Nothing—nothing at all will force me to move out!"

It was an infantile thing to say of course. The old Bilquis with her imperious, stubborn way was showing through. Nonetheless it was an attitude which did not surprise my friend at all. "That's the answer I expected, Bilquis," Yaqub said, stroking his moustache and laughing. "Just the same, the time may come when you may want to leave Pakistan. If you need help …"

"If the time does, my good friend, I will be sure to remember your offer."

Another dream: this time from Raisham, usually so reserved.

"Oh Begum Sheikh," my maid cried, kneeling her tall slender form by the divan on which I sat in my bedroom that cold night I met the Lord. "I've had a horrible dream. Can I tell you about it?"

"Of course."

I listened closely. Raisham told me that in her dream some evil men had come into the house and were holding me prisoner. "I fought with them," she cried. "I called out 'Begum, run!' And in the dream I saw you running out of the house and escaping."

The maid's dark brown eyes were moist with tears. It was I who had to comfort her. But for me this was not difficult. In the words which I spoke, I found myself listening to advice which I should take to heart. "My dear," I said, "I have been hearing much from the Lord lately about the possibility of having to flee. And this may occur. I at first refused to believe. But now I am beginning to wonder."

"It is possible," I said, lifting her pale chin upwards and smiling, "that I may have to go. But if I do, it will be in the Lord's timing. I am learning to accept that. Can you believe me?"

The little maid was silent. Then at last she spoke, "What a wonderful way to live, Begum Sahib."

"It is indeed. It is the only way. Nothing, any longer, is in my own control."

And although I did believe everything I said, as the young maid disappeared from my bedroom, I found myself not quite as in charge of my emotions as I may have sounded. Fleeing? Running away? Me?

The series of message "experiences" began to come more rapidly in the autumn of 1971. One day Nur-jan came to me breathless and taut with emotion.

"What is it, Nur-jan?" I said as she started to brush my hair, her hands trembling.

"Oh, Begum Sahib," Nur-jan sobbed, "I don't want you to be hurt."

"Hurt by what?"

Nur-jan dried her eyes. She told me that her brother, her own brother, had been to the mosque the previous day, and that a group of men had said that at last the time had come to take action against me.

"Do you have any idea of what they meant?"

"No, Begum Sahib," Nur-jan said. "But I am afraid. Not only for you but for the boy, too."

"A nine-year-old child? They wouldn't …"

"Begum Sahib, this is not the country it was even five years ago," said Nur-jan seriously, so unlike her usually bubbly self. "Please be careful."

And indeed, it wasn't but a few weeks later that it happened.

It had been such a lovely day. Autumn was in the air. The monsoon season was over and the weather was crisp and dry. Nothing untoward had happened for days on end and I found myself saying that after all we were living in a modern age. It was 1971, not 1571. Holy wars were a thing of the past.

I went up to my room for my prayer hour.

But suddenly, without knowing why, I had the strongest urge to get Mahmud and to rush outside to the lawn!

What a foolish thing to do. But the urge was so definite that I dashed down the hall, woke Mahmud up from his siesta, and without explanation hurried the groggy and protesting child down the hall.

Still feeling foolish, I dashed down the stairs, threw open the French doors and ran outside.

The moment I stepped onto the terrace, I smelled acrid smoke. Someone was burning pine boughs. We had a long-standing rule that no one was allowed to burn trash on my land. I went in search of the gardener and when I rounded the side of the house was instantly filled with horror.

There, heaped against the house, was a mound of dried pine boughs, ablaze. The crackling flames, hot and fast, raced up the side of the building, leaping high.

I screamed. The servants came running. Soon some were rushing back and forth to the streams with buckets filled with water. Others had unreeled the garden hose and were spraying the flames but our water pressure was low. For a moment it looked as if the fire was going to catch the timbers which stuck out from the end of the building under the roof. They began to smoke and smoulder. There was no way to throw water that high. The only way we could keep the house from burning down was to quench the flames themselves.

On we raced, against time. The ten servants which were on the staff formed a line to the stream passing buckets of water from one person to another, sloshing it over in their hurry.

On everyone worked for half an hour, until finally the leaping flames began to be brought under control. We stood, about a dozen of us, in a circle around the fire. All of us were perspiring, all of us shaking. In another few minutes the house would have been ablaze, impossible to quench.

I caught Nur-jan's eye. She shrugged ever so slightly and nodded her head.

I knew exactly what she was thinking. The threat had been carried out. I looked at the wooden roof beams, their ends charred black, and the soot stains on the white walls of my house. I thanked the Lord that nothing else had happened and shuddered to think of what could have happened if I had not been directed outside at that very moment.

An hour later, after the police had come to investigate, make their notes, question me and the staff, I was once again seated in my room. I picked up the Bible to see if the Lord had anything special to say to me.

One phrase leaped off the page.

"Haste thee, escape thither; for I cannot do anything till thou be come thither" (Genesis 19:22).

I put the book down and looked up. "All You have to do now is show me the *way* You want me to leave. Will it be easy, or will it be hard?"

"And above all, Lord," I said, this time with tears suddenly filling my eyes, "what about the boy? Can he come too? You have been stripping me of everything. Does that include the child as well?"

One day six months later, in May of 1972, the Lord spoke to me still again through another dream. Raisham came to me with worry written in her eyes.

"Begum Sahib," Raisham said, "is the cash box safe?"

She was referring to the portable strong box in which I kept the household cash.

"Of course it's safe," I answered. "Why?"

"Well," Raisham explained, obviously trying to control her voice, "I had a dream last night in which you were motoring on a long trip. You had the cash box with you."

"Yes?" I said. This wasn't too unusual, since I often carried the cash box with me on trips.

"But the dream was so *real*," Raisham insisted. "And the sad part is that as you were traveling, people stopped you and stole the cash box."

She trembled and once again I had to comfort her with assurance that the loss of my money would lead me into a still closer dependence on God. After she went back to her work I thought about that dream. Could it be prophetic? Could it be telling me that my finances would be taken from me? Would I soon be completely on my own, hurtling into the unknown with no means of support?

These were astonishing days. For just two months later, on a hot July day in 1972, a servant came to announce the arrival of my son Khalid.

"Khalid?" My son still lived in Lahore. Why a special trip, especially in this intense heat? What was so important that it could not be handled on the telephone?

Khalid was waiting for me in the drawing room. "Son!" I exclaimed as I walked in. "How great to see you! But why didn't you phone?"

Khalid came over and kissed me. He closed the drawing room door and, without preamble, he plunged into the purpose for his visit. "Mother, I've heard a frightening rumor." He stopped. I tried to smile. Khalid lowered his voice and went on, "Mother, the government is going to expropriate much private property."

My mind went back to the visit from my government friend who had said the same thing, more than a year earlier, back in March, 1971. Was his prophetic visit coming to pass now? Khalid told me that Bhutto was starting his land reforms and that it was very likely that my properties would be among the first to be nationalized.

"What do you think I should do?" I asked. "Will they take it all or just part?"

Khalid got up from his chair and walked over to the garden window, deep in thought. Turning back to me he said:

"Well, Mother, nobody knows. Perhaps it would be best to sell *some* of your properties in small lots. That way the new owner will be protected from a total government takeover."

The more I thought about it, the more I felt Khalid's suggestion made sense. We drove over to discuss the issue with Tooni, all of us agreeing that this was the right way to proceed. It was decided then. Khalid would go back to Lahore. We would join him there to arrange the paperwork. Tooni, Mahmud and I would follow shortly.

So it was that one hot morning in July of 1972, the three of us found ourselves nearly ready for the drive to Lahore to see real estate agents about my properties. As I stepped out of the house I was struck by the beauty of my garden. Summer blossoms were at their height and even the springs seemed to tinkle louder than usual.

"We'll be back in a few weeks," I said to the assembled staff on the front steps of the house. Everyone seemed to accept the idea. Everyone that is but Nur-jan and Raisham. Nur-jan suddenly burst in tears and rushed away.

Sadly I went up to my bedroom to pick up an item I forgot. When I turned again into the hall to go back downstairs, Raisham was standing in front of me. She took my hand, her eyes wet with tears.

"God go with you, Begum Sahib Gi," she said softly.

"And He with you," I answered.

Raisham and I stood in the hall silently together, saying nothing but understanding everything. Somehow I sensed that I would never see this tall slender person again—she with whom I had become so close. I squeezed her hand and whispered, "There is no one who can do my hair like you."

Raisham put her hands to her face and rushed away from me. I was about to close the bedroom door when something stopped me. I walked back into the room and stood there. A hush settled over the white-furnished room. The morning sun flooded in from the garden window. This is where I had come to know the Lord.

I turned my back on the room and on my precious garden, where I had so often known the Lord's Presence, and headed outside to the car.

There were people I would be extremely glad to see in Lahore. First, of course, Khalid, his wife and their teenaged daughter. Then there was the possibility of seeing the Olds. I had written that I would be coming to Lahore. Their new mission was in a village some distance from the town, but I hoped that I could see these old friends.

Lahore, as usual in July, was broiling, its ancient streets steamed with rain from the last monsoon. As we threaded our way through the crowded downtown streets, a loudspeaker on a minaret above us crackled, then broke into the metallic voice of a muezzin's noontime prayer. Traffic suddenly lightened as cars and trucks pulled to the curb. Drivers climbed down to the sidewalk, laid out their prayer mats and began prostrating themselves.

Tooni could only stay with us for a very short time because of prior obligations. After we got the necessary paperwork done and had a short visit, Khalid took us to the railroad station so that Tooni could catch her train. It was a poignant moment at the station, more poignant than I could understand. According to plan, Mahmud would be seeing his mother again in just a few days. Yet we all sensed something unusual about the leave-taking. Mahmud, lanky for nearly ten, tried to hold back the tears as he kissed his mother. Tooni cried openly as she embraced the boy. Suddenly I found myself crying too and we all three hugged each other there on the station platform.

Finally, Tooni threw her dark chestnut hair back and laughed: "Oh come on, we're not having a funeral."

I smiled, kissed her again, and Mahmud and I watched her climb aboard the coach. As the engine tooted and the cars slowly began to leave the station, a pang caught my heart. I searched for Tooni's face in the coach window. We located her and both Mahmud and I blew kisses.

Hungrily, I fastened Tooni's face in my mind, etching it in my memory.

The next day I spent time with realty men who advised me that my property sale would take several weeks. Khalid assured us that we would be welcome as long as we wanted to stay.

The one thing that disturbed me was that I would not have spiritual fellowship. I knew now why disciples went out two by two. Christians *need* each other for sustenance and counsel.

I called the Olds. How great it was to hear Marie's voice! We laughed together and cried together and prayed together on the phone. Though their schedule prevented them from coming to Lahore, they could of course put me in touch with Christians in town. Marie mentioned especially a college professor's wife, Peggy Schlorholtz.

Strange! Why did my heart beat faster at the name?

Within minutes, Peggy and I were on the phone with each other. Within hours, she was in Khalid's drawing room. When she saw me her face broke into a smile.

"Tell me, Begum Sheikh," she said, "is it true that you met Jesus for the first time in a dream? How *did* you come to know the Lord?"

So there in the drawing room I told Peggy the whole story, just as it had begun six years before. Peggy listened intently. When I finished she took my hand and said the most amazing thing.

"I wish you would come to America with me!"

I looked at her, dumbfounded. But again my heart was racing.

"I mean it," said Peggy. "I'm leaving soon to put my son in school. I'll be in the States for four months. You could travel with me and speak to our churches there!"

She was so enthusiastic that I did not want to dampen her spirits. "Well," I said smiling, "I do appreciate your invitation. But let me pray about it."

The next morning a maid brought a note to me. I read it and laughed. It was from Peggy. "Have you prayed yet?" I smiled, crumpled the note and did nothing. It was just too preposterous to think about.

Unless. … Suddenly the events of the past two years crowded into my mind in a momentous sweep. The dreams. The warnings. The fire. My determination to do whatever the Lord wanted—even if it meant leaving my homeland.

No, I had not really committed Peggy's question to the Lord. But I did now. I placed the trip in His hands. It was difficult because I knew with a part of me which I could not understand, that if I left it would not be just for four months. It would be forever.

"Lord, I will say it once again. You know how much I want to stay in my land. After all, I'm 52 years old, and that's not time to start all over again.

"But," I sighed. "But … that is not the most important thing is it? All that really matters is staying in Your Presence. Please help me, Lord, never to make a decision that would take me away from Your glory."

14

Flight

Odd, how after the Lord changed my mind about leaving Pakistan, sudden roadblocks emerged.

One, for instance, that seemed insurmountable was a regulation that citizens of Pakistan are only allowed to take five hundred dollars out of the country. As my dependent, Mahmud could take 250 dollars. How could Mahmud and I possibly live for four months on 750 dollars? This by itself seemed enough to keep us from considering Peggy's suggestion further.

Then a few days later, Peggy invited me to her home for a visit. As we chatted, Dr. Christy Wilson's name came up in the conversation. She knew him too. I was quite concerned about him since I had heard he had been ejected from Afghanistan by the Muslim government which then had destroyed the church he had built in Kabul for foreign nationals.

"Do you have any idea where he is?" I asked.

"Not really," Peggy said.

Just at that moment the phone rang. Peggy went to answer it. When she returned, her eyes were wide, "Do you know who that was?" she said. "It was *Christy Wilson!*"

After we got over our startled, laughing surprise, we began to ask ourselves if this were more than "coincidence." Dr. Wilson, Peggy said, was just passing through Lahore. He wanted to come out for a visit. Of course I was glad, for it would be good to catch up on news, but I had an intuitive sense that more than casual visiting was going to occur.

We had a marvelous reunion at Peggy's house the next day. I brought Dr. Wilson up-to-date on events in Wah and in my own life. Then Peggy told him about trying to persuade me to come to the United States. He became quite enthusiastic about the idea.

"There are several problems though," Peggy said. "The first is the regulation that Bilquis can take only five hundred dollars out of the country."

"I wonder …," Dr. Wilson said stroking his chin. "I have some friends who might. … Perhaps I could send a wire. … I know a man in California. …"

After a few days Peggy phoned, all excited. "Bilquis," she shouted. "It's all arranged! Dr. Bob Pierce of Samaritan's Purse will sponsor you! Do you think you could be ready to leave in seven days?"

Seven days! Suddenly the enormity of the idea of leaving my homeland swept over me. For I still felt convinced that if I did in fact leave, it would be forever. I understood what Rudyard Kipling meant in his lines:

> God gave all men all earth to love,
> But, since our hearts are small,

Ordained for each one spot should prove
Beloved over all …

Wah … my garden … my home … my family. … Could I seriously contemplate leaving them?

Yes, I could. I could consider nothing else if I were truly convinced that this were God's will. For I knew what would happen if I deliberately disobeyed. His Presence would disappear.

Over the next twenty-four hours another confirmation appeared to come through. Khalid told me at supper that there was only one minor detail left to cover, then all of the real estate problems would be over. "I think you can say quite safely, Mother," Khalid said, "that as of today you have divested yourself of the properties you wanted to sell."

Then suddenly doors slammed. Not by God, so it seemed, but by my country. For still a regulation came in, to the effect that no Pakistani can leave the country unless all of his income taxes have been paid. Mine had been paid, but I needed a statement to that effect. I had to get an Income Tax Clearance Certificate. Only with this could I buy tickets for the United States.

Four of my seven days before departure were gone; only three were left now as my son Khalid and I walked into the government office to get the Clearance Certificate. Khalid and I thought there would be no problems at all, since my papers were in order.

The office was on a busy street in downtown Lahore. However, when I stepped into that building, something struck me as strange. It was far too quiet for the usual bureaucratic office where clerks ran hither and yon and someone always seemed to be arguing with a staff member.

Khalid and I were the only ones in the office except for a bald-headed clerk who sat at the far end of the counter reading a magazine. Stepping up to him, I told him what I wanted.

He looked up only partially and shook his head. "Sorry lady," he said putting his head back down into the magazine again, "there's a strike on."

"A strike?"

"Yes, Madame," he said. "Indefinitely. No one is on duty. There's nothing anyone can do for you."

I stood staring at the man. Then I withdrew a few feet. "On Lord," I prayed aloud, but in such a way that only my son could hear me, "have You closed the door? But why did you encourage me so far?"

Then a thought struck me. Had He really closed the door? "All right, Father," I prayed. "If it is Your will that Mahmud and I go to America, You'll have to be the one to arrange for my clearance." A strong sense of confidence filled me and I found myself addressing the clerk.

"Well, *you* seem to be on duty," I said. "Why can't *you* give me my clearance?"

The man glanced up from his magazine with a dour expression. He seemed the type who was always happy to say no.

"I told you, lady, there's a strike on," he grunted.

"Well, then, let me see the officer in charge." One thing I had learned in my government work was that when I wanted something done, I should always go to the highest authority.

The clerk sighed, slapped down his magazine and escorted me to an office nearby. "Wait here," he grunted again, then disappeared into the office. From it I could hear a low murmur of voices, then the man emerged and motioned me in.

Khalid and I found ourselves facing a handsome middle-aged man sitting behind a scarred desk. I explained my need. He leaned back in his chair, twirling a pencil. "I'm sorry Madame … Madame … what did you say your name was?"

"Bilquis Sheikh."

"Well, I'm very sorry. There's absolutely nothing we can do during this strike. …" But suddenly a light of recognition flooded his eyes.

"You aren't the Begum Sheikh who organized the *Simple Living Plan*?"

"I am."

He slammed his fist on the table, then shot up. "Well!" he said. He drew a chair over and asked me to sit down. "I think that was the most wonderful program our country ever had."

I smiled.

Then the officer leaned across his desk in a confidential manner. "Now let's see what we can do for you."

He got me to explain precisely what the problem was and I told him that I was supposed to be in Karachi to catch a plane for the United States in three days. The man's face took on a resolute look. Standing up, he called out to the clerk on the counter. "Tell that new assistant to come in here."

"I have," he said to me in a very low voice, "a temporary stenographer. He is not part of the regular work staff and isn't on strike. He can type up the Certificate. I *myself* will put on the seal. I'm glad to help."

A few minutes later I had the precious Certificate in my hand, fully executed. As I left, I confess, I waved the paper at the surprised little clerk who looked up from his magazine just long enough to see my smile and hear my "God bless you."

As we left the government office building a few minutes later, an astonished Khalid mentioned to me that it had taken only twenty minutes to complete the entire business. "That was less than it would have taken if everyone had been on duty!" he said.

My heart singing, I tried to explain to Khalid that the Lord wants our *companionship*. When we pray, He wants to work *with* us. It was the Moses' Rod Principle. If I had just put the problem in the Lord's hands without stepping out in faith myself, I might never have gotten the Clearance. I had to step out by doing everything I could. I had to ask to see the man in charge. Just as God required Moses to strike the rock with a rod, He asks us, too, to *participate* in the working of miracles.

Khalid seemed a bit taken aback by my enthusiasm but recovered and added with a smile: "Well, I'll say one thing, Mother. I notice that instead of 'thank you' you always say 'God bless you.' And when you say that, it's the most beautiful thing I've ever heard."

Now that all my papers were in order I wondered if I could take a quick trip back to Wah to say goodbye, for by then I was convinced that this trip would be for more than four months. However, when I brought up the subject, Khalid said:

"Didn't you hear about the flood?"

Heavy rains had struck the portion of Pakistan between Lahore and Wah. Many square miles of land were flooded. All traffic was snarled. The government had taken over transportation.

My heart sank. I would not even be allowed to say goodbye. The Lord was asking me to make a clean break, like Lot being told not to look back.

I had planned to leave Lahore on Friday morning, two days off. I would fly to Karachi, the jumping-off place for the United States.

Peggy and her son would begin their trip in New Delhi. Their Pan American New York-bound plane would stop at Karachi and Mahmud and I would join them on the plane there. On Thursday morning, however, an unusually strong urge swept over me not to wait. My anxiety centered around Mahmud. Surely grapevine efficiency had taken the news back to Wah that we were not on a simple visit to Lahore but were on our way out of the country. Wasn't it probable that relatives might try to take Mahmud away from my "corrupting" influence! Would I be stopped on some pretext or other? A strong sense of danger spurred me.

No, I wouldn't wait. I would leave that very day. I would go to Karachi, stay with friends, and lie low.

So that afternoon, after a flurry of packing, Mahmud and I said quick farewells to Khalid and his family and hurried to the airport. We flew out of Lahore with a definite sense of relief. We were on our way!

Karachi was, as I remembered it, a rambling desert and seashore town nestled against the Indian Ocean. It was a hodgepodge of the old and new, of gangling camels brushing against Rolls Royces, of buzzing fly-filled bazaars next to smart shops offering the latest Parisian fashions. Perfect. The town was so large we would just be swallowed up in it.

We were staying with friends and I was shopping downtown, preparing for our departure for America the next day. Suddenly a strange oppression came over me. I closed my eyes as I leaned against a wall for support and prayed for my Lord's protection. I was given the strong leading that Mahmud and I were to move to a hotel that night. I tried to shake it off. "This is silly!" I told myself. Then I remembered the story of the Wise Men being warned in a dream to leave early by another route.

Shortly, we were checked into the Air France Hotel at the Karachi Airport. I took Mahmud to the room as quickly as possible, ordered our meals sent up, and together we simply waited. Mahmud seemed restless. "Why do we have to be so secretive, Mum?" he asked.

"I just think we ought to be quiet for a little while, that's all."

That night before the flight, I lay awake in bed wondering. Why was I so apprehensive? There was no real reason for it. Was I letting my nerves take over? Was I overreacting to the threats of the past? The fire? I slept fitfully and only for a few hours. By two o'clock in the morning I was up and dressed, again prodded by a strong sense of urgency. Again I felt ridiculous. It was unlike me. The only way I could explain it was that the hour had come for me to *leave* the hotel and I was being *propelled* by the Lord. I hustled a groggy Mahmud into his clothes, then gathered our bags, placing them by the door for the bellman to pick up.

It was three o'clock in the morning. The flight was at five. Mahmud, still sleepy-eyed, stood with me in front of the hotel waiting for a taxi to take us to the terminal. I looked at the waning moon and wondered, would this be the last time I would see this moon in my own country? An early morning breeze wafted a scent of narcissus, probably from a flower box, and my heart cried out, for I sensed that I would never see my garden again.

Finally the doorman flagged a cab. Mahmud and I climbed in. I prayed as we wove our way through traffic. Even at this early hour the airport avenues were busy. As cars pulled alongside at stoplights I nervously sank back a little deeper into the seat. "We're just being quiet for a little while," I quoted myself, trying to sound as reassuring to my own ears as I had to Mahmud. No, that wasn't the way. What I really needed to do was to pray. "Lord, do take away this nervousness. Nervousness is not founded in You. I cannot trust You and worry at the same time! And yet if this urgency is of You, Lord, there must be a reason and I will obey."

We pulled into the terminal and got out onto a bustling sidewalk where the rumbling thunder of jet engines and the cacophony of hundreds of voices blended in an atmosphere of urgency. My heart caught as I looked up and saw my country's flag, the star and crescent on its green background, snapping in the breeze. I would always respect that flag, my people, and their Muslim faith. A porter hurried our luggage over to the check-in counter where I was grateful to see it disappear into seeming safety.

Just 40 pounds of luggage each. I smiled as I thought of our family trips on other days to the interior when thousands of pounds of luggage were taken for just a few week's stay and my sisters still cried for the clothes that we couldn't take along.

We had an hour to wait before plane time. Keeping Mahmud close to me, I felt it best for us to mix in with the crowd in the terminal so we wouldn't be noticed. But I couldn't shake the sense of impending danger. Again I scolded myself for needless worry. The Lord is in charge, I told myself. He is guiding me out of this situation, and all I need to do is obey.

Then Mahmud asked to go to the restroom. We walked down the hall to the men's room. I waited in the corridor.

Suddenly the loudspeaker called out our flight.

"Pan Am flight for New York City now ready for boarding."

My heart jumped. Where was Mahmud! We must be going!

Finally the men's room door opened. No, it was a turbanned Sikh who stepped out.

I found myself edging to the door. What was I doing! Certainly no woman in a Muslim country would be caught going into a men's room even to look for a nine-year-old missing youngster.

Now they were calling our flight again. "Pan Am flight for New York City is now ready for departure. All passengers should be aboard."

Oh no! My heart cried. I had to do something. I pushed the men's room door back and shouted, "Mahmud!"

A little voice answered, "I'm coming Mum. ..."

I breathed a deep sigh and fell back limply against the wall. Soon Mahmud came out. "Where were you? What kept you!" I cried.

No matter. I didn't wait for an answer but grabbed the boy's hand and ran. Now we rushed down the long hall to the boarding gate. We found ourselves among the last passengers getting aboard.

"Wow, Mum!" cried Mahmud. "What a ship!"

What a ship indeed. The 747 airliner was huge. We were both excited. I had never seen such a big plane before.

As I was about to step aboard I hesitated for a moment, at this last touch of Pakistan's soil.

But we had to keep moving. Inside the plane, which seemed like an auditorium to me, a stewardess directed us toward our seats. Where was Peggy? What would I do in the States without her?

And then, there she was! Working her way up the aisle toward us. Peggy threw her arms about me.

"Oh precious lady!" she cried. "I was so worried. I couldn't see you in the crowd at the boarding gate!" I explained what had happened and Peggy seemed relieved. She introduced us to her son who was with her. "Too bad we can't sit together," she said. "We just had to take the seats they gave us."

Frankly, it was just as well. My thoughts were not social at that time. They were on the realization that I was leaving my homeland. I felt sad, certainly, but at the same time *complete*. I couldn't understand it.

Soon Mahmud was being Mahmud. He made friends with a stewardess who took him into the cockpit for a visit. Mahmud came back enthralled. I was pleased. The stewardess asked us to put on our seat belts. I looked out the window to see the first rays of dawn spearing the eastern sky. The engines rumbled and a surge of excitement filled me. Our ship began to lumber down the runway. I looked behind me but could not see Peggy.

But Mahmud's face was there, next to me. And it shone with excitement as the jet engines exploded into thunder at takeoff. I took Mahmud's hand and began to pray.

"What now, Lord? Again I have such a feeling of *completion!* You have brought me out of my homeland, like Abram. Not knowing what comes next, yet complete. Satisfied, because I am with You."

Even embarrassment over my fears and nervousness didn't bother me now. All I knew was that I had obeyed the Lord in every way. And I had to admit that I would never really know what might have happened if I had not followed His every command and moved as I did.

Tiny lights whisked by the windows and suddenly the rumbling of wheels beneath us ceased. We were airborne! In the light of early dawn, I could see the shoreline of Pakistan on the Indian Ocean receding below us.

I held out my hand to Him. He was my only security. My only joy was staying in His Presence. As long as I could stay there I knew that I would be living in the glory.

"Thank You, God," I breathed. "Thank You for letting me travel with You."

Postscript

Bilquis Sheikh went on to live in the USA, a woman with no country to call her own, but with more of a heart for every nation. Having had to leave behind her garden on the other side of the world, she created another one on the hillside behind the little house in California which she shared with her grandson Mahmud. She died in 1997.

EPILOGUE

After the Book

After Bilquis Sheikh moved to the United States in 1973, she spoke all over North America, and later in different countries of the world, sharing what God had done in her life. In early 1989, while living in Thousand Oaks, California, she suffered a severe heart attack. Her three children rushed to her side from different parts of the world—her daughter Tooni and son, Khalid, from Pakistan, and her daughter Khalida from Kenya. Since it was inadvisable for her to continue to live on her own, they persuaded her to return to her family in Pakistan to spend her later years.

In 1992 Bilquis' grandson Mahmud, whom she had adopted as her son, also returned to Pakistan and began a successful orthodontic practice in Islamabad.

April 9, 1997, was her final day here on earth and her entrance to the home prepared for her in heaven. She was buried in Murree,

Rawalpindi District, in an old Christian graveyard nestled in the Himalayan Mountains. Her simple white marble tombstone is engraved with a prominent cross, underneath which is written:

Bilquis
Born 12-12-12
Died 9-4-97
Loving the Lord

In September 1999 Mahmud was tragically murdered while attempting to avert an honor killing involving one of the servants working in his home. Mahmud is survived by his wife and two children, a daughter and son, who continue to live in the Islamabad area.

Remembering the Flower Lady

SYNNOVE MITCHELL

I remember the day as clearly as if it were yesterday: Thursday, November 24, 1966. David, my husband, was leaving shortly for Kabul, Afghanistan, and I would be alone with our two small children, Jonathan and Joy, in an old mud-brick Army barracks built by the British during World War II. For the past year we had been living in this small town, two miles from Wah Village, outside the gate to the Wah Cement Factory, on the road between Rawalpindi and the Khyber Pass.

I was spiritually desperate. David and I had both grown up in India as missionary children, so we had felt at home immediately when we first came to Pakistan in 1961. I was born in India, and except for eight years in Norway during World War II, had lived all my formative years on the Indian subcontinent. David and I loved living here. It was home. But we were not here just to feel at home; we were here to share the good news of the Kingdom of God.

But I was desperate because God was dealing with me, showing me clearly that, on my own, I did not have what it takes to share the Good News in Pakistan.

Early in the morning of November 24, I fell on my knees before God. His Holy Spirit, I knew, is the only One who can work deep in the heart—especially in the heart of a Muslim—to reveal the need for a Savior, the need for Jesus. I needed a fresh touch from Him myself, and confirmation that He knew where I was living and where I was spiritually.

So I cried out to Him, asking Him to do a work in me through which I would know He loved me personally, deeply. First I asked Him to let me know beyond a shadow of a doubt that He wanted me in this mud-brick Army barracks; and second, that I would not be able to explain away His work; and third, that through this work our neighbors and others living around us would see the reality of Jesus and His power to bring people to God. As a postscript to this prayer, I added, "O God, do this soon, or I will have to pack up and leave."

As I said, I was desperate. But poor David! I told him of my prayer just before he set out on his journey to Kabul. He had no idea when he left what state he would find me in when he returned. He knew only God Himself could meet my need.

Five days passed. I continued to lay my requests before God. Then came the day for my weekly Bible study. As many as fourteen women from a nominal Christian background gathered each Tuesday in our living room. But because of the dryness in my own soul, I had nothing fresh to share.

"O God," I prayed, "unless Your Holy Spirit speaks to me through Your Word, there will be no life in what I share. Please, Father, open up something from Your Word that will give life to these dear, illiterate women who don't have a chance to read the Bible on their own, or I'll have to cancel the meeting."

After that prayer I began to sense the Lord telling me, *Share with them the story of the wise men.* So I opened my Bible to Matthew 2. The simple story of wise men from the East in search of the King of the Jews, a story I had known since childhood, now opened up to me with freshness. Here were men who knew little about God but who had a deep hunger to worship Him. They knew so little that they went to Herod, a godless, ruthless Gentile ruler, to find out where to find this King who was worthy of worship.

Herod recognized them immediately as men of wisdom and stature, because not only he but all of Jerusalem was perturbed at their news and questions. King Herod gathered the Jewish leaders to find out where the Messiah would be born. Having a thorough knowledge of the Scriptures, they gave the right answer, Bethlehem. But they returned to the daily routine of their lives. In contrast, Matthew writes of the wise men, "When they saw the star, they rejoiced exceedingly with great joy!" (Matthew 2:10, NASB). They who knew very little but who longed to worship the King were filled with anticipation and joy. They recognized Jesus as the King, fell down before Him and worshiped Him.

God brought new light and life to the story for me. I was filled "with exceeding great joy" myself, and anticipation that God would do something special. I could hardly wait for the women to come. The story of the wise men would grip them, I knew, as it had me. I was convinced that all fourteen of them would come to a saving knowledge of Jesus that very day.

The women began arriving. We pushed back the cane sofa and chairs to make room for all of us, women and children, to sit on the reed matting that covered the floor. Hashmat, my blind helper, led the singing with her strong, true voice, and her fingers skillfully played her *dholki*, a cylindrical drum with skin stretched tightly over both ends. I loved the enthusiastic singing, clapping and intricate rhythms of Pakistani music.

Then, with excitement, I told these women the wonderful story of the wise men. But their reaction was the same as mine had been previously—mild interest, but no inner illumination as to its application to the heart. My exhilarating anticipation to witness God at work turned to deep disappointment, even a bit of anger—anger at the women for their lack of response, and anger at God for letting me down.

I ended the wise men's story saying something like this: "If this story had happened today, it would mean that we Christians would be like the religious leaders. We know the right answers and can give them to others, but we ourselves would go home to our regular daily routines, oblivious of our need to worship Jesus; whereas some seeking Muslims, who know very little about this story, would be like the wise men, falling at Jesus feet and worshiping Him." I closed the meeting with a prayer for God to have mercy on us all and give us seeking hearts.

I was still standing at the front door bidding the village women goodbye when Begum Bilquis Sheikh drove into our driveway. Everyone knew who she was. Who had not heard of the Wah Khans? Wasn't she formerly the wife of General Sheikh, the minister of interior under President Ayub? But was that a Bible she clutched in her hand? The village women could not help but be shocked at the timing of her arrival.

"Welcome to our home, Begum Sheikh," I said, trying to mask my surprise at her arrival, and at the amazing timing.

"I have only come to ask a question," she replied, looking flustered by the Christian village women still in the process of leaving.

I ushered her inside, seated her in one of our cane easy chairs and rearranged the rest of the furniture that had been pushed aside to make room on the floor for everyone. Then I turned my full attention to my special guest.

"Would you like tea or coffee, Begum Sheikh?" I asked, following proper Pakistani etiquette.

"Neither," she replied. "I have come to talk, not to drink tea. Where is your husband?"

"He's on a trip to Afghanistan."

"Do you know anything about God?" she asked abruptly.

Forgetting about serving tea or coffee, I settled into the other cane easy chair. "I'm afraid I don't know as much as my husband knows about God, but I do know Him," I answered.

She went on to tell me her story—about recently reading both the Quran and the Bible and being very confused. Until this time she had thought they ran parallel, and that both led to God. But now, she said, seeing differences between the books, she was confused. She had prayed, *O God, over the years I have not sought You. But now that I am seeking You, do not let me go astray. Show me Your way.*

"Last Thursday," she continued, "I had a dream. I was on a mountaintop, standing at a crossroads, and I did not know which way to go. I knew the roads had something to do with the Quran and the Bible. I did not know which road to take. Standing at the crossroads was a man wearing a long robe, with sandals on his feet. I went up to ask him which way to go to find God. Before he could answer, I woke up and heard myself crying out, 'John the Baptist, John the Baptist!' Mrs. Mitchell, please tell me, who is John the Baptist?"

In awe at the realization of what God was doing in her heart, I explained to her that John the Baptist was sent as a forerunner to prepare the way for the coming of the Messiah, and the one who later baptized Him. John was the one who pointed to Jesus, declaring, "Look, the Lamb of God, who takes away the sins of the world!"

Pain flashed across Begum Sheikh's face as she bowed her head. "That is what I was afraid of. That is what I was afraid of."

"What were you afraid of?" I asked softly.

"I was afraid that John the Baptist was pointing me to Jesus. If I choose Jesus, I lose everything!"

She raised her head and looked at me directly. "Forget I am a Muslim. Forget the problems we have with Jesus being called the Son of God. Forget about our believing that the Bible has been changed. Just tell me one thing: What has Jesus done for you?"

O God, I cried out in my heart, *why have You sent Begum Sheikh to me when I am dry in my soul? Why didn't You send her to someone who is on top spiritually, someone who could share out of strength, not out of spiritual weakness, as I am experiencing?*

But at that moment I knew that God had sent Begum Sheikh to me for my own need. Deeply awed and humbled, I reached out once again to Him. *O Lord, pour into me, so that what I share with Begum Sheikh will have come from You—words of life.*

At that moment all that Jesus did, through His sacrificial death on the cross for the sins of everyone in the world, again became fresh and real to me. I knew God loved me personally. Deeply. I can still see a picture of myself, figuratively reaching one arm up to God, stretching the other toward Bilquis, and God pouring through me what He wanted to share with her. Out of this fresh awareness, I quietly shared with Begum Sheikh what Jesus had done for me:

"For many years," I began softly, "I had only known about God. But then, through God's Spirit working in my heart, I realized I did not know Him personally. Because of my sins, I was far from God. Sins that had seemed small to me were shown for what they were—pride, rebellion, going my own way. I felt the weight of guilt; and the terrible realization that I deserved God's judgment dawned on me. But then a wonderful truth—that God loved the world so much that He sent Jesus to receive the just punishment for my sin, to die in my place, to become my sacrifice—became wonderfully real to me. I personally received forgiveness. I experienced the tremendous joy of being free from guilt. What a gift! Jesus brought me to God. Through Jesus I have come to know God. That is what Jesus has done for me. That is what He longs to do for you. Begum Sheikh, John the Baptist spoke the truth when he pointed to Jesus and declared, 'Look, the Lamb of God, who takes away the sins of the world!'"

After what seemed like a long silence, Begum Sheikh asked me to pray. We knelt on the floor together. I clearly remember my prayer: "O God, I know that nothing I can say will convince Begum Sheikh who Jesus is. But I thank You that Your Spirit can take the veil off our eyes and reveal Jesus to our hearts. O Holy Spirit, do this for Begum Sheikh, In Jesus' name. Amen."

"Yes, God, that is exactly what I want," Begum Sheikh responded.

I knew that we both sensed the quiet presence of God. Then, realizing that the book in her hand was an old-translation Urdu Bible, and since English was like a second mother tongue to her, I offered her my copy of Phillips' paraphrase of the New Testament in modern-day English. I suggested she read the gospel of John, since it clearly explained the role of John the Baptist. Then I shared with her the story of the wise men. Suddenly I knew that God had laid that message on my heart especially for her.

When I came to the part of the story where God told the wise men not to return to Herod, as he had requested, she cried out, "God *does* speak in dreams, then! If the Bible tells about God speaking in dreams, then I know He has spoken to me in my dream. I don't usually dream, Mrs. Mitchell, but I had another dream that I don't understand. I know it has something to do with Jesus, too."

And she told me her dream of the perfume salesman who had come to her house. "I have a weakness for perfume, and had just run out of my favorite kind. But the perfume the salesman showed me was the most wonderful perfume I had ever smelled. It was heavenly perfume! He told me it would spread all through my home, to my neighbors … in fact, everywhere! I know it has something to do with Jesus. Can you explain this dream for me?"

At that moment my heart was singing. He had sent her the dream about John the Baptist the very day I had prayed so desperately! God has answered my prayer! He has answered all my requests. God loves me! I do not have to pack up and leave. God has deigned to show me His awesome ability to reveal Himself to anyone seeking Him. I could think of nothing else, so I answered honestly, "I can't think of an explanation right now, Begum Sheikh, but I'll pray and ask God to show me."

After saying goodbye to her, I sat for a long time in the living room, basking in God's presence and filled with awe and wonder at His love and grace. He had answered my prayer far above what I ever could have imagined. I was deeply humbled by my anger at God in not answering my prayer by fulfilling my expectations, and overawed at His great patience and mercy shown by bringing Begum Sheikh to me in my own deep need. I knew I was deeply loved by God. I would never be able to explain away what He had allowed me to witness, and our neighbors and others living nearby would have a living, present example of the reality and power of Jesus to reveal God.

I had given Begum Sheikh the Phillips paraphrase that I was currently using, but I found a copy of Ken Taylor's *Letters to Young Churches* (which was later expanded into *The Living Bible*), which had been sent us recently. Wanting to spend time with God in His Word, I opened to 2 Corinthians. Starting from the first chapter I began to read. When I reached the fourteenth verse of the second chapter, I could not believe my eyes. Right before me was the word *perfume!*

> Thanks be to God! For through what Christ has done, he has triumphed over us, so that now wherever we go he uses us to tell others about the Lord and to spread the Gospel like a sweet perfume!

The fifteenth verse goes on to say that the perfume "is the fragrance of Christ within us, an aroma to both the saved and the unsaved all around us."

Here, straight from God's Word, was the clear explanation of Begum Sheikh's dream. She had known that the perfume had something to do with Jesus. The perfume was Jesus Himself.

Christ would be in her, and the fragrance would spread to "all around us." Oh, how great is our God! I found a sheet of paper, wrote a note to my new friend and asked our watchman to take it to her early in the morning. God's Spirit was drawing her to Himself and His Word was confirming it.

But how could I share with David in Afghanistan God's mighty answers to prayer, without endangering Begum Sheikh? How could I let him know that, instead of packing to leave, I was overflowing with praise and gratitude for the privilege of seeing Him at work? Then, remembering that David and I had visited her garden in the spring, filled with all kinds of beautiful flowers, and that some of the seeds she had given us were even now beginning to sprout, I carefully worded a telegram: *Flower Lady under great conviction, have all pray!*

On receiving the telegram, he told me later, David shouted to his friends, "Praise God! My wife isn't packing to leave. God is working in the heart of Begum Sheikh. Let's pray!"

God answered those prayers and ushered us into a very special friendship with the Flower Lady, and onto a journey of watching Him work powerfully through His Spirit and His Word.

You have already read the story of that special journey in the pages of this book. You have followed Begum Bilquis Sheikh as she came to know God her Father, learned to live daily in His presence and was used by Him to share her powerful testimony in many parts of the world. But since the final chapter of this book, first published in 1978, could not include the very last chapter of her life, I would like to describe God's grace and faithfulness to her in that closing time.

Bilquis wanted to glorify God, not only by her life, but also by her death. She wanted to be sure that, in the future, everyone who saw her grave would know that she died in Christ, following Him to the very end of her life.

Knowing how much Bilquis loved the mountains, her daughter, Tooni, her cousin and very special friend Nina and I drove up to Murree, Pakistan, in the spring of 1993 to look for a suitable gravesite. Murree, a "hill station" nestled in the foothills of the Himalayan Mountains, would be an ideal place. After much searching, we found the perfect spot in an old Christian graveyard surrounded by majestic evergreens and overlooking layer after layer of mountain ranges. There was even a blossoming fruit tree framing the idyllic scenery—a reminder to me of the Flower Lady. All three of us were in agreement and at peace. The surroundings reminded us of Bilquis—of her love for the mountains and the beauty of God's creation.

Before Dave and I left for a six-month furlough in July 1993, Bilquis called us to meet with her and Tooni to make plans for her funeral, should the Lord call her home before we returned to Pakistan. She made it very clear that she believed the Lord would let her live till we returned after six months, so David and I could be near her when her time to leave came, and we could be responsible for the Christian part of her funeral. But she wanted everything ready, just in case her Father had other plans.

Tooni took out a big sheet of paper, and under her mother's specific instructions sketched her tombstone—a white marble slab with a prominent cross, with the simple message *Bilquis, born 12-12-12, died ———, Loving the Lord*, decorated with engraved narcissus. We wrote down the hymns to be sung at her funeral that had been a source of encouragement and strength to her over the years. We also introduced her to the vicar of the

Church of Pakistan (a union of several denominations, including Anglican) who was responsible for the chosen gravesite, the Reverend Isaac Burt Paul. This tall, vibrant Christian Punjabi would be responsible for her funeral, should she leave us before our return to Pakistan.

Not only did the Lord let her live through our 1993 furlough, but she lived through July 1996, the time of our next furlough. I had an evening reception to attend in Murree two days before leaving, and decided to visit Bilquis, who now lived in a lovely home her beloved Mahmud had built just for her on a hill surrounded by pines, not far from the main road to Murree. On the way, a sudden monsoon storm came crashing down. Lightning flashed, the skies released torrents of rain and the pickup got mired in mud on the unfinished road leading up to her home. Leaving the truck, I trudged up the slippery hillside in the downpour to the shelter of Bilquis' home.

I will never forget her reaction when she saw me standing in her doorway. In utter joy and astonishment, she exclaimed, "Sanovar!" (It was her own little twist on my Pakistani name, Sanobar.) "You have come on a night like this? The best part is that you have brought *Jesus* with you!"

I was deeply moved by her greeting. It revealed her unwavering, vibrant love for her Lord.

"Yes, my dear Bilquis, and you bring Jesus to me! Didn't He promise that if even just two of us would meet together, He Himself would be there with us?"

What a wonderful time of fellowship we had that stormy evening, recounting God's grace and faithfulness in both of our lives.

The next time I saw her was after our return to Pakistan. Tooni phoned me urgently: "*Ma-ji* is with me. She is very ill with post-flu complications. Will you come and give her spiritual help?"

For the next two weeks I visited her just about every day to sing her favorite hymns, to read her favorite passages of Scripture, to pray with her and to have fellowship together. Our time of breaking bread—taking Communion at her request—just five days before her death will always be a precious memory. Because of Jesus, our focus was on eternal life, not death. In the midst of the pain of dying, she received hope from knowing she would soon see her Lord and Savior face to face.

Tooni, as a medical doctor, was able to keep her mother in her home and tend lovingly to her every need. She also had a simple but lovely casket made. Because of our preparations ahead of time, the details of the funeral were not difficult to arrange. But we had a genuine problem. It rained every day, those last few days, and if it rained the day of her homegoing, how would the grave be dug without filling up with mud? In Pakistan the funeral has to take place within 24 hours, which meant we prayed that God would graciously hold back the rain on the day He planned to call her home.

Shortly after daybreak on April 10, 1997, Tooni called to tell Dave and me the news that her mother, our dear friend, had quietly drawn her last breath shortly before midnight. We grieved for all of us left behind, but rejoiced with Bilquis, who was now home with her Father, whom she had come to know and love.

The sky was dark and threatening, but it was not raining. "That's Mum's Jesus for you!" was Tooni's comment as we prepared to leave for Murree.

A small group of between 25 and 30—a few of the many who had known and loved her, both Muslim and Christian—gathered for a graveside service to celebrate Bilquis' life. We read passages from the Old and New Testaments, reminding us of the glorious promises awaiting those who belong to the Lord Jesus. And we sang her favorite hymns—"Great Is Thy Faithfulness," "How Great Thou Art" and "I Know Whom I Have Believed," the song based on 2 Timothy 1:12 that will always bring back for me memories of her life. She first heard it with tears running down her cheeks: *I know not how the Spirit moves, convincing men of sin, revealing Jesus through the Word, creating faith in Him. But I know whom I have believed and am persuaded that He is able to keep that which I've committed unto Him against that day.* On first hearing this song, Bilquis had exclaimed, with emotion, "Someone else has gone through exactly what I have experienced!" Now *that day* referred to in the song had arrived.

Before the service started, those of us gathered at the grave had an unforgettable experience: The upper portion of the simple wooden casket, covered and lined in white, was opened for all of us to see Bilquis' face for a last goodbye. Her head was surrounded by beautiful white flowers, and on her face was a serene look of peace, almost a smile, belying the struggle and pain of the last few days.

Suddenly, before the casket was closed, the dark cloud above us parted briefly, and a bright ray of sunshine, almost like a spotlight, shone directly onto her face. I could hear from the audible reactions of others surrounding her casket that they were as taken aback as I was. It looked like a beam shining directly from heaven, God's benediction on her unwavering trust in Him, whom she had dared to call *Father*.

Enriched by the East

SYNNØVE MITCHELL

My husband, David, and I are grateful for the privilege of having been raised in both Eastern and Western cultures. The pungent smells and brilliant colors of an Eastern bazaar—curry spices piled high, brilliant yellow turmeric, bright red and black peppers, dark-brown cinnamon, light-brown cumin, and the gray-green of powdered coriander—evoke childhood memories as intensely happy as a cold, crisp, white Norwegian winter snow scene with the scent of pine and fir and the welcoming aroma of strong coffee in a ski chalet. Very different, but we love them both, and have been greatly enriched by both.

For the average Westerner, the sights, sounds and scents of the East are fascinating, but their thinking patterns, their worldview, their values and their decision-making methods often baffle us. We do not always realize that the Easterner experiences the very same bafflement when first encountering the West! But most of the bewilderment is removed through personal relationships. Through the sheer fun and eventual bonding with friends, understanding replaces fear, suspicion and the initial awkwardness of trying to break the ice.

Over the nearly forty years Dave and I lived in Pakistan (our childhood years in India not included), we have enjoyed noting some of the contrasts between East and West. Many of these we learned from Begum Sheikh and the patience she displayed with us. I spent hours with her, sitting cross-legged on her bed or *takhtposh* (a low, wooden, table-like platform), leaning against an oblong pillow for comfort, learning the proper etiquette when eating her delicious curries with my fingers instead of with knife, fork and spoon, and listening spellbound to her stories of political intrigue, such as the communication struggles between Eastern and Western officers during World War II. Those were unrushed times, no goal or agenda in mind except to enjoy one another's company and get to know and learn from each other. It was here that the Phillips translation of the New Testament (and later the complete Bible) became worn, as we enjoyed not only social interaction but learning to know God in greater depth.

Since Begum Sheikh herself had been drawn to Jesus through dreams, it was not surprising, over the years when we were together in Wah, that God brought several seekers to hear her story who had also received dreams and visions from Him. I watched how carefully she brought attention to Jesus by praying for them and claiming the promises He Himself had made, and applying those promises in simple faith to their specific needs. She was concerned not only to give her visitors truths about God, but to bring them into the presence of Jesus, the Truth.

The fact is, it is much easier to talk to Easterners about spiritual things. They are willing to take the time because, as a rule, they believe in the supernatural and are very aware of the spiritual realm. Most secular Westerners, on the other hand, believe primarily in what can be seen or proven by the scientific method. Often the Westerner feels that to talk about spiritual matters and "myths" is a waste of time.

Jesus was an Easterner. He flowed with what His heavenly Father had orchestrated for each day. He walked dusty roads, rode on donkeys, sat by wells and taught spiritual truths by telling simple stories that had powerful application to daily life—very much like life in the East, even today.

One of the most frequently heard words in the Urdu language is *izzat*. Woe to the person who does not understand not only its linguistic meaning but also its cultural importance. *Honor*. David and I will never forget the near-tragedy that happened to an insensitive Westerner we knew shopping in a Pakistani fruit market. Instead of enjoying the fun of learning to bargain, he called the fruit vendor dishonest for asking too high a price for his fruit. The word *dishonest* dishonored the vendor in front of his other customers. A near riot took place as they moved to the vendor's defense. Had not a quick-thinking Pakistani driver pulled our friend into his car, who knows what could have happened?

An Easterner could probably forgive any sin more easily than public dishonor, whereas Westerners think in terms of right and wrong. As Christians we believe God is either pleased or displeased with us, according to how well we follow the biblical standards of right and wrong. Over the years, however, David and I have learned from our Eastern friends that the God of the Scriptures puts great emphasis on His honor. Over and over in the Bible we read that everything

God does is for His name's sake, for the glory of His name. It all boils down to God's honor. If we truly long to honor Him, we will automatically want to do what is right.

The frontiersman of the American West, who could do everything on his own and pull himself up by his own bootstraps, is still highly admired across the U.S. We seek privacy and are individualistic, following the motto *Do your own thing*. How very different from the East! There a person finds his identity in the group, the "brotherhood" or tribe to which he belongs. The emphasis on doing everything together, rather than on the individualistic "I can do it myself, thank you," creates strong bonds to family and community. Decisions are made within the group setting. The roles as defined by the group—mother, daughter, wife, grandmother, sister, niece, hostess—and the events that take place within that framework set the agenda for daily living.

That is why it was so excruciating for Begum Sheikh when, after her conversion, the family made the decision to boycott her. The honor of her own family, and her place within their close-knit bonds, was of vital importance to her. How different from the personal goal orientation of the West! Our God-given roles within the family often play second fiddle to the goal of individual material success.

I am aware of how difficult it is for Western women to understand the restrictions in independence, in dress and in freedom of choice and movement in which some of our Eastern sisters live. The tradeoff is found in a sense of security and belonging. The male head of the family is responsible for the safety, welfare and honor of the women in the household. (But I will let you in on a secret: Women have a lot more power within the confines of the courtyard than we Westerners realize! Many times the woman is the neck that turns the head.)

I will always be grateful for our Pakistani friends who not only took us into their homes, but into their hearts. When David had to be gone for an extended time, I was always welcomed into the protection of our friends and neighbors.

Westerners cherish punctuality. To be on time is of utmost importance. But for the Easterner, hospitality trumps punctuality.

Once I found myself in a section of Rawalpindi after a long absence, and on impulse decided to drop in on friends I had not seen in several years. When they opened the door, they were all dressed up, about to leave for a wedding. We greeted each other warmly, but when I tried to excuse myself, promising to see them the following week, they would hear nothing of it! I had come to their home as their friend after a long time. They would fix me *chai* and find out not only about my own health, but the health of my family as well. Whereas I was uptight about their arrival at the wedding, they were intent on honoring me as their guest.

"The wedding won't start on time," they explained. "And as long as we get there to congratulate the bride, groom and their families, and can celebrate with the guests, that's all that matters. We are so glad and honored that you have come to our home."

Then I enjoyed their fellowship and warm hospitality, putting aside my need for being on time. Yes, they *were* late for the wedding, but not for the festivities. And they were able to attend a very important event without neglecting their duty to show hospitality to a friend.

That incident also illustrates the courtesy of the East as contrasted with the casualness of the West and our emphasis on efficiency. Westerners, wanting to accomplish our own agendas right away, are content with a perfunctory greeting: "Hi, buddy. How ya doing? Could you help me fix my car?" Our Eastern friends, on the other hand, use endearing and honorific titles (Mrs. Mitchell, Sister or Aunty Sanobar), and will engage us in regular conversation only after inquiring about our health and the health of our family members.

My Western upbringing and training have taught me to be analytical; to collect cold, hard facts; to depend on verified statements; and, if possible, to chart these statements statistically on a linear graph. This is the way to track progress! To be truthful, I love to see lists of projects completed, goals met. But I am grateful, after living in the East, to have learned (especially in interpersonal relationships) to be more intuitive, to hear the heart questions behind what is shared verbally, to take the time to absorb what is happening. Cold facts are not always as they appear, nor can progress in heart matters be graphed linearly. Making connections and building deep, warm relationships is what life is all about.

The face-to-face, blunt, direct dealings of the West, moreover, can deeply offend our Eastern friends, who are used to a gentler, more indirect manner of relating. Many times the Eastern choice of an intermediary or mediator can help bridge a broken relationship. As Westerners we are prone to want to confront the person who has hurt us, to "tell it like it is." It might make *us* feel better, but often it makes the situation worse. Western Christians have been taught to deal with painful relational breakdowns according to Matthew 18, in which Jesus urges us to go directly to the person involved. But going directly isn't God's *only* way! Sometimes we forget that Jesus is God's chosen Mediator in the broken relationship between God and man, and He can be a powerful model for us in building bridges.

I am grateful that, through Begum Sheikh, I had the privilege of learning some of the nuances of the East while being fully accepted as a Westerner enjoying and learning from the East. She herself had learned to appreciate many Western ways, not only because her education was in English, but also from her father's position in the British government and her extensive travels abroad.

I like to think of the intermingling of East and West as a tossed salad in which each ingredient maintains its own color, texture and taste, rather than blending into the bland sameness of the more frequently used analogy of a melting pot.

Despite many elements of the Eastern way of life that enrich Westerners, we know that, due to Adam and Eve's choice, every virtue in every person and culture has been twisted. But Jesus has bridged the gap between God and man. He can straighten those contorted virtues, and there is hope for every person and every culture.

I love the contrasts and beauty of different cultures! So does God. In fact, the Bible reveals that the untwisted virtues of each culture will be displayed in heaven. Can you imagine how glorious that will be? Revelation 21:24–26 (NIV) puts it this way: "The kings of the earth will bring their splendor into [the heavenly city]…. The glory and honor of the nations will be brought into it."

That is what God is doing today! Through the Good News of God's love in sending Jesus as our Mediator—the One who can straighten the twists—the ugly, frightening side of each culture can be removed. In the Kingdom of God, the West needs the

East and the East needs the West. As we learn to see each other as God sees us in Jesus Christ, we are preparing for that day when the unique beauty of every culture will be fully restored, displaying the glory our Creator planned from the beginning of time.

THE SHAMING OF THE STRONG

To be pregnant with a much longed for child is a joyful experience for most women. But if you know that this baby is so grossly deformed that she cannot be born alive – what then? Do you carry her tenderly to term and love her while you can, or do you terminate a life that is, in the eyes of the medical profession, of no worth? In this heartwrenchingly honest book, Sarah Williams and her husband face these issues with shining faith and courage that challenges us all to reconsider what we value and to understand more clearly what is precious to the heart of God.

Marion Stroud

Sarah's moving and authentic account shames our feeble excuses for treating the vulnerable as though they were less than human. Reading this made me feel more human.

Heather Gemmen

I didn't mean to read this. I hadn't wanted to cry. I certainly wasn't in the mood to be moved or challenged. But I found myself confronted by a beautiful attitude to people.

Anne Atkins

THE SHAMING OF THE STRONG

SARAH WILLIAMS

KINGSWAY PUBLICATIONS
EASTBOURNE

First published 2005
This 2-in-1 edition 2008

Cover design: PinnacleCreative.co.uk
Front cover photo C Paha_l | Dreamstime.com

ISBN 978 1 84291 401 4

KINGSWAY COMMUNICATIONS LTD
26–28 Lottbridge Drove, Eastbourne BN23 6NT, UK
www.kingsway.co.uk

Printed in Great Britain

Contents

CONTENTS

1

The Day of Trouble

There are two ways into the Women's Centre at the John Radcliffe Hospital in Oxford. We took the far one. I glanced at my watch as we entered the lobby. My calculations had been precise. I had ten minutes to spare before my routine 20-week ultrasound scan in the Prenatal Diagnosis Unit. I had dropped the children at school, driven to the supermarket to do the week's shopping, rushed home, crammed the food into the cupboards and begun preparations for Hannah's birthday tea later that afternoon. All day I had been reminiscing about the birth of our eldest exactly eight years before. Hannah was born in Canada on Vancouver's North Shore in a room which overlooked the white-capped mountains of Grouse and Seymour. I remembered the mountains as I struggled to find change to purchase my hospital parking ticket.

My neighbour was on the seventh floor of the John Radcliffe having given birth to her third baby 36 hours earlier. I headed straight for the lift, abandoning my mother in the lobby. Adrienne was sitting up in bed like a queen, radiant with the relief and joy of her son's arrival. I held him in my arms and realised with a surge of excitement that this would soon be me. I laughed out loud as I headed back to the ground floor. Next time I visited the seventh floor I too would have my baby with me.

It was surprisingly full in the waiting room for a Monday afternoon. My mother set up her laptop to catch up on some work. Paul would have done the same if he had not been in a client meeting in London. He and I had never been sentimental about ultrasounds. The first time we had seen Hannah on the screen in the Lion's Gate Hospital in Vancouver, we both reacted to the bizarre unreality of first seeing our child through the intrusive medium of technology. It was disconcerting to observe someone as intimately close as our own baby under the auspices of a total stranger who busily recorded obscure measurements.

Our friends told us this would be the moment of initial bonding, but we struggled to tell the difference between a head and a foot. We had to be persuaded that the mass of black and white, which shifted back and forth between graphs and cursors, bore any relation to the increasingly clear mental picture we were drawing of our little one. We made a vow not to find out the sex ahead of time and we eagerly discussed the ethical pros and cons of pregnancy screening all the way home in our clapped-out Dodge Omni. 'I will never have another ultrasound scan,' I asserted stridently. 'What's the point? I would never have an abortion.'

'But what if the identification of a problem allowed medical intervention?' Paul's rapid retort did not surprise me. Such conversations came naturally during our student days at theological college.

Perhaps I was becoming mellow with advancing age, or maybe the exhaustion of two small children had taken the edge off my romantic idealism. Either way, I really wanted to know the sex of this third child and I could barely read the magazine in front of me because I was so excited at the prospect of seeing my baby, by whatever technological means.

The doctor called my name and I got up to follow him. He asked if my mother wanted to join us. She was reluctant at first, not wishing to overstep any grandmotherly boundaries, but, sharing my excitement, she did not take much persuasion. I made her promise she would leave when I asked the doctor to tell me the sex of the baby. It was dark in the room and I remember the dull pattern on the curtain round the bed and the sharp cold of the jelly as the doctor squeezed it onto my bump. I made a joke about how much I wished it were twins to save me the pain of future pregnancies.

And then we saw the tiny foot. I caught my breath, silenced by the sudden rush of love and connection which gripped my attention. There were no shifting lines this time. I could see the foot as clearly as my own; even the toes were distinct. The baby turned and seemed for an instant to look straight at us. I could see the detail of the face. It was as though the baby waved, desiring to bond as much as I did. Something stirred inside my heart at a level far deeper than my emotions. I felt as if my spirit had been captivated and my whole body yearned to embrace and protect this child.

I now knew what those friends meant by bonding. With Hannah it had happened when I saw the bright blue line on the home pregnancy test. With Emilia it happened when I first held her in my arms after an arduous labour. This baby had moved, within the space of minutes, from the realm of a future idea to a visible person with whom I had a relationship in the present. I smiled contentedly, thinking how unashamedly sentimental I had become as I lay there silently oozing love at the screen. All my scruples about scans were firmly relegated to my youth.

'That makes it all worthwhile, doesn't it?' said Mum, reflecting my own thoughts and referring to the long weeks of acute nausea which had preceded this day.

But the doctor was being slow; his cheery voice had given way to a clipped monotone. When he left the room and returned with a woman technician, I reasoned that he was simply inexperienced at doing ultrasounds. I had seen what I had come for and I wanted to get home to make the party tea. I was irritated when the woman redid everything the doctor had already done. If we did not leave soon I would not have the tea on the table in time to allow Paul and the girls to play an extended tickling game and to read an extra chapter of the Narnia Chronicles before bed.

Then the woman put her hand on my arm and said the words that every expectant mother hopes she will never hear: 'I am so sorry, there is something wrong with the baby. We need to fetch the consultant.'

'But there can't be,' I responded immediately. 'I saw the face. The baby looks fine to me.' Slowly she shook her head and squeezed my arm slightly. I went cold all over. An unfamiliar constricting sensation descended on me. I observed its creeping paralysis with the rational part of my brain, which seemed to be standing at a distance watching the proceedings with a strange forensic clarity. How could this be? God knew I could not bear this, not after I had given my heart away.

'Mum, I'm terrified,' I whispered.

'We are going to ask God to come,' she replied. The edge in her voice suggested she was no less afraid than I was, but the discipline of years had made prayer reflexive. 'Lord Jesus, we invoke your presence right now.' I remember the gratitude that shot through me when I thought of how awful it would have been to be alone. My mother had not planned to come with me to the hospital. I had told Paul and her that I was quite content to have some time to myself. My mother's decision had been spontaneous and last minute. She was sick of typing and ran after me as I shut the front door. 'Hang the e-mails – why don't we make a jaunt of it? I'll sit in the waiting room while you go in. Let me drive so that you can relax and get your energies up before the great party tea.'

I heard footsteps in the corridor and the lowered tones of serious discussion. I knew I had to pull my mind into gear, rousing myself from the obliteration of the shock to ask all the right questions – the questions Paul would have asked had he been there. The consultant sat down beside me. He glanced at the notes to check my name before greeting me. Evidently, my name had not featured in the rapid relay of information behind the door. There were a number of people peering over his shoulder, but they were just moving shadows. My eyes were fixed on the screen with an intensity of concentration that startled me. The consultant murmured a long succession of incomprehensible numbers to the gathered group at his shoulder. They nodded and ummed and ahhed in knowledgeable unison. Then, using the tiny white arrow and his finger for reinforcement, he showed how the person I had come to adore had a massively deformed body.

'I have to tell you, Mrs Williams, that this baby will not live. It has thanataphoric dysplasia, a lethal skeletal deformity that will certainly result in death shortly after birth. The chest is too small to sustain the proper development of the lungs. When the baby is born it will not be able to breathe.'

I concentrated on the medical terms, repeating *thanataphoric dysplasia* over and over again under my breath. I wanted to stop him speaking, but I was frightened of forgetting the words. 'You must be mistaken…' I shouted at him in my head. 'This can't be true, you have muddled my body with someone else's. This is not my baby. It must be a fault on the screen.' But the consultant spoke with a certainty that I had never heard in a medic before. He was leaving me no room to misunderstand the implications of what we were observing. Instead of stopping him I found myself nodding like everyone else in the room, intimidated by the finality of his words. 'I suggest that you and your partner come back in the morning so that we can talk further about what you want to do.'

It was not until we sat in a side room with a second female consultant that I realised that deciding 'what you want to do' meant having a termination. I felt dizzy and dazed like a sleep-walker as I made my way back through the waiting room amidst the clamour of bumps, siblings and grumpy fathers. It is strange the detail one remembers in moments of crisis: the blond child on the floor playing with a tractor, the girl in the bright red maternity dress drinking from the water fountain, the look of pity on the receptionist's face as she watched us leave. At the exit I caught sight of a woman leaning her arm lazily on her heavily swollen stomach between long drags on her cigarette. I could not speak. I was numb all over. My mother took my arm and steered me to the car.

As I crumpled emotionless into the passenger seat I thought of Paul on his way home, unaware of what he would face when he got off the train. I remembered his look of pure delight when I told him I was pregnant for the third time. I thought of Hannah and Emilia bursting through the front door with party balloons already taped to the letterbox. I thought of Adrienne in the park with her baby in the buggy. A kind of aching emptiness enveloped me. Every line of thought ended with the same conclusion: 'Thanatophoric dysplasia, this child will not live, it will not live…' Round and round it went in my head, like a mantra.

I started to shiver uncontrollably. I wrapped my arms around my body in the hope that I would somehow disappear into the car seat. Slowly I began to absorb the fact that I was going home to face the most difficult decision of my life.

2

Pineapples and Amethysts

If praying somehow constitutes a spiritual beginning, then Christmas Day was certainly the start of it all. It was then that we asked God to give us the gift of another child. The 25th December has particularly romantic connotations for Paul and me. We first set eyes on one another on Christmas morning in a small church in Kent. Paul's uncle was the pastor and his family had come up from Dorset to celebrate together. My family had been attending this church for some years and I had heard a great deal about 'the nephew' who was studying politics, philosophy and economics at Oxford. What I did not realise at the time was that he had also heard a great deal about the serious girl with long blonde hair and masses of brothers and sisters who was also on her way to study at Oxford. Paul was sitting four pews in front of my sprawling family. We were so vast in number that we took up two rows, forming a kind of human bloc on one side of the church. Half of us were presided over by my mother and the other half were supervised by my harassed father. I was sandwiched between Naomi and Justyn on that particular morning and my youngest brother Richard was squirming on my lap. At the end of the second hymn Paul turned round and looked straight at me. My eyes met his for a second only, but with that momentous glance he stole my heart away. I hid behind Richard for the rest of the service, overcome by shyness.

Exactly 16 years later, we were standing in the pouring rain halfway up a Welsh hillside searching for an ancient Celtic pilgrim site at which we were intending to pray specifically for an extension to our family.

'Can't you pray by the woodburner in the holiday cottage?' pleaded my entire family.

'Of course we can,' I said, 'but it wouldn't be…' I struggled to find the right word, '…as historic.' The fact that Christians had been praying on this particular hill for the best part of two millennia seemed entirely irrelevant to our freezing family hungry for their Christmas turkey. My historical zeal was matched by Paul's keen sense of Welsh ancestry, however, and we pressed on up the hill regardless. After all, we had been waiting five years for this day.

After our second child Emilia was born, the doctor told us that we would be extremely unwise to contemplate having any more children. A long-term back injury had become acute as a result of the pregnancy and the strain of lifting two small children. I spent three months in bed, but it was a year before I could lift Emilia into her cot at night. If my disc were to prolapse again I was likely to face major back surgery. We waited and we prayed for five long years.

Young children and physical incapacity are not a happy mix. I watched my friends have their thirds and fourths, lifting them effortlessly one after another from car seat to pushchair, into swings at the playground and out of trees, wielding hoovers and stooping at the end of the day to pick up toys without even having to bend their knees. Some of them began to ask if we had given up on having more children. Slowly I began to reassess my expectations and to re-evaluate the unquestioned assumption Paul and I had harboured since we were first married that we would have at least four children.

It was a declaration of defeat when I finally admitted that I needed more sustained help to cope with the basic routine of family life. It was at this stage that Emma came to nanny for us on a part-time basis. We had known Emma since she was 18. She and her family had been part of our church in Oxford. We had observed her gentle consistency over the years as she had nannied for one family after another. I could hardly believe our good fortune when she agreed to come and work for us. With inimitable efficiency she began to pick up a large part of the physical work of caring for the children. I immersed myself in work, spending three years teaching at Birmingham University before returning to Oxford to take up a history fellowship at one of the university colleges. All the time I did my back exercises dutifully and continued to hope that my dreams would not always elude me.

After five years there were signs of considerable improvement in my back condition and so we reached Christmas Day and the wet Celtic pilgrim site. I know that God can hear our prayers anywhere, but there was something special about that hillside and no doubt God saw the funny and earnest side of our kneeling there in the mud with our frosted hands holding the cross which more patient pilgrims had carved in the rock 1,600 years before.

A month later, when we had fully recovered from the colds we contracted in Wales, I was able to tell Paul that he was going to be a father again. Hannah and Emilia were delirious with excitement and so was Emma, who, after five years of looking after us, had become a trusted friend and an integral part of our family.

It was with a touch of triumph that I told my closest friend our news. 'Janet, I'm pregnant,' I said abruptly in the hope that I might surprise her.

'I thought you might be,' she replied, as astute as usual. Her slow smile and the twinkle of humour in her eyes betrayed a coincidence of timing which reduced us to helpless laughter. 'So am I,' she whispered.

We had had our first children together. We had read all the same books to prepare. We wanted the same things for them and we worried about them with similar levels of intensity. We enjoyed the fact that Hannah and their eldest daughter Josie were now in the same class at school, as were Emilia and their third daughter Becky. Our husbands relished the long-established tradition of enjoying a celebratory drink together after the birth of each of our five daughters. When Hannah was born Mark and Janet flew all the way to Canada with three-month-old Josie to fulfil this custom. Any other friends requesting a three-week-long stay in our small student apartment just after the birth of a baby would have met with a flat 'no', but not these friends. We had known them since our undergraduate days at Oxford. We had been part of the same church ever since. They were more than family to us. The appropriateness of having our third and fourth children within a month of each other was more than we could contain.

We spent the rest of the day making plans, discussing due dates and anticipating the exploits of the next two. We talked with such rapidity and at such length that the children retreated to the sandpit at the bottom of the garden, and Mark suddenly found urgent business to attend to elsewhere.

But then I started to be sick. I vomited first whilst teaching a tutorial on Gladstone's foreign policy. I just caught a glimpse of the student's bewildered face as I fled from my college room at high speed. Having covered my mouth lest the worst should happen, I could offer no explanation for my seemingly crazed behaviour. I sprinted down the corridor past the Senior Common Room. To my horror the Principal, the Senior Tutor and the College Secretary were assembled for a meeting with the door open. They looked up disapprovingly, probably expecting to see an unruly student. I tried to slow my pace to a composed walk and to wave lightly with the hand that was not pressed to my mouth. Little did I realise that first time how many more embarrassin moments were to follow.

When I returned to my room, I told the startled student that it was something I had eaten. 'Shall we carry on?' I mumbled, still tasting the vomit in my mouth with the distinctive metallic aftertaste of pregnancy. 'Where were we? Yes … to what extent can Gladstonian Liberalism be defined in terms of a distinctive foreign policy?'

'Are you sure you're all right, Dr Williams? Do you want me to come back later?'

'Not at all,' I said rather too brightly. 'I'm absolutely fine.'

When the same thing happened twice in the following week's tutorial, the student began to eye me with great suspicion and I began to wonder if I could negotiate my way round the late nineteenth century while the room heaved and my bookshelves swam in front of my eyes.

By the eighth week of pregnancy work had become an impossibility. I barely moved except from my bed to the toilet to empty my sick bowl.

'Be thankful,' people kept saying. 'Nausea is a sign of a healthy baby.' So I tried hard to be grateful, imagining the baby literally brimming with good health while I wasted away. When I started to be sick on my own saliva there was little else I could do but lie in hospital being intravenously rehydrated. It would not have been so bad if I could have read, but the words would not keep still on the page as I reeled like a novice sailor on the high seas.

'Why is this happening, Lord?' I remember asking after days of staring at the hospital ceiling.

One spiritual visitor was quick to give me an answer. 'God says you need a special anointing to carry this baby. His call is on this child and that is why you are suffering so much to bring him into the world.'

I don't think she heard me mutter disdainfully, 'He'd better be a prophet to the nations to justify this amount of vomit,' and I sincerely hope she did not hear the unrepeatable expletive that followed.

When I look back, I am surprised to find that this period of intensive and incapacitating sickness lasted only three months. It felt like a lifetime. Perhaps if I had known then that this is exactly what it was, I might have treasured those days more.

All this time to pray, I wrote in my journal, *but I don't know what to say*. I asked God to stop the sickness nearly as many times as I was sick. Pregnancy nausea is one of those things which is hard to describe to people who have not been through it.

'You feel so absolutely ill. It is like the worst sick bug you can ever remember having, lasting for months on end,' said

Sissel, my Norwegian friend, who even 20 years since her last pregnancy had not forgotten the horror of it. 'What man do you know could cope with that? But technically you are not ill and everyone thinks that you are just complaining. It is so frustrating.'

'It's just not fair!' I stormed at her. 'I thought we were meant to bloom in pregnancy!'

She laughed. 'Another of those myths that people put on women, I'm afraid.'

I cursed the person who propagated the myth and I resented the fact that the statistical minority upon whom that myth must have been founded seemed to cross my path with a frequency that compounded my frustration. Sometimes I would rant at Paul at the injustice of men who, from my perspective, were happy to enjoy the best moments of the process of procreation but managed to avoid altogether the painful consequences. His eyes would crinkle into an ironic smile after such outbursts as he quietly washed out the sick bowl at the end of the day and prepared for yet another scintillating evening listening to my lament, fetching glasses of water and filling hot-water bottles late into the night.

Dependence was not a word which entered my vocabulary easily, and perhaps it was the sense of helplessness and weakness more than anything else which made those early days so uncomfortable and disorientating. I ordered my life. The only way to juggle the various commitments of home, work and church was to fine-tune the organisation of my diary. Endless vomiting did not fit with my plan. My inability to stop the sickness, whether by prayer or by tablets, frustrated me beyond the resources of my humour. I found myself lower than I had been in years and yet guilty for feeling low about something I wanted so much and had prayed about for so long. I hated hearing how others were teaching my students at college. I watched members of our church cook our meals and clean our house with a mixture of gratitude and irritation that I could not do it myself. The girls ran to Emma when things went wrong and I had no energy to engage Paul in conversation. All I could do was reflect, and most of the time this made me feel even bleaker.

I thought a lot about my own childhood, wondering how on earth my mother had managed to have six children in ten years seemingly without batting an eyelid. I remember the riotous fun of family walks, or debating round the kitchen table, or acting out a play that one of us had written. Perhaps it was these memories which fuelled my own desire for a big family. My mother had revelled in it and to me that represented the pinnacle of true femininity. I guess I assumed that my future would naturally follow the pattern of my past and I would be a capable mother in the mould of my own. Yet the truth was that I had difficult pregnancies every time. My back injury had made the early stages of child-rearing a test of physical endurance, not a pleasure. I had found it hard enough to admit that I struggled to cope with two children, let alone bringing a third into the world. This confusion of mind simply reinforced my bewilderment. Busying myself doing things for people was a far more comfortable role than being on the receiving end of other people's kindness. And filling my head with historical data was easier than allowing my mind to free-wheel and take me in directions I was not sure I wanted to go.

Pineapple will for ever remind me of this confused feeling of dependence. Liz, our pastor's wife, phoned one day to ask if there was anything she could do.

'No,' I said. 'We're fine, thanks.'

She was wise enough to add, 'Are you sure?'

'Well,' I murmured after a few moments' thought, 'I really do fancy some pineapple. When you next go shopping, would you buy me a fresh pineapple?'

I expected Liz to call round with my pineapple after a couple of days, so I was quite taken aback when, an hour later, our pastor Mike arrived on the doorstep. I had always found myself tongue-tied in Mike's presence, so there was nothing new when I stammered my thanks. His pastoral professionalism intimidated me and the fact that I was standing there in my old dressing gown feeling like death only exaggerated my sense of smallness.

The pineapple arrived in Liz's best glass bowl. It was cut into tiny pieces so I could eat little bits when I fancied it. 'Go and lie back down on the sofa,' Mike instructed. 'I'll bring you some in a small bowl.'

I did as I was told. I took the bowl from him, muted, and I ate three pieces. To my horror and humiliation, there and then in front of him, I threw up in the green washing-up bowl I kept constantly by my side. I hardly dared look up. But Mike did not flinch. He did not walk out and he did not offer any platitudes. Instead he picked up the sick bowl, silently took it to the toilet, emptied it, cleaned it out and laid it back down beside me on the sofa. He then went and played with the children, who were rioting. I was so stunned at the simplicity and tenderness of his actions that I stayed on the sofa, dazed. When Paul got home and took charge of the children, Mike prayed with me. There was a gentleness which I had never seen in him before. My 'busy self-important pastor with large black diary crammed full of pressing meetings' stereotype evaporated there and then. My dependence had drawn care from unexpected places.

My one comfort in the morass, both emotional and physical, was anticipating the person I was struggling to bring into the world. I got through vomit after vomit by saying over and over again, 'It will all be worth it in the end.' I used to get to sleep at night imagining the baby in detail and thinking how I would look back and laugh at all the sickness when I held the child in my arms. Janet came often during those weeks, taking the girls off to play or just sitting with me, cheering me up with the anticipation of shared joy.

'Hello, darling, it's Wren,' came the voice at the other end of the telephone. My mother called herself Wren with all the family these days. Paul had first adopted the nickname as a way of avoiding the difficult decision of how to address his new mother-in-law. Should he call her 'Mum' like her own children, 'Jen' like the rest of her family, 'Jenny' like her friends, or 'Jennifer' like the bank manager? He opted for 'Wren', as in 'Jenny Wren', and thereafter the name stuck. Now she said to me, 'I've been praying for the baby and I had a vivid picture. Can I tell you about it?'

'Of course, go ahead.' I needed all the encouragement I could get.

'There's a little mountain stream behind the family home in Scotland where I used to play as a child. Hard granite boulders containing layers of amethyst come tumbling down into the surging water and the amethyst layers are exposed. These layers are very soft and fragile and they break into little chunks when the rock encasing them is smashed. These get washed to the sides of the river and lie there among the shingle. They don't look like amethyst; in fact it's hard to tell them from any other little stones. But if you put them in a pebble polisher and spin them round in different grades of polish grit they come out looking like jewels. I felt this baby would be one of these; a special unexpected treasure. The beauty of his or her personality may not be easy to see at first, but deep inside there's something that is unexpected and intensely beautiful but also very fragile. This quality will need to be recognised and appreciated for what it is and then very carefully honed before its beauty is apparent to others.'

When our conversation ended I searched for the amethyst necklace my father had given me when I was nine. He had made it from a polished stone taken from this same stream in Scotland. I kept it by my bed to remind me of the treasure and to help me appreciate the beauty in spite of the vomit.

By week 20 I no longer vomited quite so regularly and I had some of my energy back. Apart from the unrelenting feeling of sickness I was much recovered, if a little thinner than normal. I even ventured into the attic to take a sneak preview of the baby clothes. Somewhere inside me I harboured the belief that I had earned an easy second half to the pregnancy. I began to anticipate cashing in the credit due from the suffering for a late bloom. I was even cheery when Paul lay in bed with pneumonia, glad that I could do something for him at last. I remember with a shudder of irony writing in my journal, *The worst is over now. I can start to look forward.*

3

Father's Question

I sat bolt upright in bed, my hair soaked with sweat. I clutched my tummy out of instinct. It was still dark outside, although I could just hear a few birds starting to sing. Paul was fast asleep next to me. I crept out of our room and fumbled through the darkness, making my way downstairs to the kitchen.

I made myself a cup of tea. At first I could not remember my dream, only the atmosphere of it. It was the overarching sense of foreboding which had woken me more than the images themselves. The house was coming down on my head, or to be more precise it was bending under the strain of a most terrific hurricane. In my dream I had been standing under the archway between the kitchen and the back door, where I now stood waiting for the kettle to boil. The entire building swayed and bowed, forcing me to the ground, where I lay praying that the storm would pass but expecting the roof to collapse on me. And that was it. I woke up, sure that it had been real.

I laughed at myself as I hugged my cup of tea and rubbed my tummy, yawning. I had always dreamed vividly during pregnancy.

Emilia had heard my descent. Like me she is a morning person and in her toddlerhood rendered all alarm clocks redundant and challenged my morning prayer routine to the limit. She trundled into the kitchen with Teddy under her arm, snuggled onto my lap and sipped the cooling dregs of my tea. It took a surprisingly long time for her to remember that it was Hannah's birthday and burst into the inevitable flurry of excited activity. Together we attached balloons to the light over the table, laid out the breakfast with birthday napkins and arranged cards and small presents around Hannah's place, putting the larger ones carefully to one side to be opened that evening.

By six o'clock we were ready for Paul and Hannah to wake up and join in our fun. We had to resort to the smell of chocolate to rouse them both. It was some time before we were all sitting up in our bed, Emilia and I with considerably more enthusiasm than the other two.

'How are we going to fit five in this bed?' Paul groaned.

'Say Happy Birthday to your sister, baby!' Emilia shouted with her mouth to my tummy.

Hannah put her head on my shoulder and asked me quietly at exactly what time she could accurately say she was eight.

'Not until 7.23 tonight,' I said.

'But that was Canada time,' Paul interjected. 'If you really want to be accurate about it, you were born early on the morning of the 14th May English time, not the 13th at all.'

'But I *am* Canadian, Daddy,' Hannah retorted firmly, proud as always of her birthplace. He grinned and winked at her from the other side of the bed.

As I took the girls off to school that morning I could never have anticipated how much could change in just 12 hours. I think now as I write of a man whose wife of 30 years collapsed on the bathroom floor and died two days later, and of my friend who waved goodbye to her husband after breakfast and by teatime was a single parent with four children under ten. I think of Tanya, who packed her son's lunch and two hours later brought the same sandwiches home in a crumpled backpack after having identified her son's body at the local hospital. He did not reach school. He was crushed along with his bicycle by a passing lorry. I never used to think about such things in the safety of my own well-crafted routine. But that night I pondered on the phrase in the Psalms which speaks of 'the day of trouble':

> For in the day of trouble
> he will keep me safe in his dwelling;
> he will hide me in the shelter of his tabernacle
> and set me high upon a rock. (Psalm 27:5)

Within five minutes of my phone call on our return from the ultrasound scan, Mike and Liz were there. My brain was addled from the shock.

'The baby will not live. It has thanataphoric dysplasia. I can't get through to Paul. His mobile isn't responding. I don't know whether I should leave a message on his voice mail. My mum's gone to collect the children. It's Hannah's birthday. I don't want to see anybody. What am I going to say to them? I don't want to be alone. I have to decide what to do. I can't decide what to do.'

Others with less wisdom would have filled the place with words or been drawn into the temptation to give answers and follow thoughts to their end. But Mike and Liz knew enough to wait with me in the shock and let the pieces fall to the ground before identifying which ones needed to be picked up and in what order. Liz wrapped me in a blanket and Mike let me talk in broken sentences, sifting what needed to be done from the kerfuffle of my anxiety. I expected them to tell me I could not have an abortion; but when they did not say anything, despite my questions, I began to relax in the safety of their presence.

When Paul came through the door they slipped away; but we knew they would come back if we needed them. Wren had taken the girls straight to a cafe for tea. This was a better option than me trying to cook. Paul and I were alone. A garbled telephone message had put him in the picture. He looked very tired and for a long time he stood in silence with his arms around me.

The hours that followed were a blur. All I remember is Paul's determination to fend off the shadow which had fallen over the day, to prevent it from invading Hannah's celebration. 'I don't want her birthday to be for ever after associated with this. We don't need to tell them until tomorrow.' He read the girls a story and tickled them as usual as he put them to bed. It is strange how you can do such normal things when you are first in shock. I sat in the lounge cuddling my knees.

Once I would have been quick to register my opposition to abortion. Like most evangelicals, I knew the 'right answer' to this ethical question. But as Paul and I stared at our dilemma, sitting in the lounge after the girls had gone to bed, we realised that the stark ethical principle was not enough to carry us through the rest of the pregnancy. It was not enough to enable us to cope with the ongoing nausea, the threat of my back problem, the possibility of watching our baby die in great pain. Principles, however sound they might be, were simply not enough to give us the capacity to go on. They stopped short, leaving a great wide chasm of pain.

I was shocked to find that the only thing I wanted was to get the foetus out of my body as quickly as possible. I wanted the pregnancy to be over. 'It's the kindest thing to do, isn't it?' I said.

Paul said nothing for some moments. His face was white and his tired eyes stared blankly across the room. 'I think,' he whispered slowly, 'we need to ask God that question and find out what he wants us to do in this situation.' His face disappeared behind his hands as he hunched forward and began to pray. I too closed my eyes and lost a sense of everything but the movement of my lips and the aching cry of desperation in my heart.

I have often heard people use the phrase 'God said to me' and I've never been entirely sure what it meant until that evening in May, when I can only say that we felt God the Father speak a message to our hearts as clearly as if he had been talking with us in person. 'Here is a sick and dying child. Will you love it for me and care for it until it dies?'

With these words God gave us a taste of his heart. It seemed as though for him it was not primarily a question of abstract ethical principle but the gentle imperative of his overwhelming love for this tiny, deformed, helpless baby. Before we finished praying the chasm between the principle and the choice had been filled with God's love. As I lay down in my bed that night I realised the decision had already been made and I was at peace. I turned in my Bible to the Psalms and I read:

> Because you are my help,
> I sing in the shadow of your wings.

> My soul clings to you. I stay close to you.
> Your right hand upholds me. (Psalm 63:7–8)

I underlined the words *sing*, *clings* and *stay*, writing the date in the margin. This is how I would get through what seemed the impossible challenge of the rest of the pregnancy. God would be my help.

4

Sanity

The peace did not go away as we returned to the hospital early the next morning. A large man in his late fifties greeted me with a broad smile and a firm handshake.

'I hope you slept well,' he said, ushering me into a windowless examination room, leaving Paul standing bewildered on the threshold. It seemed a strange comment to make, given the circumstances. The consultant parked himself on a stool in front of the computer. His bulk dwarfed the stool like a parent perched on a little red plastic chair tying a child's shoelace at the end of preschool. No one addressed Paul and, being unsure of what to do, he rounded the white screen which shielded the bed from the door and made for the corner. When the nurse settled me onto the bed he had to flatten himself against the wall to avoid her backside. He looked grim and out of place.

'Now, Mrs Williams – Sarah, if I may. We are going to repeat the examinations that we carried out yesterday. I am going to record some more information. Then I will show you and your husband the findings and we can deal with any questions you may have.'

I put out my hand in an attempt to draw Paul closer so that he could at least see the screen. His hand felt cold to my touch.

'Please can you also tell us the baby's sex?' Paul asked. The doctor looked up with a hint of surprise. It was unclear whether this arose from the nature of the question itself or from the fact that Paul had spoken for the first time.

'That may or may not be possible. I will see.' His head was firmly bent over the keyboard. The nurse stood behind him with a clipboard. Another man, whose identity was a mystery to us, half leant, half sat on the desk with his arms folded. Occasionally he roused himself in response to a changed tone in the consultant's murmuring. At these points he leant over the consultant's shoulder and nodded his agreement.

I watched Paul's face as our baby appeared on the screen. His eyes were riveted on the tiny form, as mine had been the day before. He held my hand more firmly. There was motion and life in the figure before us. The doctor moved the cursor swiftly from one part of the skeleton to the next, highlighting the abnormality.

'The most important feature to note here is the severe global limb shortening. There is also long bone angulation and a marked alteration in bone echo density, all of which point to thanataphoric dysplasia. And there, you see,' he continued as if in passing, 'even the head is abnormally large as you would expect in these cases. There is likely to be brain damage, of course.' The doctor's voice was loud and he seemed to be speaking to a large general audience.

'Thanataphoric dysplasia is best described as a form of severe dwarfism. It is a congenital abnormality, which occurs in about 1 in 700,000. Problems in the genetic structure may be inherited from one or both parents, or they may be caused by an initial random error in the arrangement of the chromosomes. We are looking at the latter here. This particular chromosomal abnormality will result in death either immediately or soon after birth.'

'Is the baby in any pain now?' Paul asked above the flow of the doctor's words. The consultant carried on speaking for a few moments before he stopped to absorb the question.

'That is hard to say,' he said eventually. 'Sometimes the bones break in utero and there is some suggestion that this can cause foetal distress.'

'Do you see any evidence of this now?' Paul urged him.

The consultant spent some time reviewing the measurements before he said, 'The bones are thin but no, I do not see signs of fracturing. Fracturing is more usually associated with osteogenesis imperfecta type II … and I am 98 per cent certain this is a case of thanataphoric dysplasia. No, I do not see evidence of fracturing at present.'

'So there is no pain now.' Paul turned to me with relief in his voice. 'The baby is not in pain now.'

'Not now at least,' the consultant continued as if to dispel any shred of unreality from our understanding. 'But the pain will come as soon as birth starts. At that point the skeleton will probably be crushed as it moves down the birth canal.'

'Is there anything wrong with the heart?' Paul asked. 'It looks all right to me.'

'No. Not as such. But if you look here you can see there is significant chest compression indicated by a relatively large cardio-thoratic ratio. This is consistent with a poor prognosis, but it does look as if the heart itself is OK.'

'Did you hear that?' Paul said to me as the doctor moved the cursor back over the different areas of deformity, showing us again the different parts of the skeleton that would eventually rob the baby of life. 'There, a healthy heart,' Paul persisted. 'Look at that heart. There's nothing wrong with the heart.' He was right. You could see the heart pulsating with life.

'And the sex?' Paul asked eagerly, not moving his eyes from the screen.

'It's hard to tell in these cases. Sometimes the foetus is androgynous. But it looks female … yes, there you are, female, although you can never be certain, of course, but it does look female.'

I felt Paul squeeze my hand almost imperceptibly. 'Our daughter,' he whispered.

There was something surreal about seeing her there, comfortable, warm and surrounded by my body, but hearing the doctor's voice in the distance describing her death. I remember thinking distinctly as I watched her with the consultant's voice behind me, 'But hold on a minute, this is her life. She isn't dead. She's alive now. She can hear my heart. She can hear Paul's voice and her sisters' laughter. She can experience different foods as I eat them and most of all she can know the presence of the Holy Spirit while she's in the womb.'

'What would a termination involve?' I heard myself say abruptly. My voice sounded strange above the noise of the consultant's murmuring. The man on the desk stood up and leant back against the wall.

'A very simple procedure, Mrs Williams,' the consultant replied at once.[1] 'The normal method is to give an anaesthetic and then inject the foetal heart under ultrasound guidance. Once the foetus is confirmed dead, drugs are given to induce stillbirth.' He paused and looked up at Paul, whose eyes had not yet left the screen. 'Of course you are welcome to a second opinion before making that decision. We can have you examined at Great Ormond Street within a few days.' He turned back to me when he saw that Paul did not respond.

'That won't be necessary,' I said quietly. 'How quickly would I need to decide?'

'Whenever you want to,' the consultant said. 'You can choose to have a termination right up to 38 weeks gestation,[2] but obviously you would want to make the decision as quickly as possible. I will ask my colleague to come in and talk to you further if you wish. She deals more directly with this than I do. My area is really research, which brings me on to another

---

[1] About 180,000 abortions take place in Britain each year, making it one of the most common operations performed on the NHS. Recent estimates suggest that 1 in 3 British women have had abortions.

[2] The 1990 Fertilisation and Embryology Act reduced the legal limit for an abortion on social grounds from 28 to 24 weeks. However, under this law no restrictions are placed on the termination of babies in the case of foetal handicap at any stage in pregnancy, in spite of the fact that the government's Science and Technology Committee are still reviewing the accusation that many handicap abortions happen unnecessarily, mistakenly and for reasons that are not scientifically justified. At present political pressure is being brought to bear to further reduce the legal limit for social abortions. But there has been no equivalent pressure to alter the existing legislation with regard to cases of abnormality.

issue. I know it's a little early to be thinking about this, but you will need to think about whether you are willing to grant us permission to do a full post-mortem examination on the baby at whatever stage this is relevant. Given the rarity of the disease, this would be of great help in research.'

'I want to carry the baby to term,' I said very simply.

The leaning man sat back down on the desk. The consultant took his glasses off and swung them to and fro between his thumb and forefinger. He did a poor job of masking his surprise. I wondered how many couples rested in his professional medical judgement.

'Well, of course there's no pressure to make the decision quickly,' he said. 'You can come back in a week or a month. You may need more time to consider.'

'Thank you,' Paul said. 'We would like to take some of the pictures with us if we may. And do you have anything I can read on this condition?' The nurse began to shuffle papers awkwardly on the desk.

'I'm very sorry, this child will not live,' the consultant said firmly. I wondered if he thought we were in denial as to the severity of the situation.

'I would find it helpful to read something if I may,' Paul continued, 'and then we would like to come back and discuss the birth with you.'

The consultant turned round and said something about a research paper to the leaning man. He left the room and returned soon after with a ten-page booklet. 'This is about a range of skeletal abnormalities including various kinds of dwarfism, so you will have to wade your way through it, I'm afraid. It's basically an assessment of the diagnostic and prognostic accuracy of sonographic prenatal screening procedures, but I hope it will contain information about the condition which will be of use to you. I suggest you phone my secretary when you are ready to come back and she will arrange an appointment for you. Goodbye, Mrs Williams.'

I think the doctor doubted our sanity when we left the hospital smiling and clutching our baby pictures.

5

Sticky Bun Tea

Emma was angry. She was at our house waiting for the children to come back from school. I knew she was angry because of the way she laid the table. Things banged and she moved abruptly.

'Shall we go for a quick walk, Emma?' I suggested.

She looked at the clock. 'The girls will be back in five minutes. I haven't finished the tea yet.' She did not look at me.

'I'll do it,' said Wren, emerging from the utility room. 'Go,' she whispered as Emma went to get her coat. 'And don't rush – she needs you.'

I had phoned Emma the night before to tell her about the initial scan. She was distraught and unable to speak for tears. I had not yet told her what we had decided.

'It's not fair. Not after all that sick,' she said before I could even open my mouth. 'Why would God let such a thing happen? It's not … it's not … right.' She shoved her hands deep into her pockets and I was glad it was God she was angry with, not me. 'Why did he let you go through all that sick just for this? You've waited so long. It's not … it's not fair. I prayed so hard that you would get better from the sick. It makes me wonder why I pray. And now look what God's done!'

I didn't know what to say. I looked at her as we walked along. Her faithful companionship had been like a firm bedrock for me over the last five and a half years. Her unwavering friendship provided the consistency factor in our family life and it struck me how characteristically unselfish it was of her to think first of me. We are nearly the same age, Emma and I, but life has taken us down different routes. I have a husband and children, she does not. Paul and I have always known that she loves our children with a strong protective love that covers over the many irritations which must have arisen from working for us and with us for so long. I found myself saying, 'I'm sorry, Emma. I know you were looking forward to this baby as we were.' She started to cry and I saw that her abrasiveness was a smokescreen to hide her grief.

'Yes, I was.' I realised that it was not just me and Paul who were going to lose someone precious. I thought about Wren back at home with the girls. She would lose a grandchild. Emma would lose someone who would have been as dear to her as Hannah and Emilia are. Family is not something you take for granted when you are single.

'Sorry about all the sick, too,' I said.

Emma cried more loudly, but with a fleeting laugh. 'It was flipping hard work – all that sick.'

'Thanks for looking after me,' I said. 'Seems to be the story of our lives, doesn't it?' We both laughed, remembering the days when I would direct Emma from the floor cushions where I lay, irritable from the back pain. Her dreams had not worked out either and it put things in perspective for me. We made our way back to the house.

'We've decided to carry the baby to term, Emma.'

'That doesn't surprise me,' she said. 'How will you cope? What about your back? What happens if your back goes again?' I did not know how to answer. There were no guarantees. She could tell from my face that these questions were not going to go away in one short walk. 'Well, I guess we'll just have to cross that bridge when we get to it, won't we?' Her voice was beginning to sound normal again and her use of the familiar word 'we' comforted me with its implications of team work. I was glad that we had weathered a few storms together before this one.

'Thanks for explaining,' she said as we went through the front door. 'It helps.'

The girls were leaping around the kitchen, full of the day's events and excited that Wren was still there, even though they thought she was only staying one night for Hannah's birthday.

'Hannah, Emilia, we want to talk to you in the lounge for a moment,' Paul said in a tone which strangely stilled their leaping. Wren brought us a tray of tea with some sticky buns. We sat together on the green sofa. We did not eat the sticky buns.

'Mummy and Daddy have got some bad news, I'm afraid. Mummy went to see the doctor and the doctor looked at the baby.' Paul was white. I could see how profoundly it was paining him to say this to them. I held his hand. 'The baby is sick. The doctor thinks that she will die when she's born.'

He waited, giving them silent space to allow his words to sink in. I forced myself to say nothing. I would have filled the quiet with words to try to structure their responses. Paul is wiser than I am.

They both began to cry. 'Is the baby alive now?' said Hannah finally.

'Yes, and she's a little girl.'

'What's wrong with her, Daddy?' Emilia wailed.

'The bones in her chest are too small and when she's born and she tries to breathe, she won't be able to.'

Emilia wailed again, throwing herself against Paul.

'Is she in pain?' Hannah asked, unwittingly echoing Paul's question from earlier that day. I smiled through my tears at their similarity and the integrity of their concern.

'No, she's not in pain now,' Paul said very definitely.

'Can we always love her?' Hannah asked after a long pause.

'Yes, she's your sister and you can love her now while she's in Mummy's tummy and you can always love her even after she dies.' Somehow this seemed to be enough for Hannah. She wrapped her arms round the bump and cried into my tummy.

Emilia gripped Paul's arm. 'I don't want the baby to die. God must make her better.'

Paul let her go as she squirmed off his lap and he did not respond as she lurched and stood on the corner of the tea tray, spilling the contents. 'We're going to pray that she will get better. I don't want her to die!' Emilia stormed.

'Of course we'll pray that she will get better. We'll pray that every day; but even if she doesn't, she's still part of our family now and we can love her.'

'I don't want the baby to be sick,' said Emilia. 'I want her to sleep in my bedroom with me.'

'We don't want her to be sick either,' I said, beginning to cry again myself. I felt guilty that I was failing them. I knew how Emilia had prayed faithfully since she was three that God would give her a younger brother or sister. I did not trust myself to say anything else. I looked at Paul helplessly. Emilia went to find Wren and tell her to tell Jesus to make the baby better. Hannah clung to me for a long while. She would not leave my side when we eventually moved into the kitchen to pick at our tea.

There were lots of things we could have said that might have made it easier for the children in the short term. 'Maybe she will get better.' Or, 'We will have another one.' Or perhaps we could have kept it quiet and just told them at the end. I thought about those scenarios. But I remembered how angry I had been with my father when he did not tell me how sick my mother was when I was 14. I found out afterwards that she had nearly died. I had felt betrayed by him because he had not told me the truth. Paul never traded in any currency but the truth and so it did not surprise me that he had been straight with the girls. I found it hard not to try to use words to cover over the aching sense of emptiness. Often parenthood is about using words to make children feel better. I wondered what had happened to all Wren's words over the years. These days she said increasingly little to us, but much more to God. I went to sleep that night praying that God would turn this for good in the children's lives.

Paul told Mike and Liz of our decision that night. 'You have made a good and difficult choice. We will support you. The church will be praying for you.' Since the pineapple incident

I trusted Mike, and I knew that they would support us and the church would pray. It was sad that it took a vomited pineapple to bring me to that understanding.

The next day I phoned Mark and Janet. I had been putting it off. I could not stop thinking about their baby. When Josie answered the phone I asked to speak to Mark. I thought it would be easier for Janet to hear it from him.

'Mark, I had my scan. The baby is deformed. It isn't going to live beyond birth.'

There was silence, not a word. 'Mark? Are you there? Mark?' All I could hear was a strange muffled sound. 'What's the matter, Mark? Are you all right?'

It was some time before I realised that he was crying and although he was trying, he could not make words come out. And I had thought it would be easier to tell him than Janet!

'I'm so sorry,' he said. 'We'll phone you back.'

Fifteen minutes later Janet rang. 'Can we come over?'

'Yes of course,' I said, and then I hid in my room dreading their arrival. I did not want to see them. What was I going to say? How would they handle it? How would I feel about seeing Janet in maternity clothes, remembering our last happy and hope-filled conversation? There was no escape from seeing them.

They stood in the kitchen while I made them a drink. There was an awkward formality that seemed all the more exaggerated by the fact that there had never been any such restraint between us before.

'It's a little girl,' I said at last as we seated ourselves in the lounge. 'Paul wants us to name her soon.' They both began to cry. I could not cry. I wanted to, but I felt stiff and uncomfortable.

I was pushing them away. I did not want their intimacy now. My eyes looked everywhere in the room but at them.

Janet was sitting next to me on the sofa and she turned round and looked straight at me, brushing her tears to one side. 'I guess we've got a choice, haven't we?'

I frowned, unsure what she was about to say. I had had my fill of choices lately. 'What do you mean?' I asked.

'Well, we can either walk through this together or we can walk through it separately. We can either choose to share the pain together or we can choose not to. We can choose to love one another's babies or we can choose not to.'

I was stunned. I could not have taken that kind of directness from anyone else. But I knew exactly what she was saying and her straightforward clarity and her bravery in confronting my distance cut right through all the layers of emotion and defence. It appealed directly to my heart and to the integrity of our friendship. She was not going to pacify me with words that hid the gulf which had developed between us as a result of this news. It was not without reason that I had respected her for so many years.

From that moment on we could talk. She had broken down the barrier of my silence. I often wonder whether, without the risk she took, we would have been condemned to a friendship of distance and platitudes. She, Mark and I wove in and out of prayer and conversation for three hours. By then we had talked about every angle and aspect of the situation, praying, crying and even laughing by the end of it.

When they left I thought about the scripture that commands us to grieve with those who grieve and rejoice with those who rejoice (Romans 12:15). Both grieving and rejoicing are choices we must make actively out of love for one another within the resilience of community. There were few days when Janet and I did not call each other during that summer, and certainly no week went by without us journeying through the pregnancies together. Janet chose to grieve with me. Later I would have to choose to rejoice with her. Both choices were costly.

6

Two Big Roads

In the weeks that followed I wished that every relationship could have been as open as this. It was a different scenario with many people at church. I remember watching one person run back into the toilet when they saw me coming because they did not want to meet me in the doorway. Perhaps they did not know what to say; but something, even the quickest 'I'm so sorry', was always better than nothing – nearly always, at least.

The same lady who had prophesied over the baby when I lay vomiting in hospital was unwilling to let the matter lie. 'You must pray that God will heal this child. I believe God wants to heal in this situation. Think what a testimony you would have if he did.' Every time I saw her she would say the same thing. 'I am praying that God will do a miracle and heal the baby. It has to be his will to heal her.'

She told me about a couple from another church who were fighting cancer. The husband was in the advanced stages of the disease, but still he clung to 'his healing'. She told me in admiring tones of how they had travelled the length and breadth of the country and even as far as South America to be prayed for by various people with healing ministries. She would leave a deliberate pause at the end of her descriptions during which I think I was meant to repent of my own passivity. The one word she never mentioned was death.

After a good six weeks of these conversations I could remain silent no longer. I sat down next to her at the back of church. 'Thank you for praying for the baby,' I said. 'We need prayer very much indeed and we really appreciate your concern. I know it may sound strange, but I see this pregnancy like two big roads. Each road has a large sign over it and I have to decide which route to take. The first one says "Healing" in big letters.' I heard her purr next to me at the sound of the word. 'The other sign is a bit more difficult to read, but I think it says "God himself". This path doesn't look nearly so inviting. It's dark and unknown.' I turned to look at her, a little nervous. 'I don't want to spend the precious time I have with the baby searching for healing. I want to spend it seeking God and loving the baby as she is. Paul and I do not feel that this baby will live and we trust that we will find God in the pain, not in the avoidance of it.'

I do not know that she really understood what I was trying to say, because she carried on saying the same things to me for the rest of the summer. It was only months later, when the man she had told me about finally died, that she began to ask if it had really been God's will to heal him. The man's widow was questioning the entire basis of her faith in the wake of his death. If God had not healed, perhaps he did not love, and if he did not love, perhaps he was not good or perhaps he did not even exist. It was a dangerous path to travel, and it had certainly made the last days of this man's life fraught with tension and questioning.

I returned to work a week after I had discovered that the baby would die. The College Secretary had relayed the news to my colleagues via an official e-mail, but few people said anything. Those cards I did receive were precious. I found that empathy came from unexpected quarters. A senior member of faculty who had spoken to me only infrequently wrote me a long letter describing how he and his wife had waited for many weeks after discovering that their child was likely to have Down's syndrome. When their son was born he was severely handicapped, but the letter managed to convey with great simplicity and emotion the supreme delight their son had been to them over the years, not merely in spite of his disability but also in fact because of it. That letter comforted me.

What I did not anticipate in making the decision not to have an abortion was the anger that it would provoke in some people. In one conversation with a university medic the moral arguments in favour of abortion were presented to me in a robust fashion. 'To fail to abort in the case of proven foetal abnormality is morally wrong, because in doing so one is deliberately and wilfully choosing to bring avoidable suffering into the world. It becomes an ethical imperative to abort in the case of suboptimal life.'

I felt like an undergraduate who had been duly chastised for a weak line of argument in a badly written tutorial essay. I knew the argument was not intended personally. Arguments rather than people tend to prevail at Oxford and although I tried only to muse on his argument with the distance of theory, it still kept me awake at night. I knew there was something wrong with the argument; something which made me want to ask if he thought the same logic should be applied to the elderly and if by this definition euthanasia should not also be seen as an ethical imperative. But I could not, as yet, find a defence and the force of my colleague's case led me to consider whether I was in fact being selfish in prolonging the baby's life for as long as I could. As a historian of the nineteenth century, I could not help but remember how John Stuart Mill argued in his essay *On Liberty* against the freedom to reproduce.

To bring a child into existence without a fair prospect of being able not only to provide food for its body but instruction for its mind is a moral crime both against the unfortunate offspring and against society.[3]

Mill's idea became enshrined in liberal thought, introducing a philosophical case against harming people by bringing them into existence under adverse circumstances. Mill could not have foreseen the arenas in which these ideas would be deployed in the twenty-first century – the wrongful life cases being upheld in Californian courts,[4] for example, or the use of such utilitarian arguments in the defence of prenatal testing with a view to

[3] J. S. Mill, On Liberty, (1859), chapter 5.

[4] There has been a recent proliferation of legal cases in the United States in which children have brought actions against their parents or parents against doctors alleging so-called 'wrongful birth' or 'wrongful life'. The alleged wrong is that a child has been brought into existence in less than optimal circumstances. Initially such actions did not succeed. For example, Gleitman v. Cosgrove (1967) involved a child who had been born a deaf mute and almost blind because his mother had contracted German measles during pregnancy, but the Supreme Court of New Jersey would not accept the plaintiff's claim for damages against doctors who allegedly told the mother that German measles afforded no

aborting defective embryos. The word 'suboptimal' rang in my head for days afterwards.

I heard other arguments which were both more insidious and more personal. A feminist colleague, whose expertise in linguistics made her a formidable combatant in any discussion, saw me as a traitor to the cause. 'Are you sure you're making the right decision?' she said to me one day on the way out to the college car park. 'What if against all the odds the baby should live but be severely mentally and physically handicapped? It will ruin your career, your life. Don't you think it's irresponsible to run that risk? You do have the right to choose, you know.'

I was so stunned by her candour that I temporarily lost the power of speech. She sidled closer to me and whispered in covert tones, 'Is your husband putting you under pressure?'

She had never met Paul. I nearly laughed. She looked a little disappointed when I said finally, 'Paul has not put me under pressure either way. This is my choice. I simply want to enjoy my baby for as long as I can.'

---

risk to her child. But courts in California, Washington and New Jersey have all now recognised the right of an infant with birth defects to collect damages in a wrongful life suit. In the case of Curlender v. Bio-science Laboratories (1980), for example, the case involved a child born suffering from Tay-sachs disease. The parents were awarded damages for having negligently been told they were not carriers of the disease. The claim made in a wrongful life suit it is not that the negligence of the physician was the cause of the impairment, but that the physician failed to inform the parents adequately and is, therefore, responsible for the birth of an impaired child who would otherwise not have been born and would not, therefore, have experienced the suffering caused by the impairment.

My colleague said nothing for some weeks after that conversation, though I felt her eyes on me every time we passed each other. I thought a great deal about what she had said to me. In many ways I greatly admired her brutal honesty. I thought about what she meant by 'the right to choose'. What did this phrase mean? As far as I could see, for her it meant the ability to practise a principled life of preserving feminine independence at the cost of all human intimacy. I spent a long time thinking about what the law really implies when it allows a woman to have an abortion right up to full term. What effect does that have on a culture? I began to consider from a Christian perspective what it means to have freedom to choose. I wrote these words in my journal:

Rather than being a liberty of autonomy, freedom from obligation or the power to mobilise resources for our own ends, biblical liberty is first and foremost freedom from the consequences of sin, the freedom to enjoy the space to choose to serve others and most of all to choose to serve the living God. Biblical liberty is the Spirit-empowered ability to choose to fulfil our obligations, to lay aside comfort for the sake of another, and to use all our resources to honour and fulfil our created function.

I wished I had the courage to say those words to my colleague's face.

7

Suboptimal Life?

I think the phrase goes, 'It never rains but it pours.' It was the 22nd May, nine days after we discovered that the baby would die. I was just settling back into work. Emilia had been unwell for some time. From February onwards she had started to show signs of an unnatural tiredness. She rarely seemed to want to eat and there was blood in her stool. At first I put the fatigue down to starting school and the disruption to our normal routine caused by the pregnancy nausea; but when the symptoms persisted and then worsened and she began to complain of acute abdominal pain, we became concerned.

Hospitals are all too familiar to Emilia. She was born with a malformed windpipe which required surgery at the age of one, while a hearing problem necessitated regular hospital visits to fit hearing aids and to discuss her partial deafness. I had almost forgotten our preliminary appointment at the children's department, eclipsed as it had been by more recent events, when the registrar himself phoned with the results of Emilia's blood tests and asked us to bring her back to the hospital immediately. Paul was inundated with work, having taken the best part of a week off in the immediate wake of the scan, and it was impossible for him to accompany us to the hospital. Wren drove up from her home in Kent once again.

'I'm not leaving you to go into that place again on your own…' she said on the phone, unwilling even to utter the word 'hospital' after the horrors of the week before.

'We'll be all right,' I insisted. 'We'll take lots of games to play in the waiting room. We don't have to go near the Women's Centre this time. I'll make sure I don't park in the same car park so that it doesn't remind me of last week.'

But Wren came all the same and once again I was glad she was there, in the right place at the right time with her prayerfulness. This time she left her laptop at home.

Emilia needed a general anaesthetic for a colonoscopy, but they told us she would only be half an hour in the examination room. Wren could see that I was anxious when after an hour and a half she still had not emerged from the room where they had taken her on a trolley with magic cream on her hands and Teddy still stuffed under her arm. We chatted too brightly in the waiting room. Wren tried desperately not to let me see that she too was anxious.

When the consultant himself came into the waiting room still wearing his green surgery outfit, I nearly collapsed in terror. After the discovery of the previous week, the unexpected and the tragic now seemed plausible.

'Mrs Williams? I wonder if I might have a word with you, please?'

I followed him out of the waiting room into a side ward. 'Have a seat, would you, Mrs Williams.' He pointed to a plastic chair in the corner. 'I'm afraid I have some rather bad news.'

I was convinced he was going to tell me she was dead. 'Emilia has severe Crohn's disease. We're going to have to keep her in hospital until we can get the disease under control.'

The relief was immense and, to the perplexity of the doctor, I laughed. 'Thank goodness,' I said.

He did not laugh. I went red with embarrassment at my inappropriate response. I tried to explain that I had just had a big shock, but my words trailed away and were replaced with a large lump in my throat.

The consultant embarked on his explanation. 'Crohn's is an inflammatory bowel disease, which in cases as severe as this and so early on in childhood can have long-term implications on growth and development. It's a chronic illness for which there is no cure at present. It's characterised by the inflammation of areas of the digestive tract. In Emilia's case this inflammation is happening from the mouth all the way to the anus. The inflammation is causing ulceration; there are abscesses and some strictures in the bowel.' He continued in a monotone, 'It's caused by an overreaction of the body's immune system. No one knows what triggers it off. It could be environment; it could be the result of a genetic susceptibility.' He paused for a moment. 'She's a brave little girl. She must have been in a lot of pain for some time. She's not at all well. She'll take a while to come round and she's likely to be quite sick and uncomfortable. I'll come and see you later when we get you up to the ward.'

Bewildered, Wren and I made our way to the children's ward. 'Two daughters,' I kept muttering. 'What's going on?'

Emilia vomited three times as she came round. She lay on the trolley looking disarmingly like Paul with her bright eyes and her quizzical expression. They took us to a small side room on one of the children's wards, where they rigged up her drip and began an intensive course of intravenous steroids.

Ringing Paul and then Emma brought back bad memories of the week before. I could hardly believe I was doing it again. Paul abandoned his work and caught a taxi straight to the hospital, where he spent an hour questioning the doctor about Crohn's disease. There was something darkly comic about phoning our fellowship group that evening for the second week running and asking them to pray for us in yet another crisis.

For over a week Paul, Emma and I took it in turns to sit at Emilia's bedside and sleep on the floor in her room. She charmed every doctor in sight and soon there were nurses in abundance who emerged from nowhere to play with her or to say goodnight before going off duty. Each child in her class had drawn her a picture and they covered the walls and the windowsill. One of my students even sent her a teddy bear wearing a university sweatshirt.

Cocooned as I was from the shock of the previous week, it was a while before I could take in the implications of Emilia's illness. My mind could not get round the thought of long-term persistent illness and the effort she would face in battling through. It had been hard enough with her hearing problem. As I lay in the hospital beside her listening to her breathing and watching the red light on the drip, the word 'suboptimal' kept coming back to my mind. Did Crohn's make Emilia suboptimal as well? She would not die of the disease, but where most children would surge across a level playing field in their growth and development Emilia was likely to face an uphill assault course. The doctor had laid great stress on lifestyle challenges. He had even correlated quality of life with the course of the disease, and a long shadow had fallen over her future.

I wondered if, with the rapid development of pre-implantation genetic diagnosis (PGD), couples would be able to screen and predict the genetic propensity of a baby towards autoimmune diseases of this kind, as well as serious hereditary conditions, and in so doing preselect and implant only the healthiest embryos. Why, if this technology is used for serious life-threatening illnesses, should it not also be extended to chronic illness such as Crohn's? Indeed, I had read that the same technologies were already being used in a number of countries to allow parents to choose the gender of the embryo at pre-implantation stage and in some cases to attempt to anticipate how likely a baby was to possess certain desirable physical or mental attributes. I recalled how in a recent budget the government had announced that they intended to spend 40 million pounds on stem cell research over a three-year period to make Britain one of the leading countries in the world in prenatal research of this kind. I looked around the children's ward and wondered if such procedures would eventually empty half its beds.

I lay there thinking about these things in the stifling heat of the hospital, exaggerated as it was by the oven effect of pregnancy. I looked at Emilia, remembering the special award she had just won at school for 'persistent cheerfulness'. There was nothing suboptimal about her spirit or the amount of love she drew from our hearts.

Silently, I formed a counter-argument against the position adopted by my medical colleague. Both his argument and all the practices I had been pondering presuppose a particular definition of normality, health and quality of life. But what happens to the argument if the definition on which it rests is dubious? After all, whose definition of normality is it anyway? And on what basis is it assessed? Is the normal person one who has physical attributes within a particular range? Do normal people have a certain intelligence or skin colour? Are there normal habits one must have, or normal speech patterns? In the 1870s families of 12 regularly lived in one-bedroom cottages with outside toilets. J. S. Mill might raise a philosophical eyebrow, but most of the time this was considered perfectly normal. Today overcrowding of this kind would be considered an intolerable suboptimal cruelty, in the Western world at least. Surely lifestyle and quality of life are entirely arbitrary concepts? Normality is a relative scale with no set of accepted criteria in all cultures. At one end of the scale lie those restricted by intellectual function, illness, age or accident to dependence on others for their survival. At the other end are those with efficient minds and bodies who are not only able to provide sufficiently for their own needs but also to serve the needs of others. The baby, Emilia and Hannah sit at different points in the spectrum of 'normality' so defined; but could I, as a parent who loved them equally, decide which one of them had the best quality of life and which one was, therefore, most normal and most worthy of their place on the planet? Could I tolerate the idea that Hannah and the baby, for instance, were subject to different legal rights while in the womb on the basis of some arbitrary standard of normality? Later I listened to a tape in which Canon John Hughes seemed to summarise these musings by quoting Jürgen Moltmann:

> In reality there is no such thing as a non-handicapped life. But ideas of health set up by society and the capable condemn a certain group of people to be called handicapped. Our society arbitrarily defines health as the capacity for work and a capacity for enjoyment, but true health is something quite different. True health is the strength to live, the strength to suffer, the strength to die. Health is not a condition of my body, it is the power of my soul to cope with the varying conditions of the body.

Strangely it was Hannah, who had never seen a day's illness in her life, who struggled with her sister's illness more than Emilia did herself. Emilia's humour and determination carried her through the pain of toilet trips, the indignity of examinations and the smarting agony of injections. But Hannah was tortured by anxiety. She said very little, but her tension was palpable. When she came to the hospital she sat sullenly kicking the chair. We could not get her to eat. Finally, after many days, she voiced her fear, just as I walked out of her bedroom having said goodnight. 'Is Emilia going to die too?'

'Oh darling, no, of course not,' I said, returning at once to kneel at her bedside so that my face was close to hers. 'Is that what you've been thinking?' She nodded, hiding her face in the pillow. For days she had carried that thought, unable, or perhaps too timid, to articulate it to anyone. Some people say that children are very resilient and they cope with things better than adults, but I am not so sure. Children can make connections which adults do not make and, unless we allow them to talk, those connections get silenced and buried. They can lead to untold damage and fear, which can sometimes take decades to unravel. I thanked God that this had come out into the open and we were able to pray with her.

There was an odd comfort in being able to do things for Emilia. The busyness of going to and from the hospital distracted us. I could read to her, I could cut up her food into bite-sized pieces. I could wrap her in a warm towel after her bath in the hospital bathroom. I would never do any of those things for her little sister. When Emilia eventually came home from hospital, we decorated her room with cards and put little treats on her bed. It was a straightforward and tangible kind of loving.

'I don't know how to love the baby,' I said to Paul that evening. 'What can I do for her?'

'How do you think I feel?' he said. 'You can do so much. You have her inside you. I could envy you that. All I can do is look after *you*.'

I had not thought about it like that. *I want to love this baby*, I wrote in my journal, *but I do not know how to*. I knew how to love Emilia when she was sick and Hannah when she needed to talk; but how should I mother this one whom I might never hold alive? I used to sit on the sofa and gaze at the ultrasound pictures. I was sure I could see her face clearly. I could not help but think of the verses from Psalm 139:

> For you created my inmost being;
> you knit me together in my mother's womb.
> I praise you because I am fearfully and wonderfully made;
> your works are wonderful,
> I know that full well.
> My frame was not hidden from you
> when I was made in the secret place.
> When I was woven together in the depths of the earth,
> your eyes saw my unformed body.

All the days ordained for me
were written in your book
before one of them came to be. (Psalm 139:13–16)

As I pondered on these verses in June and early July I realised that, if this were true of my child, if God had indeed purposed her and loved her as this passage suggests, then not only did this have profound implications for how I judged 'normality', but it also had profound implications for my role as a mother. I began to think long and hard about what it means to be a mother. I realised increasingly that I wanted this child for myself. I wanted a baby to hold, a toddler to laugh with, a child to teach, to meet my dreams for my family and to fulfil some of my ambitions. I did not want a deformed baby. I certainly did not want a dead one. God began to challenge me: what if *his* definition of life and health was different from *mine*? What if this baby's destiny was simply to be with him for ever? What if the days ordained for her did not include a birthday? Did it make those days any less precious or meaningful? What if my role as a mother was to co-operate with God's dreams for my child – his plans for her – even if they did not fit with mine? If the job God had given me to do was to help her to live her life to the full while it lasted and to prepare her for heaven, then by remaining in a place of prayer and worship close to the Father I could familiarise her with the atmosphere of his presence, so that she would know him when she went to be with him.

But how can I do this, I wrote in my journal in June, *when I know I am going to lose her? Won't it hurt more if I give my heart away?* Almost at once a verse from Isaiah came to mind: 'He grew up before him like a tender shoot' (Isaiah 53:2). I looked up the verse. I knew that it was talking here of the Messiah, who would come into the world as the suffering servant to carry the sin of the world to the cross. But the 'him' in this verse was a parent. The Father watched Jesus grow, knowing he would see him suffer and ultimately die. God was not asking me to do anything he had not already done himself. It helped me to picture the circle of unbreakable love existing within and between the persons of the Trinity. I saw myself being drawn into this circle and then it became less a question of my loving the baby and more a case of my watching how God loves and then following him in his love.

This image had two profound implications for me. First, I saw how God the Almighty loved with complete self-giving. Moreover, because of that love, Jesus the Son's redemption unconditionally covered the baby as it did me, and the presence of the Holy Spirit drew us right into the heart of this communion. I began to rest with the baby day after day in this quiet place of love. Second, as I began to picture the Trinity in this way I found it took away the dislocation of death. Death would change the way I could share love with my child, but it would not take away the love itself. Neither of us need stop being part of the fellowship which exists for ever between the persons of the Godhead. Jesus' separation from the Father on the cross means that we need never be separated from the eternal nature of God's love. When I saw us in God like this, I was no longer afraid to love her. And I wished I had seen all my relationships like this before, especially when I had been bereaved in the past. From this perspective death really is more transient than love.

8

Loved One

'We need to give the baby a name,' Paul said, and I knew that he too had been thinking about how he could love her. That weekend Hannah and Paul scanned every baby name book they could find. They read out name after name, often with great hilarity.

'We need a name that expresses her spirit.'

Hannah nodded pensively, agreeing with Paul. 'Yes, some names tell you what people are like and what they do. She needs a name that says what she means.'

Paul and I looked at each other, amazed to hear an eight-year-old putting ideas as complex as this into words. This experience was deepening us all.

'I want something Welsh,' said Paul. Paul's sense of heritage was at the fore again. I remembered the cold stone, the rain and the feel of the wind on the Welsh hillside. December seemed so long ago. I groaned – that just made the search for a name even harder. All day they worked.

That night Paul had a dream. He was sitting up in bed when I woke the next morning. He had been crying. 'I saw the baby in my dream.' Paul does not remember dreams often, so I listened intently. 'She was about three or four years old. Her hair was long. She was running fast through an open field towards the mountains. She was so free.' He added quietly, 'I feel connected with her now.'

He and Hannah continued their search for a name. 'What do you think of this?' Paul said finally, passing one of the name books to me.

'Cerian…' I read.

'What does it mean, Daddy?' said Hannah.

'It's Welsh for "loved one". It means "loved".' His voice was a bit wobbly.

'That's perfect,' I whispered. And so we called her Cerian.

With her name, Cerian moved from an idea to a person who was part of us all, and we began in our own ways to celebrate her presence. Hannah and Emilia started to address the bump regularly. Hannah would snuggle close and put her arms around my tummy and talk to Cerian when she thought that no one was looking. We proposed a toast to her at the end-of-term meal. Hannah showed off my bump to her friends at the Junior Sports Day, insisting on taking endless pictures of me with her little camera. Emilia drew pictures for the baby and Hannah even wrote a song. Paul put his arms around me and the bump at night.

For me worship became the active expression of my motherhood. Cerian and I just stayed together in a place of intimacy with God day after day, surrounded by worship and other people's prayer. This was an intimacy more rich and precious than any I had known before. The verse from Psalm 63 became real. I literally clung to God because he was my help and he enabled me to sing in the shadow of his wings. His right hand upheld me. Just as Cerian was totally dependent on me for everything with which to sustain her life, so I was totally dependent on God for the grace to live through each day and to carry Cerian for him. I was full of peace.

Peace, however, was utterly distinct from ease. Those remaining 16 weeks of Cerian's life were both the most wonderful and the most awful. I guess 'peace that passes all understanding' (Philippians 4:7) would not mean anything if it was not the peace of a lighthouse in the middle of a horrendous storm.

9

The Tape Recorder

'I hate being fat. I hate it. I hate it. I hate it.' I was stomping round our bedroom. 'I'm not eating any differently, and I'm just swelling up. It will take me the rest of my life to lose this much weight. I hate it.'

'Well, you are pregnant. People normally get fat when they're pregnant. Isn't that the whole point?' remarked Paul, not looking up from his book.

'But you don't understand,' I stormed. 'It's horrible! It's horrible to be this fat, and for what? Nothing. Look, even these maternity trousers are tight on me and I'm only 28 weeks.' Paul sighed and put down his book. How many times had we had this conversation? 'Why do I have to keep putting on weight? It feels like my body is out of control.'

There was a knock at the front door. 'Blast! The midwife's here. She's early. Just what I don't need right now. I am *not* in a good place this morning.'

'No, I can see that,' Paul muttered, picking up his book again.

Hannah and Emilia opened the door to Lois, the Scottish midwife. She came into the hall with her enormous bag.

'Why have you got such a big bag?' asked Emilia at once. 'Do you keep babies in there?' She peered inside.

'No, not babies exactly,' said Lois, 'but everything to deliver them.'

I could see that Emilia was wondering what 'deliver' meant, and I pre-empted questions about postmen by adding, 'Lois has to help when babies are being born.'

'Can you show me what's in your bag?' Emilia asked, fascinated.

'I will,' said Lois, following me into the lounge. She had been thoughtful in arranging to come round to our home to carry out the routine prenatal checks. 'It will save you looking at all those other pregnant mums, lovie.' I was glad of this. A room full of maternity dresses, copies of *Parenthood* magazine and crawling siblings was my idea of a nightmare. It also allowed the girls to hear the baby's heartbeat and to connect with the development of the pregnancy.

'How are you feeling?'

'Fat,' I said.

'Mmm…' She looked at me. 'Yes.'

'Great,' I muttered under my breath. 'I look it as well as feel it.'

'Can I look in your bag now?' said Emilia.

'Well, as a matter of fact, you can.' Lois let Emilia find the blood pressure monitor and she explained to both girls how it worked. After taking my blood pressure she took each of theirs and both girls took her blood pressure in turn.

While she filled out various forms she told the girls of her adventures as a midwife. Their eyes widened as she described the time she was called to a houseboat on the River Thames at two o'clock in the morning. She had to climb across fences and wade through muddy fields before she found the boat.

'Did you have a torch?' asked Hannah.

'Yes I did, but only a small one and I had to carry my bag.'

'Wow!' said Emilia, awestruck. She glanced down once more at the sheer size of the bag. 'What happened next?'

'They had a dog and it bit me.'

'You should always keep dog biscuits in your bag,' said Emilia authoritatively, probably remembering Wren's handbag, which always seemed to carry such provisions.

'Was the baby born?' asked Hannah.

'Oh yes,' said Lois, 'but we had to light candles so that we could see.'

'I definitely want to be a midwife when I grow up,' said Emilia, not taking her eyes from Lois's face.

'It was a little boy.'

'What did they call him?' said Hannah.

'Do you know, I can't remember.'

Hannah and Emilia thought of suitable nautical names while Lois started to examine me. 'You are carrying a lot of fluid. A bit too much, I think. When did you last weigh yourself?'

'This morning. I've put on ten pounds in a week.'

'Hmm,' she mused, still feeling my tummy. 'Ten pounds in one week is not good. You're carrying too much fluid. I think you may have developed polyhydramnios. The baby's deformity may be stopping her from swallowing enough amniotic fluid and consequently your tummy is literally swelling up like a hot-air balloon.' That was certainly what it felt like. 'You're likely to go into premature labour at any time. You need to prepare yourself.'

I felt sick, as though she had punched me. I did not want these days with Cerian to end. I had been pacing myself, expecting the pregnancy to last for at least another ten weeks. I had not thought about the end yet. I had only just come to terms with the beginning. I lay on the sofa feeling faint while Hannah squeezed the green gel onto my tummy ready for the Doppler machine.

'Now, where's this heartbeat … There it is!' cried Lois almost straight away. 'Baby's head is here. This is her back and here is her heart.' She turned the monitor right up and the sound filled the room.

Paul had come downstairs. He was standing in the doorway, as eager as the rest of us to hear the heartbeat.

'She sounds like a horse running,' said Emilia.

And she did. Her heart sounded just like the wild pounding of hooves. It was loud and free and so alive. We listened for a long time. None of us spoke. Then Emilia ran upstairs. We thought she might be upset until we heard the crashing of objects flying round her room and her little legs thumping back down the stairs.

'Here we are,' she said. 'My tape recorder!'

'What a great idea,' we all said at once.

'Yes, it is a great idea,' said Lois. 'If you want to make memories, make them now.' She glanced at Paul.

When the girls had finished helping her put all the objects back into her bag, she sat them down on the sofa next to me. 'Have you got any questions?'

Silence. I could see the girls were thinking. Finally Hannah shook her head. 'I don't think so.'

'Yes, I have a question,' said Emilia slowly, fixing her level gaze on the midwife. 'Why doesn't Jesus make the baby better?'

Lois went red. The atmosphere tensed. That question had obviously not featured in her training. She shuffled on her heels as she knelt in front of us.

It was Hannah who broke the silence. 'That's a good question, Emilia. I would like to know the answer to that question too.'

'So would I,' I said flatly.

'We all would,' Paul added. But we knew there was no answer to that question. Emilia went to sleep that night listening to her sister's heartbeat over and over again.

10

Awkward Questions

In the wake of the midwife's visit Paul phoned the hospital and arranged another scan. When we arrived at the John Radcliffe I was surprised to see that he had his briefcase with him this time. 'I've been doing a bit of homework,' he said. I knew what that meant.

It was a different consultant this time. He looked lean and fiercely intellectual. His hair was grey and his glasses sat on the end of his nose. He shook our hands briefly and stooped over the computer. 'My colleague has shown me the images of the last scan. I understand that there was some debate as to whether this is an instance of osteogenesis imperfecta type II or thanataphoric dwarfism?'

'The conclusion reached was thanataphoric dysplasia on the grounds that the bone density and the global limb shortening were less consistent with osteogenesis,' Paul replied briskly. I looked at him. Where did that come from? The consultant looked at him too before his eyes re-engaged with the screen in front of him. He worked silently for some time. We were content to look at Cerian.

His voice intruded all too quickly. 'Yes, Mrs Williams, you certainly do have polyhydramnios. The uterus is already distended and the fluid levels exceed those expected at 28 weeks. This is a normal corollary of skeletal dysplasias of this kind. Polyhydramnios is one of the most important signs of serious congenital abnormality. Abnormalities make the baby's swallowing mechanism ineffective, so that large quantities of liquor accumulate in the amniotic sac. You are likely to go into premature labour at any time.'

'So what happens now?' I said. He did not seem to understand the question. 'Will I just get bigger and bigger?'

'Yes. The uterus will continue to enlarge with the pressure of the amniotic fluid and eventually the pressure will be so great that it will force the uterus into contraction and you will go into labour. You could have an amniocentesis, to drain off some of the fluid, but it would need to be done daily in order to keep the levels down.'

'And there's some risk to the baby in this procedure.' It had been on these grounds that I had resisted the option of having an amniocentesis test earlier in the pregnancy.[5]

'That is true,' replied the consultant, 'although with a foetal condition as serious as this the situation is somewhat more complex.'

'Does polyhydramnios present any risks for Sarah?' Paul asked.

'No, not usually.'

---

[5] Amniocentesis involves the insertion of a hollow needle through the abdominal wall and uterus into the pregnancy sac, thereby allowing the removal of amniotic fluid surrounding the baby. An amniocentesis test can be carried out routinely at approximately 15 to 16 weeks gestation. The test is generally offered to women over the age of 37, those with a history

'Only discomfort,' I added weakly.

'Yes, it can cause pain and discomfort and in some very rare cases it is potentially dangerous. Have you thought any more about the question of termination? I would be willing to carry out a termination for you at any point.'

There was silence. He busied himself at the keyboard. I felt scandalised at the thought of killing Cerian and incredulous that they were still raising this as an option. I did not trust myself to speak.

'I read the paper you wrote on prenatal sonographic diagnosis.' Paul's voice was calm and measured. 'I found it very interesting. What are the statistical chances of the baby living?'

'Approximately 1 per cent,' said the doctor.

Paul touched my arm lightly as if to say, 'Trust me.' I wondered what other couples did when they were unable to put questions into words, intimidated by the authority of the white coat and the weighty atmosphere of scientific knowledge.

'And by what means are you arriving at that statistic?' Paul asked.

'On the basis of a study of 35 cases of skeletal dysplasias considered over a seven-year period from January 1989 to December 1995.'

'How many foetuses were terminated within this sample?'

'Termination occurred in 22 of the 35 cases. Spontaneous abortion or intrauterine death occurred in two cases; there were six infant deaths, and five, that is 14 per cent, of the infants survived the first year.'

---

of genetic disorder in the family or those who have previously had a child with particular congenital abnormalities. It is commonly used to detect chromosomal abnormalities such as Down's syndrome. Ultrasound scanning is used to guide the positioning of the needle so as to avoid damage to the placenta or foetus. In rare cases the procedure can cause miscarriage.

'How many of those cases terminated would have lived?' Paul persisted.

'That is impossible for us to ascertain other than by forming an opinion as to likely prognosis when a post-mortem examination was permitted.'

'So really, you do not have adequate data to make the 1 per cent survival judgement, because 63 per cent of women with babies in this condition abort?'

'Well … yes,' he conceded. 'If you put it in those terms, yes.' I could see that the men had forgotten me. The consultant was no longer talking to Paul as a patient. He asked him if he was a medic.

Paul pressed his point further. 'Even if we were to concede that there is only a 1 per cent chance of survival – let's talk about the 1 per cent.'

'But…' the doctor tried to interject.

'What provision will be made for the 1 per cent chance of survival?'

'But this baby will not live.' He adopted the same mantra as the previous consultant.

'We have just agreed,' said Paul in the same dignified tone, 'that there is, even by your statistics, at least a 1 per cent chance of survival. Therefore, as a father it is my responsibility to ensure that all provision is made should that 1 per cent chance come about.'

'Well, theoretically, yes, but we're talking about a theoretical scenario here.' The consultant was starting to look annoyed.

'No, we're not talking about a theoretical scenario; we're talking about my daughter. What will the procedure be if the baby is born and there is a chance that she will survive?'

I groaned. This conversation was beginning to make me panic. Facing Cerian's death was bad enough; I had not begun to absorb the scenario of living with her in a critical state. I wondered if Paul was in denial. I felt sick and put my head back on the pillow. The men talked above me.

Paul continued, 'I have spoken to a friend who is a surgeon at Birmingham Children's Hospital. He has told me of an operation that is done to enlarge the chest cavity. Could this be done in the event of Cerian surviving birth?'

'This procedure would not work in a case of this kind because of the inadequate development of the lungs.'

'I wouldn't want any invasive medical intervention,' I said, sticking my head up from the pillow. 'I only want her to be given palliative care, in the room with me so that she can die quietly.'

The consultant was looking quite red now. 'Mr and Mrs Williams, if this theoretical scenario were to take place and the child were to survive any length of time, which I do not for one minute think will happen, then the decisions that are made regarding the baby's care will not be yours to make.'

Paul and I looked at each other. This was a red rag to a bull. Paul spoke again. 'You mean to tell me that we have, or rather Sarah has, the right to decide whether or not to terminate the life of this baby right up to the moment of its birth, but thereafter we have no rights as parents over the medical care of our child?'

'Of course we would inform you of everything we were doing, but we are legally obliged to do all that we can to sustain the child's life.'

'That is a philosophical and a legal contradiction!' said Paul.

'I would not put it in those terms,' said the doctor. 'There are just two legal systems which operate: one which applies to the mother carrying the unborn child and one which applies to the legal standing of the child after birth.'

'That's ridiculous!' I could see that Paul was losing it. The conclusion was plain. The unborn child had no legal rights and nor had the parents of a severely disabled child. We were dealing with systemic injustice here. But at the time all I could think about was just how fat my tummy was going to get.

'What do we do now?' I asked again, lamely.

The doctor seemed to have forgotten I existed. 'It's best if you talk to your midwife about that. Technically this is not an obstetric problem. Do you have any other questions?' he said warily.

'No,' I said, looking meaningfully at Paul. I had to get out of the room. I was going to throw up.

'No,' said Paul through his teeth. 'We don't have any more questions, for the moment. But we'll contact you if we do.' I bolted out of the room.

I could almost see the steam coming out of Paul's ears. 'I can't believe it!' he said. 'How can something as illogical as that be allowed to happen and people don't even know about it? I hate this place!' So did I, but not for exactly the same reasons.

'Do you really think she may live?' I asked, trying to keep up with Paul as he stormed to the car.

'No, of course I don't,' he blazed.

'Then why on earth did you ask all those questions?' I knew I was playing with fire to try to discuss this when he was in such a state. 'It makes me panic when you talk about her living but being so deformed.'

'Why does it?' Paul shouted as we climbed into the car. 'What would it be like if she lived and she needed care and we weren't ready to give it because of some warped research finding by a couple of old men who've spent their lives looking at bodies on computer screens? What would I feel like then?' I was mute. 'Don't tell me what I can and can't ask them. The whole system excludes fathers and it intimidates people into not asking awkward questions.' Paul turned on the ignition, but he made no move to start our journey home. He sat crumpled in the driving seat. 'Just let me love my daughter my way. This is my way of loving her – making sure that we've explored and thought through every option.'

I put my head on his hot shoulder. 'I'm sorry.' He shrugged, but I would not take my head away. Finally, he put his arm around me.

'It *is* wrong, isn't it?'

'Yes, it's utterly wrong,' I said, not sure whether he was talking about the legal system, Cerian's deformity or life in general. We looked out across the car park at the white building.

'In that part they sustain life at all costs,' I said, pointing to the upper end of the building, 'and in that part they dispose of babies. If you want a baby but can't have one you go in that entrance, and if you have a baby but you don't want it you go in up there. In the middle they rob the aborted foetuses of cells to help the other lot of would-be parents.'

'And there's a different legal code governing both ends and no one ever asks about the contradiction,' Paul added. 'It's utterly insane.'

'What are we going to do about it?' he said, reversing the car slowly out of the car park. We drove home feeling tired, sad and small.

11

The Labour Bag

I tried to pack my labour bag many times, but I could never quite finish the job. I would lay out my brand-new towel and my dressing gown and my carefully selected toiletries and as I did so my thoughts would swing. At one end of the pendulum there was wild hope and anticipation that we might in fact find that the doctors had got it wrong after all and out would come a miraculously healthy little girl. At the other end there was an engulfing terror which centred around the thought of her dead, misshapen form. Then my mind would go blank and I could not remember what I had or had not packed and I would end up in a heap of desolation.

'How *do* you prepare for a birth and a death at once?' I asked Liz at the end of a morning service in mid-July. 'Can anything be more unnatural?'

'We know of some people in Northern Ireland,' she replied. 'They carried a child to term knowing the baby would die. Why don't you ring them?'

It seemed a good idea at the time, but both Paul and I felt nervous as we picked up both telephone handsets. Our trepidation evaporated, however, the moment David answered the phone. 'I'm glad you called,' he said. 'Tell us about your baby.' We were off. It could not have been easier to talk to them and the relief of finding people who understood was immense. Our questions poured forth. Most of them – such as 'What happens to the body after we leave the hospital?' or 'Should we take our own blanket for the baby?' – had seemed too detailed and bizarre to ask anyone else. But these details mattered and David and Sally understood exactly why.

'How did you prepare for the birth?' I asked Sally.

'I sewed the baby a little blanket. This helped me anticipate him as a person and it was something to hold on to afterwards.'

'Did you take pictures?'

'Oh yes, these were so very precious. I had a friend who had a stillbirth right at the last minute. They offered to take pictures at the hospital, but she refused. She was so shocked and confused she just wanted to get home as quickly as possible. Afterwards she deeply regretted having no image of the baby. She could not face holding the baby either and this was a far bigger regret. They let her see the baby two days later in the hospital mortuary, but it wasn't the same and she always felt guilty for not having held the baby close to her. My memory of holding our son is very precious. We took our photographs to a local artist and from the face they drew a wonderful charcoal etching of the baby. It's in our lounge. We also took a lock of hair and we had a footprint made with a mould.'

'What was it like watching the baby die?'

'Terrible, but also beautiful, in a strange sort of way,' Sally said. 'And … full of God. He lived for nine hours. I held him in my arms and told him how I loved him and what I would have liked to do with him if I had a chance, and we prayed our thanks to God for him.'

'And the deformity?' I was afraid to ask this question and my heart raced. We knew their child had died of a structural abnormality called anencephaly, in which parts of the brain and the flat bones of the skull are missing.

'It's important,' she said slowly, 'to let yourself explore the baby's deformity. It leaves no room for fear to grow and afterwards you may always wonder and wish you had. For us the imagined appearance was actually much worse than the reality.'

'How did your other three children grieve?'

'Differently. There is no mould. The older one showed a lot of emotion at the time and the younger one none at all. The middle one just kept on asking questions until we were weary of it. It takes time for them and the important thing is to let them do it their way.'

'Did they come to the hospital and see the baby?'

'Oh yes. That was vital. Although it was important to prepare them well beforehand. In order to avoid unnecessary distress the staff wrapped the baby in a blanket so that they could only see the face. They needed to say goodbye to their brother and to let him go. It seemed almost more painful at the time, but in the long run it was much better for them.'

'What was it like for you, David, watching the labour?' Paul interjected. His voice sounded distant, even though he was only sitting upstairs using the other phone in the study.

'Hard,' David said. 'I felt helpless. It wasn't until the baby was born that I really bonded with him. It's hard when you're a bloke; you don't get to know them as the mum does, carrying them as they do. And then he was gone too soon. You kind of distance yourself before the birth. You have to in order to survive, I guess, but then when they're there in your arms there's no distance to protect you any more and the grief kind of hits you. Afterwards people kept asking me, "How's Sally? Is she OK? How are the kids? Sally must be feeling dreadful." No one ever asked me how I was or how I was feeling. I was pastoring the church at the time and I had to say all the right things to people, but inside I felt like punching them and shouting at them, "Can't you see I'm hurting too?"'

After an hour and a half we started to say our goodbyes. Within 20 minutes of the call I had packed my labour bag, fortified by the sense of companionship.

12

An Angel in Yorkshire

'What am I meant to do now?' I wailed at Paul on the last day of the children's school term. I had packed my bag thanks to David and Sally and we had written a birth plan in case I went into labour. Even the car-parking money was in my purse and the numbers to ring for prayer and to notify people after the birth were in a prominent place on the pinboard. The university term had finished. Finals results were out and I was officially on maternity leave. There was nothing left but the suspended animation of anticipation and dread.

'Are we just meant to sit around and wait for the baby to come? Do we go on holiday, or do we stay here? Each day I wake up and I don't know if it will be today, tomorrow or two months' time. I don't know how to plan, how to shop, how to respond to invitations. I don't even know how to dress. I think I may go mad.' The last days of both the pregnancies with Hannah and Emilia had felt like months and the agonising state of limbo I was experiencing could in reality continue for another eight to ten weeks. Paul nodded pensively.

'Fun!' he said suddenly. 'That's what we need. Something that will be relaxing for us and fun for the girls.'

I looked at him gloomily. 'Fun' was not a word which I could in any way associate with the rack-like tension I was experiencing. 'And where exactly are we going to find that?'

'No! You cannot be serious!' said Emma when Paul told her later that day that we had decided to go camping with the whole church in Yorkshire. 'What will Sarah sleep on? She can barely sleep in her own bed, let alone on the floor of a tent.'

'Well, it won't make much difference then, will it?' Paul grinned at her. 'It's me you should be worrying about, Emma.'

'What happens if Sarah goes into labour at the camp?'

'There's a hospital in Harrogate. And my rally driving techniques are superb, as you know.' Emma looked at him doubtfully. 'I've rung them,' he added. 'I even got through to the maternity ward. They were very friendly.' Emma scowled.

'We have to do something with the children,' I said, trying to add a touch of practicality to the reasoning.

'They'll love it.' Paul's enthusiasm grew with Emma's agitation. 'All their friends will be there. There are children's groups for them. Mark and Janet are going. Come on, Emma. It'll be fun.'

Emma shook her head. 'I've heard that one before. Insanity, that's what it is – pure insanity.'

I had used the same word in earlier discussions that day, but I was now hurling myself at the idea with abandon. After all, the probability of insanity was high either way. Staying at home I would go insane, and in going camping I might at least stand a chance of going insane with a degree of hilarity.

'Well,' Emma said at last, 'I guess I could bring my one-man tent and put it up next to yours… You may need a bit of extra help.' We all laughed and the girls cheered and danced in delight at the prospect.

For the next few days I almost forgot the shadow of future events in the upheaval of organising camping stuff, packing saucepans and cleaning sleeping bags. Paul had wild ideas of taking portable camping fridges, heaters and barbecues, but he was at work so Emma and I cleaned the barbecue, searched for utensils in the attic and shopped for waterproof matches and tent pegs. It would be more precise, in fact, to say that Emma did the work, because she kept on insisting that I rested, yelling at me when I attempted to climb the stepladder into the attic. 'Don't even think about it! You are *not* going up there. You won't even fit through the hatch.' This last comment at least made me hesitate. 'Insanity, that's what it is,' she muttered. 'Utter insanity. For goodness' sake, go and lie down!'

The car was full to overflowing. Our car is affectionately known as Rocket, or less affectionately by Paul as 'the West Wing'. It is, after all, bigger than his study!

It is a seven-seater which, I recalled as I put the last few bits on the back seat, we had bought in anticipation of more children. I sighed and leant against the door. Plans … perhaps I should give up making them.

'Look,' I said to Emma as we finally shut the front door ready to leave. I held up a pocket-sized first-aid pack. 'Just in case we need it!'

She roared with laughter. 'Fat lot of good that'll do us.'

And so we set off with a great feeling of irresponsible freedom. By the time we reached North Yorkshire Paul had finished his last work call and the mobile was ceremonially shut down. 'We're on holiday!' he proclaimed to the motor-way.

'We are, are we?' said Emma sardonically, sandwiched on the back seat between the two girls with sleeping bags stuffed round her legs.

Mark and Janet arrived before us. Their pitch was comfortably close and all five girls disappeared on bikes with much merriment. After helping Paul and me to unpack our belongings, Emma erected her own little yellow tent. Paul made the first cup of tea and sat in a deckchair at the tent entrance like a nomadic patriarch. We gazed at the prospect of a happy week.

Janet was forced to use crutches because she had developed painful symphysis pubis dysfunction, caused by the instability of the pelvis during pregnancy. We both rejected the hard-backed seats after the first prayer and praise meeting and Mark and Paul carried our comfortable sun-loungers into the auditorium and parked them next to each other near the front. Janet and I between us moved so slowly that we would barely make it back to the tent before it was time to set off for the next Bible study.

It was hot. In fact, for the pregnant it was unbearably hot. Janet and I sat outside our tents fanning ourselves with programmes while Paul and the children had long and messy water fights. The worst moment for Emma and me came when, in order to exact revenge for a dastardly act during one water fight, a youth worker burst into our tent and tipped an entire washing-up bowl over Paul's head, the table, the stove, the clean towels and our lunch. 'That's the end of water fights,' said Emma categorically.

The children threw themselves into their 'big groups' with much enthusiasm. Between meetings they roamed the campsite on their bikes with their friends, returning only to hear Paul read the next chapter of *The Hobbit* at bedtime.

And then, halfway through the week, it began to rain. It did not stop for two days. The days of Noah seemed to be upon us again. Tents flooded and caravans leaked, awnings were washed away and wellington boots filled up with water. People abandoned the camp in droves, some seeking shelter in nearby hotels and others just making a beeline for home.

'You call this fun?' Emma remarked as we trudged back from the toilet block, feeling very little difference between the downpour and the cold shower we had just queued half an hour for.

'Well, on a relative scale this could be called a comparatively light and momentary affliction, don't you think?' I said, rather enjoying the spectacle of near hysteria and despair which we witnessed inside every other tent. To our amazement our tent did not flood and neither did Emma's. We felt like the Israelites watching the Red Sea close over the Egyptians after they had walked through on dry ground – relieved, triumphant, but a tad guilty too. Although we had no dry garments left, we did not fare too badly. Most of all, good humour did not fail us. In fact the deluge itself became a place of encounter, particularly for Emilia.

Hannah, Josie, Becky and Mary ran into the tent just as the lightning cut across the sky for a second time. They counted three between the flash and the ominous rumblings of thunder.

'Where's Emilia?' I asked, handing them mugs of hot chocolate. They looked at each other blankly.

'I thought she was following us,' said Josie.

'So did I,' said Hannah.

'Where were you?'

'We were down at the bottom of the field by the big gate that doesn't open. The thunder started and we all got scared so we came back.'

'But not Emilia?'

'We thought she was with us.'

I resisted the temptation to berate them. They knew only too well that Emilia neither responded nor moved as quickly as they did. I saved the irritation for myself and my fat tummy, which prevented me from even walking down the hill with the children, let alone riding back up again. Emma and Paul put on their boots.

'You stay here with the girls,' they said as they pulled back the door and dived into the rain. I tried not to look worried. The gate marked the furthest boundary of the campsite. It was some distance from any of the tents. Emilia's little legs would not have carried her up the hill at the pace of the others. I knew she was frightened of thunder.

Eventually Paul returned with Emilia on his shoulders. Emma followed behind, dragging her bike up the hill. The gaps between the lightning and the thunder were lengthening, but still the storm prevailed and it was almost dark at four in the afternoon. Paul put the freezing child down on my lap. I wrapped my arms around her. I felt her sodden clothes deposit their wetness through the layers of my jumper and maternity trousers.

'You're soaking, Emilia,' I said. 'Have some hot chocolate. It'll warm you up.'

Paul handed her a large chunk of Cadbury's Dairy Milk to dip into her drink. 'She was very intrepid,' he said. 'Tell Mummy about your great adventure.'

Emilia polished off the chocolate before she would speak. 'There was a big storm,' she began.

'I know, darling. I could hear it. It was so loud.'

'Hannah left me behind and I was all alone. I was very frightened. I thought I might get struck by lightning if I went on my bike and I couldn't remember which way to go back.'

'So what did you do?' I asked, hugging her more closely, feeling like a wretchedly neglectful mother for letting my sick five-year-old child roam the campsite alone.

'I sat down and curled up in a ball and I cried. But then I saw an angel and I wasn't frightened any more. I just waited there until Daddy came and got me.'

'An angel?'

'Yes, an angel.' She was still sipping her hot chocolate contentedly.

'What did he look like?' I enquired.

'Like a normal angel, of course.'

I did not want to sound ignorant of such things, but I could not stop myself asking, 'What does a normal angel look like? How did you know he was an angel, Emilia?'

'He smiled at me and I felt all warm and I didn't feel frightened any more. I knew it wasn't an ordinary man because he wasn't a man, he was an angel.' She talked with a simple nonchalance that made me feel cumbersome in my sophisticated adulthood with my prompt dose of scepticism.

'Have you seen angels before, then?' I asked.

'Of course I have,' she said, looking at me as though it were an odd question. 'I've felt them at school in the playground when no one plays with me, and when I was at the hospital and my tummy hurt. They're always looking after me. Can I go and play with Becky now?' She slipped off my lap, put her boots back on and ran out into the storm to find Mark and Janet's caravan. Paul and I looked at each other dumbfounded. I prayed for childlikeness to meet our storm with faith.

On the final and wettest morning of the camp the speaker took his text from Psalm 22 and he preached a word which was decisive and formative for me.

> My God, my God, why have you forsaken me?
> Why are you so far from saving me,
> so far from the words of my groaning?
> O my God, I cry out by day,
> but you do not answer, by night, and am not silent.
> Yet you are enthroned as the Holy One;
> you are the praise of Israel.
> In you our fathers put their trust;
> they trusted and you delivered them.
> They cried to you and were saved;
> in you they trusted and were not disappointed…
> O Lord, be not far off;
> O my Strength, come quickly to help me. (Psalm 22:1–5, 19)

He spoke of a king on the cross. He spoke of the glory of God revealed in and through suffering, and he spoke of the strength of this king made manifest through ultimate weakness and vulnerability.

It was not a theme we usually hear much about from the pulpits of our churches. Mostly our themes revolve around strength, triumph and wholeness. This was new and I listened with avid concentration to every word. 'The kingdom came through suffering and death. Consequently, there is room for us to lament before God. In fact we need to learn to lament. What Jesus dreaded most was the absence of the Father and that is exactly what he got. Sometimes God is silent and when he is silent God wants to know if we will trust him still. As we walk through suffering and we face the silence of God we can show others that God can still be trusted. Have we got room in our understanding of God for his absence – and the maturity that comes from continuing to trust? The cross was the place of Jesus' enthronement. If Jesus is our master, then should we not also expect to face suffering? But if we trust God in our frailty, we too are vindicated as Jesus was ultimately.'

I sat still at the end of the talk for a long time. When I began to weep, I let my long hair fall over my face so that people would not see my tears. I wanted to be alone to think. My tears were not just of sadness, they were also tinged with relief – relief that the message provided me with a theological structure through which I was able to mediate and interpret my experience. During the time of worship which followed a very clear picture came into my mind. I saw a rider on a great black stallion charging towards me with force and haste. *I am coming to deliver you*. The words impressed themselves on my heart. I tried to draw the image in my journal, but failed and resorted to words instead. Both the talk and the image meant a great deal to me at the time, but I could have little idea then just how profoundly important they would be later.

We survived the deluge, but by the time I sank into a hot bath at home, the thought of more 'fun' had lost its attraction. We were glad to be home. Another week had passed. *Thirty weeks*, I thought, looking at my tummy protruding above the surface of the bath water. Who would have thought? I heard the phone ringing in the distance. Hannah brought me the handset.

'Mummy, your tummy is huge!' she said, skipping away.

'Thanks, Han,' I said, putting the receiver to my ear.

'Why don't you come down here for the rest of the summer? Paul can commute to London from Hildenborough station,' said Wren at the other end of the line. God was providing for us. I climbed out of the bath, repacked, and we set off again, this time to Wren's house in Kent.

13

The Cerian Summer

Everything in Wren's house is conducive to peace. She opens her home to individuals, groups and churches for quiet days and over the years the building itself has adapted to a pattern of worship. At the side of the house is a room dedicated to prayer. There is a cross on the bureau forming a focal point and a beautifully formed figure of Christ on the cross wearing a crown of thorns, which my brother Justyn made for Wren as a gift. The chairs are comfortable. Music is always to hand, as are tissues, and warm fleece blankets to curl up under. Two full walls of the room are glass. They are covered in part with well-tended houseplants and there are views on both sides. In the summer the back window is usually open and you can feel the breeze from inside and smell the fragrance of the garden.

I know of no other garden as full of flowers as Wren's. In amongst the flowers there are interesting places to sit. .There are statues, a pagoda, a huge swing which Wren seems to use as much as the children, a wooden chalet filled to overflowing with readily accessible craft materials.

Beyond the trees at the bottom of the lawn is a wooded area where, if you look carefully, you can just make out the children's camp. Further on there is another more secret garden. The path winds down through the orchard to the woods. The four dogs usually show people the way.

After dropping Paul off at the sleepy local railway station, I used to sit most days in the prayer room, reading my Bible and listening to music. The girls never grew tired of the garden. They made a bivouac in the woods and created fairy castles out of the roots of the trees. Paul made them a seesaw and from there they carried out intrepid adventures to the watery islands in the middle of the pond. The midsummer midges were unbearable, but they did not seem to notice. They improved the tree house and swam in the huge paddling pool which Wren borrowed from her friend. When they grew tired of it she slipped out and bought a slide. She attached the hose to the slide and the girls hurled themselves down into the paddling pool at high speed. She also set the hammock up on the lawn under the shade of the largest oak tree. I often sat there in the afternoons. Wren cancelled all her engagements so that she could be at home with us, weaving an environment of peace.

Each day Wren and the girls walked the dogs through the surrounding countryside. Emilia found a hiding tree and jumped out at people as they walked past. When Paul came home in the evening we would sit on the terrace and eat our supper together as it grew cool and dark in the garden.

I tried to accompany Wren, dogs and children on their walks, but the more my tummy continued to grow the less I was able to walk. On one of these outings a car approached us just as we turned into the lane. 'Car!' Wren called, pulling the dogs on the lead to restrain them. 'Mind out, girls,' I called. In a flash, Emilia rushed into the road, came up behind me and pushed me with all her strength into the ditch, throwing herself in behind me.

'What on earth did you do that for, Emilia?' I exclaimed when the car had passed.

'Because I thought you were going to die. You might have been squished by the car.'

'I think it's more likely that the car would have been squished by me. Think of the dent my fat tummy would have made in the bonnet!' It took both girls and Wren to pull me out of the ditch.

By the end of August it was too painful to walk. One afternoon, on my drive to the station to collect Paul, I stopped at the garage. I was having a happy day until then. As the cashier took my card her eyes slid from my face and rested on the bump. 'You're huge! You must be overdue – are you having twins?' The incredulity in her voice was as alarming as the words themselves.

'No,' I muttered grimly, 'I am not.' I did not tell her I was still only 32 weeks. I walked out without saying 'thank you'.

After we had been at Wren's house for three weeks, Emma arrived. She quickly blended into the quiet rhythm of the summer. She too sensed the safety of that prayer-filled place.

Sunday by Sunday we had our own services in the prayer room. I could not face meeting strangers at Wren's church who invariably smiled excitedly at the bump and asked me when the due date was. Our little family services were incredible times. We would each bring a reading or a song, a piece of artwork or a prayer. Sometimes as part of our worship we would go out into the garden and each of us would find an object through which God was showing us something of his character. On one occasion Hannah read the words from Revelation 21 which she had copied into her journal some weeks earlier.

> Then I saw a new heaven and a new earth, for the first heaven and the first earth had passed away, and there was no longer any sea. I saw the Holy City, the new Jerusalem, coming down out of heaven from God, prepared as a bride beautifully dressed for her husband. And I heard a loud voice from the throne saying, 'Now the dwelling of God is with men, and he will live with them. They will be his people, and God himself will be with them and be their God. He will wipe every tear from their eyes. There will be no more death or mourning or crying or pain, for the old order of things has passed away.' (Revelation 21:1–4)

Emilia did an obscure drama at one point in which I died, went to heaven and then came back again. We laughed at the time, but I could not help connecting it in my mind with her extreme efforts to ensure that I was not hurt by the passing car.

We found a liberty to pray and worship as a family that we had never known before. We spent many hours talking in different configurations of relationships. Hannah sat next to me on the hammock and sewed a delicate pair of boots which she designed and made for Cerian herself. She was proud of her work and I could barely look at her as she sewed the final touch of two minute pink roses, for fear that I would not be able to stop crying if I started. Wren also tried to make something for the baby, but the shawl she was crocheting would not turn out as she had pictured. In the end she threw her efforts down in disgust and went to Tunbridge Wells, where she bought a shawl as light and delicate as a spider's web. I moulded a cross from clay in the craft room and Emilia spent all her savings on a tiny bright yellow dress which she caught sight of in a shop window.

When Emma arrived she brought with her a beautiful cotton quilt made by her mother. Cerian's initials are embroidered on the corner. She also handed me a small tissue-paper package. 'I've been keeping this in my bottom drawer. It doesn't look like I'll be needing it. I want Cerian to have it.' I opened the tissue paper. Inside was a hand-sewn cotton bonnet of the kind that I associate with the late nineteenth century. It was beautiful.

'Thank you,' I said. That was all I could say, but I knew how much it meant for her to give me this.

Afterwards, Wren remarked that one of the things that she was grateful to the baby for was the 'Cerian Summer' we spent together. Our memories are crammed full of beautiful things. On the 10th August I wrote in my journal, *What can I do but press on to hear the voice of God and listen to every intonation of his heart? I will press on to appreciate what is beautiful and do what is lovely*. Wren helped me to do these things.

It is strange, however, how one can operate on two levels, particularly in times of grief. The Cerian Summer could not have been more beautiful. It was full of rare and beautiful treasures (Proverbs 24:4), as well as the treasures of darkness mentioned in Isaiah. I was calm, even placid, on the outside; but inside I was in a turmoil of agony. I could not bear to part with Cerian. I had given her my heart. The polyhydramnios was causing increasing tenderness – my stomach was painful to touch. I needed help to get out of a chair. Day or night, I could not sleep for more than 45 minutes at a stretch, finding it impossible to get into a position that brought relief from the pain. From four in the afternoon the nausea was unbearable and I would pace round the house not knowing what to do with myself. My back began to hurt very badly. When I did sleep I dreamed, anticipating Cerian's death through vivid and troubling images. I had to fight to stay calm some days, actively putting my trust in the promises of God. One whole page of my journal is covered with the words, *Even though I walk through the valley of the shadow of death, I will fear no evil*. The *will* is heavily underlined. *Your rod and your staff, they comfort me.* I prayed that Jesus the Good Shepherd would walk with me through this dark and frightening valley.

On the next page of my journal I glued in the quote, *Courage is not the absence of fear and despair; it is the capacity to move forward confidently trusting the maker of the heavens to cover us with the shadow of his mighty hand even if the sky should fall.*

Soon after we arrived at Wren's house I went to see the local doctor. I had to register at the nearby health practice and with Pembury Hospital in case the baby should be born while we were staying in Kent. Wren dropped me off at the surgery on the way to the swimming pool with the girls. I had barely begun to read the magazine article in front of me when my name appeared on the screen above me. I was startled and disarmed when the first question the doctor asked me as I walked into her office was, 'Did you decide not to have a termination on strong religious grounds?' There was something in the manner of the question that made me hesitate. I sensed she wanted an explanation in order to compartmentalise my decision and so to shut it down.

'I do have strong religious beliefs,' I said after a pause, 'but I'm not sure that those principles are the main reason why I decided not to have a termination.'

She turned to face me and raised an eyebrow. I thought to myself, *Cerian is not a strong religious principle or a rule that compels me to make hard and fast ethical decisions. She is a beautiful person who is teaching me to love the vulnerable, treasure the unlovely and face fear with dignity and hope.* 'How can a person grieve a termination?' I said simply. The doctor looked down at my notes. 'This baby is alive now and I want to welcome her into our family. This may be all the time I will get with her and I want to spend it well. When she dies I will have the comfort of knowing that I did my best for her and I left God to decide the rest.' I could not believe I was saying these things to a total stranger.

'What have you told your other children?' she asked, paying careful attention to what I said.

'The truth, the medical truth that they're going to lose her. They helped us give her a name and they love her.' This was not my normal style of conversation with doctors. I was expecting her to start shuffling papers and drawing the meeting to a close even though I had not yet told her why I had come. But she kept on asking questions.

'What have you named her?'

'Cerian,' I said.

'That's an unusual name. I haven't heard it before.'

'It's Welsh for "loved one". We wanted to choose something unique because she's a unique person whatever happens to her.'

To my amazement and embarrassment, the doctor began to cry. 'What a beautiful attitude towards people,' she sniffed. 'I think you should write a book about this one day.'

I thought it was time to start talking about my back. This meeting was getting very intense. 'To be honest, I've come not only to register but to say that I'm terrified of having an epidural because of my back problem, but I'm wondering if my back will cope with labour if I don't.'

The doctor blew her nose. 'I'll arrange for you to go and talk to the consultant anaesthetist at Pembury Hospital. He will talk you through the options.'

I thanked her and left the surgery in some haste. What an extraordinary conversation! And her response intrigued me: 'a beautiful attitude towards people'. The connection she had made fascinated me and I started to think about how true it is that the way in which a culture treats the weak tells you all you need to know about its attitude towards people. Perhaps, in a culture which disposes of the abnormal and contains the weak so that they are unnoticed, the choice not to have a termination does need an explanation.

14

Thai Green Curry

I despaired last night. I feel utterly undone. My journal entries for the 24th and 25th August are not a happy read. *The pain increases every day. Every day she grows inside me. Each day it hurts my back but how much more it hurts my heart. Every day I love her more. In one moment I want the physical pain to end and for the delivery to happen and then in the next I pray for just one more day with her. I can't go on like this. If the baby doesn't come soon, I think I will lose it altogether. I wonder if a medieval rack is more comfortable than this? My brain is pulverised. I can't pray any more. I asked God to take the nausea away but he didn't answer my prayer. I asked God for mercy in letting her come prematurely and I have been waiting every day since early July. I asked God to take the back pain away but the more I pray the worse it gets. In January I even asked him for an easy pregnancy. With this track record how can I trust him with the labour? I pray abstract prayers about his presence but I find it hard to really trust him to be good to me in the detail. My faith and trust are stretched to the limit. I am angry with you, God. The sheer physical discomfort is making me cross and I am wearied by the never-ending nausea. I can't be positive any more.*

P.S. Please help me! I added at the end.

'Mum, I can't go on like this much longer,' I said, abandoning my journal in the prayer room and walking into the kitchen.

'I know,' she said. 'It's hideous. I can't bear it for you.' She turned round, having put the kettle on, and looked at me. 'Are you feeling all right, darling?'

This seemed a strange question. Of course I did not feel all right at one level, but at another I felt no worse than normal. 'What do you mean?'

'You're … you're…' She came over and turned my face to the window. 'You're blue. I don't like the look of you. I think I should call the doctor.'

'Mum, I'm fine. I just feel fed up and a bit faint, that's all.' I sat down at the kitchen table. Come to think of it, I did feel rather strange. 'I have a specialist appointment with the anaesthetist at Pembury tomorrow. They'll check me out then.'

'I don't like the look of you,' Wren repeated. 'I'll take you to Pembury in the morning. Emma has already said she'll look after the girls. Paul is in London again tomorrow, isn't he?'

'Yes. He has a meeting in the Curzon Street office. Where is he now, by the way?'

Paul was fixing the girls' bikes. They were planning a major bike ride for that afternoon. I went out on to the drive to find them.

'Hello!' Paul greeted me, looking up from the bike pump. 'I've booked a Thai restaurant in Sevenoaks for tonight. We all need a bit of a treat and it's a good way to say thanks to your mum for having us here for so long. We'll have to go home to Oxford on Saturday.' It was now Tuesday. I was all too aware that our time was nearly over.

'That sounds good.' I stood still. I was feeling decidedly faint.

'Are you all right?' said Paul. 'You look a bit blue. I'll get you a chair.' I tried to put my head between my knees, but my bump was in the way. I felt very odd.

By the evening I had recovered a little. I washed my hair and put on my favourite maternity smock. A large ornamental fish pond lay just inside the entrance of the restaurant and a model waterfall cascaded down a channel to one side of the staircase. Emilia's best dress was drenched within seconds, and Paul nearly impaled a tropical fish with the car keys as he tried to wrestle Emilia's arms out of the tank. Hannah walked ahead demurely, trying to pretend that she did not know the rabble in the doorway. The sodden dress was forgotten, however, as soon as the meal arrived. We were all absorbed in attending to a choking fit which overtook Emilia as soon as she swallowed her very first mouthful of Thai green curry. Hannah, traditionally the less adventurous of the two when it came to food, quietly chomped her way through three courses.

In between frequent toilet trips to deal with wet dresses, rejected curry and Crohn's symptoms, we proposed toasts to Wren. We each took it in turns to describe one thing we were grateful to Cerian for. Wren talked about the Cerian Summer. Emilia said how grateful she was that Cerian was now the youngest in the family, not her, and Emma described how Cerian had made her want to learn more about God. I wrote these memories down at the back of my journal on what I called the 'goodness pages'. I did not realise as we left the restaurant that this was the last time the seven of us would be together.

15

Cold Tea

I knew Pembury Hospital of old. I had spent a week there when I was eight suffering from a rheumatic virus. Wren had given birth to two of her children in the labour ward. As we drove into the hospital car park I wedged my hot Starbucks tea into the container by the glove compartment. 'I'll drink that when we get back.'

'Good idea,' said Wren. 'This should only take a few minutes.'

The waiting room was full of pregnant women. I thought they ought to have looked happier than they actually did. I could not take my eyes off the bumps, thinking of all the joy of anticipation and the well-prepared nurseries.

'Mrs Williams? Do come this way … You're a new patient? From Oxford? Is this your first visit to Pembury?' The nurse chatted all the way down the corridor to the consultant's room. 'The doctor's very nice, you'll like him. Don't worry, he knows all about your little one. I made sure he had the notes in advance.' I thanked her profusely.

The doctor invited me in. I told him about my long-standing terror of epidurals and the nature of my back problem. He drew a diagram of the spine and showed me how they would inject the epidural into the spinal column above the injury in the disc between L4 and L5. At first I thought it was the diagram and the talk of injections that was making me feel hot and dizzy. But when my vision started to fill with bright shiny stars and the desk seemed to move round the room in front of me and three identical doctors talked to me at once, I began to think that perhaps something was wrong. I lowered my head onto my chest. The doctor carried on speaking.

I felt decidedly strange as I made my uneasy way back down the corridor, leaning my hand on the cold wall for support. Wren took one look at me and jumped up. I managed to say, 'I'm not feeling well,' but I could not keep my eyes open properly. Wren beckoned to the nurse and together they guided me to a sofa. I closed my eyes. The whole room was spinning now. I just caught a glimpse of another nurse bringing over a blood pressure monitor.

'Her blood pressure is very low. I think we should get her down to the Labour Suite and get one of the doctors to look at her.'

I remember being pushed in a wheelchair and taking large gulps of fresh air in the hope that this would wake me up. I held the metal armrests tightly. We were greeted by a senior midwife called Marilyn. I remembered her name distinctly through the spinning because she said it so loudly. I sensed that her pristine efficiency was disorientating Wren.

'This sounds like an anxiety-induced migraine to me,' she said, as she and another nurse helped me onto the bed. 'Nothing to worry about at all. Let me take your blood pressure. What was it when you took it?' she asked the nurse who had brought me down to the Labour Suite. Marilyn pinched my arm into the black canvas band with a rip of Velcro. Suddenly she went very quiet and her previous manner gave way to a swift professionalism. 'Call a doctor immediately. We need a drip here. Her blood pressure is too low and it's still falling. Emergency equipment please…'

The last thing I heard her say was, 'Where is her husband? We need to contact her husband.' She raised her voice and called across the room, 'Can someone call her husband, please? He needs to come immediately.' I tried to say 'Please get Paul' to Wren, but she was scrabbling in her handbag trying to find his mobile number. The oxygen mask was over my face by then and she could not hear me. I was aware that they were taking her out of the room. I tried to call her, but I could not keep my eyes open any more. I heard someone shouting at me from behind, 'Stay with me, Sarah, stay with me. Try to concentrate on staying awake.' I could not open my eyes. The staff were moving me. We were moving fast down the corridor. People swarmed around me from all directions, pushing equipment. I saw Wren standing with a nurse. They were trying to make her sit down. I tried to speak to her, but I was drifting off again. I started to go through Psalm 23 in my mind. I focused on the words. I wanted Paul to be there. It felt as though I was on a great lake of water. The trolley stopped, but I was still moving. I was going up. I was up above them all, looking down at myself. There were people all round my body. It did not look like me. Still they were running. They were wrapping me in a large foil blanket. There were electrodes all over my chest. They were scanning my stomach. Someone was shouting at me, but I could not hear them. Everything was quiet in my head now. I was drifting again. I could feel the presence of God, or maybe it was unconsciousness. Whatever it was, it did not hurt and I felt full of peace. *Am I dying?* I thought. *Well, this isn't so bad. It doesn't hurt*. Then nothing.

Later Wren described how she had run outside the building to use her mobile phone. She could not find Paul's number and so she called Emma at home. Emma was in the garden playing with the girls when the phone rang. At first she thought she would let it ring on to the answer machine, but glancing at her watch she decided it could be Wren apologising that she and I were late. 'Emma? We need to get an urgent message through to Paul. Can you do that for me?' The tension in Wren's voice made Emma clutch the back of the chair. This did not sound like the onset of labour. 'His office number is written out on the piece of paper above my desk. Can you see it?'

'Yes, I have it.' Emma's hands were shaking.

'Sarah has collapsed. They think the baby is pressing on a main blood vessel. They've rushed her into the High Dependency Unit. The hospital needs him to get here as fast as he can. Things are not looking good.'

While Emma waited for the secretary to answer the office phone she looked across the garden at the children. They were taking it in turns to crash at high speed down the slide and into the paddling pool, oblivious of all but their game. She felt sick. How was she going to get through this day giving nothing away? Having left the message, she took a deep breath, closed her eyes and prayed. God and sheer determination carried her through the afternoon. She played with the girls. She walked the dogs, administered Emilia's medication, cooked tea, bathed the children and read them bedtime stories before she heard any further news.

As soon as Wren had finished the call she ran back to find me. But they would not let her into the High Dependency Unit. The nurse was kind but firm, and made Wren sit outside in the corridor. She kept patting Wren's shoulder and murmuring calming words, but gave away no information. All Wren could see were people running in from different directions, looking grave and wheeling equipment. She thought she was losing me. She prayed that Paul would get there quickly.

Paul was in a meeting in Curzon Street in London. It was unusual for meetings to be interrupted and the assembled crew looked up in surprise when Paul's PA knocked and walked in. 'Excuse me, Paul. I have an urgent message for you from Pembury Hospital.'

'Is she in labour?' he asked, beginning to shut down his laptop. Something in the PA's pause made Paul abandon his laptop and step straight out of the meeting.

'I'm sorry, Paul, it's Sarah. There has been a complication and the doctors request that you come immediately.'

Paul remembers trying to figure out the quickest route home as he hastily grabbed his things. On the way to the station in the cab he called Mike and then Mark, asking them to pray. He prayed frantic broken prayers that I would be all right and that the train would go faster than ever before. When he reached Tonbridge he dived from the train and threw himself into a taxi. 'Pembury Hospital, please. I need to get there quickly.'

The next thing I knew, a nurse was telling me not to move. 'You must remain in this position on your side. The uterus is compressing the main aorta.' I tried to lift my head, and passed out.

'Your husband is here;' I heard someone say in the distance. When I finally caught sight of Paul sitting on the seat beside me I could not understand why he looked so white and covered in sweat. He did not smile. He clutched my hand without moving. I could not speak through the oxygen mask and the drip was obscuring my view of him. Two nurses remained at the end of the bed checking my blood pressure every five minutes.

When the consultant entered the room I do not think either he or Paul thought I could hear them. They spoke to each other over the bed. 'What happened?' Paul asked.

'Your wife had a serious vasovagel attack. The polyhydramnios is causing vena caval compression. This is reducing the return of blood to the heart and brain and causing a dangerous reduction in blood pressure. I have to be honest with you, Mr Williams. We have something of a dilemma. We need to induce the baby for your wife's safety, but until her blood pressure rises we cannot risk an induction, which at 35 weeks may not be straightforward and could require either an epidural or an emergency Caesarean. Your wife's blood pressure is too low to permit either. Consequently, we are in a state of limbo. All we can do is wait.'

Paul looked exhausted when he sat back down next to me. We still did not speak. I could not make the words come out, and nor could he.

The Starbucks tea was stone cold when Wren returned to the car seven hours after she had left it. She drove back home to fetch Paul an overnight bag. Paul did not want to leave my side. The nursing staff put a mattress on the floor of the High Dependency Unit for him.

It was hard to sleep when the cramp was stealing up one side of my body and the nurse kept taking my blood pressure every

15 minutes. I woke from fitful sleep at 2.30 a.m., sweating. I thought about the girls. I remembered how Emilia had pushed me into the ditch to avoid the car and her odd drama the Sunday before. I wondered if she had some instinct that I was in danger. I thought about Paul. How would he have told the children I was dead? It was only by 'chance' that the appointment had been scheduled for that day. What if I had been at home? Would an ambulance have reached me in time? I began to shake as the reality of what had happened hit me. I lay awake for the rest of the night full of terror. What would it be like to die with Cerian? I felt very ill.

Paul woke at four. Not being able to move, I could not see if he was awake, but somehow I sensed it. I pushed the oxygen mask to one side. It was the first time we had spoken.

'Are you awake?' I whispered.

'Yes.'

'What are you thinking?'

'That I nearly lost you.'

'It was the one thing we didn't anticipate, wasn't it?'

'Yes. Nothing could have prepared us for that. I prayed in the train that you wouldn't die. I was frightened.'

'I thought I was dying.'

From then on we began to talk. We talked until they brought Paul some breakfast. While he went to wash I thought about the distinction between death and the fear of death. I had come face to face with death the day before, but in the night I had tasted the fear of death. The latter was far more dreadful than the former. The fear of death is an enemy. It seeks to rob us of our confidence that at our end God will be there to enfold us in all the glory of his person. We have no control over the timing of death itself, but I could let God come and help me rule the fear of death.

When Paul returned from the bathroom we prayed together. It was awkward to pray with the nurse in the room, but our need of prayer was greater than our reserve. We asked God to banish the fear of death and give us courage to face whatever happened next.

We had prayed, but fear is insidious. It was not done with us yet.

16

The Garrison

By the time Wren returned to the hospital at ten the next morning I no longer needed the oxygen mask. She helped the nurse to give me a sponge bath. I had been in the same clothes for 28 hours. I felt ill and weak. They moved me to the ward later in the day, but when my blood pressure dipped again in the late afternoon the doctor left swiftly to organise an induction.

'The induction is booked for early tomorrow morning, Mrs Williams. We'll take you down to the labour ward at 7 a.m. to start things off. Clearly we cannot have a repeat of this. We need to get things moving before your blood pressure goes down again and it becomes impossible to intervene should it become necessary during the labour.'

I felt very afraid. Paul had gone home with Wren to fetch the children and I was alone. I lay precariously suspended, as if on a tightrope, between two fears. On one side there was fear for my own safety and on the other fear for Cerian. What would happen if my blood pressure collapsed again during labour? What would it feel like for Cerian to have her tiny bones crushed as she left the safety of my body? I had to rally all the discipline of mind I could muster just to allay the panic which threatened to overwhelm me on both sides. I held Cerian through the bump. This would be my last night with her.

It was unbearably hot in the ward and the sweat became indistinguishable from my tears. Someone had painted the windows shut years ago. I fixed my eyes on the ceiling. I did not know how to pray. Tears poured down my face, filling my ears and soaking the sides of my hair. The curtain moved at my side. I did not look round. I had nothing left. At that moment I wished I had died the day before so that I would not have to face the ordeal that awaited me.

The chaplain sat down beside me. 'May I pray for you?' I nodded, not moving my eyes from the ceiling. He took a tiny bottle of oil from his pocket. He poured some onto his finger. Then he gently put his finger on my forehead and with the oil he made the sign of the cross. 'May the peace of God which transcends all understanding guard your heart and mind in Christ Jesus. May it garrison your mind, like a strong and resilient defence. In the name of the Father, the Son and the Holy Spirit. Amen.'

He slipped away, but the calm he brought did not. That verse of Scripture was like a rescue harness, lifting me from my tightrope to a place of safety. I stretched my arm up in the air as if to grab hold of God. It was easier than praying with words.

In my heart I gave 'the Cerian days' back to God and through my tears I thanked him for giving them to me as a gift. I asked him to protect me through labour and to help Cerian to die well.

I felt like a soldier in the midst of a war, temporarily defended in the garrison but preparing on the eve of the final battle for every eventuality. An old memory verse I had learnt in Sunday school came to mind as I silently considered my situation before God:

> Therefore put on the full armour of God, so that when the day of evil comes, you may be able to stand your ground, and after you have done everything, to stand. (Ephesians 6:13)

This was an evil day – there was no doubt about it. Yesterday I had nearly lost my life. Tomorrow I would lose my daughter. If ever 'fight the good fight of faith' meant anything to me, it was now. I did not look like a soldier in my white nightie, and the hospital did not look like a battlefield. But the thin line between the spiritual and the material dimensions of reality was blurring as it so often does at moments of birth, of death and of intercession. At these times we are afforded a glimpse of just how thin this line really is. Indeed, we see perhaps that there is no line at all. We take a second look at the mundane black-and-white plateau of our existence and we see that it is, in fact, a textured blaze of colour, contoured with wonder and mystery. And with this glimpse we see that here good and evil are sharply defined; faith and unbelief are locked in mortal combat.

Before the chaplain's visit, the fear of death had been pounding on the door of my mind, terror threatened to seep right into my heart and despair had been encircling me. All were enemies whose one objective was to undermine my faith in our Commander-in-Chief. Therefore, I did as the verse requires. I dressed myself in the belt of truth, I put on the breastplate of righteousness, I covered my head with the helmet of salvation,

I slipped my feet into the shoes of the gospel of peace, and I took up the shield of faith in one hand and the sword of the word of God in the other. Then I stood my ground, praying that after I had done everything I would still be standing.

Afterwards, I washed my face and brushed my hair. I propped myself up on the pillow and ate some supper. Then I waited for the family.

Paul made the girls wait while Emma popped in to see me. 'Am I glad to see you!' she said, sitting down beside me. 'Don't do that to me again in a hurry. I think yesterday ranks as one of the worst nightmares ever.' She recounted the story of having to ring Paul's office whilst looking out over the garden at the girls, wondering how they would react if they discovered that I was dead.

'You got more than you bargained for with us, didn't you, Emma?'

'Just a bit,' she grinned. 'Don't you worry about the girls. They're fine.' She went back out to the corridor to make space for Hannah and Emilia.

'Cerian will be born either tomorrow or the next day,' Paul told them after they had greeted me. The 48 hours I had been away from them felt like a year. They had no idea that this reunion might never have happened.

'This will probably be the last time you're with Cerian when she's alive,' Paul explained. They both put their heads on the bump and cried their goodbyes, telling their sister they loved her. We held hands and prayed together as a family.

I heard Emilia crying in the corridor as she left with Emma. There was nothing I could do to comfort her.

17

Horse and Rider

'How would you two like to sleep in a double bed tonight?' said Marilyn, sticking her head round the curtain. It was not the first thing we were thinking about, it has to be said. The girls had left an hour before. We were dazed by a mixture of grief and dread and Paul was preparing for another uncomfortable night on the floor. 'I've arranged for you to have the Hope Suite for as long as you need it,' she announced triumphantly. We had no idea what the Hope Suite was, but 'double bed' sounded good and Marilyn's commands were hardly something one would wish to argue with. I was wheeled from the ward just before 9 p.m.

'You'll like it in here,' said Marilyn, proudly turning the key to what looked like a flat. She stood back and let us enter. The floors were solid wood, soft curtains hung at the windows. There were flowers in the hallway. We made our way past a small kitchen and a larger bathroom to the main room at the end. The staff had drawn the curtains and switched on the four table lights that were positioned tastefully at different points in the spacious room. There was a rug on the floor, a pine chest and bookcase, a rocking chair and a large, luxurious terracotta-coloured sofa. The bed was pine with traditional head and end boards, and it was covered with what looked like a home-crafted patchwork quilt.

If I say it was like a hotel, that would be right at one level; but the description does not accurately convey the atmosphere of peace, home and tranquillity that filled the place. There were no hospital smells or sounds, only the faint cry of seagulls in the distance. The sense of refuge after the horror of the last 48 hours was overwhelming. Not only was my mind garrisoned, but I felt as if I was physically safe in the beautiful walled garden of a fortress. I lay very still for a long time. Paul unpacked our things.

We found out later that the suite had been given by a couple and a grandmother who had lost their tiny baby, Hope. They wanted to create a place where people like them could grieve in comfort and peace. The grandmother was a Christian and on the bookcase there was a moving tribute that she had written to her granddaughter. Wren later discovered that the mother too had found faith through the death of her child. We wrote to them afterwards, expressing our thanks for the beautiful legacy they had left for others – a haven in the middle of the ugliness of bereavement.

'One day, I'll have a room just like this in our house where people who are going through bereavement can come and stay and feel safe,' I said.

'Let's get through this thing one step at a time,' Paul replied, handing me a cup of tea.

I slept more deeply that night than I had in months. I woke at five to an unfamiliar sensation in my stomach. I hugged the bump instinctively. Cerian was kicking; not one kick but many. I had rarely felt her move. The excessive quantity of fluid, along with the tininess of her form, made it nearly impossible to feel any movement. I savoured the moments with a mixture of joy and agony. She had woken me up. Did she know that this was her day?

'It's your birthday,' I whispered.

Wren came at 6.30 and made us breakfast. I managed to walk down to the Delivery Suite, where Marilyn began the induction process. 'You're all remarkably peaceful this morning,' she said, slightly disconcerted. 'You must have slept well.'

Wren, Paul and I spent the morning reading, listening to music, and talking through the highlights and lowlights of Cerian's short life. We also prayed. We prayed for Cerian. We prayed for God's mercy upon her. We prayed about the birth and we prayed for the staff with whom we would have contact that day. Paul phoned Mark and Janet on the mobile. It was Becky's birthday.

'We're planning to come to Wren's tonight,' they told us. 'Janet's sister is having the girls. We'll be there when you want us.' We had not dared to think they would come all the way down to Kent, let alone on a family birthday, but the thought of seeing them was like a beacon. 'We're praying you through,' Janet remarked as I said goodbye, and I knew it was not just a platitude.

I picked bright yellow flowers in the afternoon while we walked through the hospital gardens in the rain trying to speed up the contractions. They seemed like a promise that one day the sun would shine again. They sat on the locker by my bed throughout the delivery. I fixed my eyes on them during contractions.

By the middle of the afternoon the contractions began to be sustained and painful. The more painful they became, the more I withdrew. Paul and Wren sat in the lounge adjoining the delivery room, which together formed a private area the staff referred to as the 'Home from Home'. I lay down on the bed with my face to the wall. I felt completely helpless.

'I simply do not know how to do this, Lord,' I prayed. 'Every contraction is taking Cerian further from me and every inch of my body is resisting labour. I can't do it, I can't do it. Just let me out. I can't go through with this.' But I knew there was no way out. I could not run away, and I could not move forward through the experience. I curled up round the bump, immobilised. 'God, show me how to cope with this!'

I lay still for a long time.

Then quite suddenly into my mind came the image I had seen during the worship at our church camp. I saw the rider on a great black stallion at full gallop. There was sound, movement and power in the sight. The hooves were pounding on the earth, sending mud flying in the wake of the creature. The mane streamed and the hair of the rider was full of sweat and rain. I knew then that it was Jesus. He was riding towards me with incredible urgency. I could see it in my mind as clearly as I could see the yellow flowers beside me. He was coming for Cerian. I remembered the words I had written in my journal: *I am coming to deliver you*. The sheer energy of the image stilled my sobbing. The rider was both warrior and lover, frantic for his loved one, coming to rescue her. I knew without a doubt that there was something in Cerian that was running with similar spirit to meet him. I remembered Emilia's comment when she had heard the heartbeat: 'She sounds like a horse running.'

'And me, Lord?' I whispered. 'What do I do?'

I barely needed to ask it as a question. I knew I had to release her to him. It was as though I had to hand her over the walls of a besieged city in the thick of battle so that she could escape unharmed with him. The urgency of the picture galvanised me. Now I knew my role, I had to rise up with discipline and maturity like one who is trained for battle. And so with every contraction I began to say, 'Lord, I trust you and I entrust her to you.' I began to find grace for each wave of pain. Instead of fighting the contractions I began to work with God towards his end, in spite of my desire to keep Cerian safely inside my body.

I realised as I went out to find Wren and Paul that this was the mental preparation I needed and through it I could garrison my mind with the courage and peace that the chaplain had prayed for the previous night. I saw myself rolling up my sleeves and getting to work in obedience to the Commander-in-Chief. The immediate sense of intimacy with God began to flow again and it did not leave me. I marvelled at the tangible reality of finding strength in weakness.

Paul lay down on the floor next to me. 'How's it going?' He fixed me with his eyes so that I could not escape the question. Paul knows I am a tortoise by nature and he was not going to let me retreat into my shell. I find solitude easier than company, even company as close as Paul's. The deeper I feel something, the more aloneness I seek. I had to make myself communicate with him. I looked at his tired face and I knew that he wanted to do this with me. Cerian had felt more mine than his because I had carried her. But he had carried me.

I told him about the picture of the horse and rider, forcing out the words between contractions. I will never forget what he said to me.

'You are only doing what every parent has to do. We have to let Cerian go and give her back to God. One day we'll have to let Hannah and Emilia go too. That's the goal of parenthood: releasing them to God. They are his anyway; we are merely guardians. Every contraction may be taking us further from Cerian, but they're taking her closer and closer to God, where she belongs.'

He grabbed his Bible and then for many hours he read me verse after verse of Scripture between each contraction. I meditated on the texts he fed me instead of focusing on the pain. Later Wren took over to give Paul a break; and so between them they carried me. When they ran out of accessible verses, Paul read us a Gerard Manley Hopkins poem.

> As a dare-gale sky lark scanted in a dull cage
> Man's mountain spirit in his bone house, mean house dwells –
> That bird beyond remembering his free-fells;
> This in drudgery, day-labouring-out life's age.
>
> Though aloft on turf or low stage,
> Both sing sometimes the sweetest, sweetest spells,
> Yet both droop deadly sometimes in their cells
> Or wring their barriers in burst of fear or rage.
> Not that the sweet fowl, song fowl needs no rest –
> Why hear him, hear him babble and drop down to his nest,
> But his own nest, wild nest no prison.

Man's spirit will be flesh-bound when found at best but
uncumbered
Meadow-down is not distressed
For a rainbow footing it nor for his bones risen.

Soon Cerian would be released like a skylark from the prison of her 'bone cage' and one day God would give her a fully restored body to live in with 'uncumbered' freedom. Death was not her end but her beginning, as it will be for me one day.

18

An Elastic Band

'The staff are just changing over for the night shift. Come and say hello to the new midwife.' Paul put out his arm like a gallant gentleman to a fine lady emerging from a carriage. The only trouble was, having rolled my bulk across the bed and heaved myself up into a sitting position, I did not have the grace to meet the image. Paul had to haul me off the bed in the end, but I did appreciate the dignity conferred by the gesture all the same.

Hand in hand we went back into the lounge, to find the new midwife standing formidably in the doorway. Stella was about my age. Her jet-black hair was cropped unevenly and it shot up in irregular tufts under the influence of some powerful hair gel. Her stud earrings extended from her right lobe all the way round the rim of her ear. She wore battered trainers, incongruous against her uniform. It was the atmosphere she brought with her into the room, however, which struck me more forcibly than her person. She stood across the room almost defying us to speak to her. When she came towards us her movement was abrupt and her manner harsh.

'How's it going, Sarah?' She left no space for me to answer. 'Marilyn's gone home. I'm in charge around here tonight. Anything you need, just give me a shout.' Then she left the room. Wren, Paul and I looked at one another. I could see Wren's knuckles were white against the arm of the chair. 'In charge…' she muttered. 'I'll show her who's in charge!'

By 11 p.m. the pain in my back was becoming excruciating. The contractions were regular and intense and with each one the agony in my spine was reducing me to the edge of blackout. I could not believe it when the doctor announced that I was still only three centimetres dilated. 'We'll have to do an epidural.' There was no point in disagreeing. The doctor was only stating the obvious.

Stella checked my blood pressure again. Above the rhythmical pain of the contractions I felt the jagged abrasion of her touch. An anaesthetist I did not recognise, wearing a green cap and gown, appeared at Stella's side and together they towered over me. Without any verbal preamble the anaesthetist took my wrist and patted the veins on the back of my hand to see where to insert the cannula.

What I feared has come upon me. These words from the book of Job moved across my mind like the message on a screen-saver. Wren used to quote the verse when we were children and she discovered that we had done something frightfully naughty. I turned my head towards Paul. He was scrutinising the blood pressure monitor.

'Can I just check that you're aware of her spinal injury?' he asked the anaesthetist anxiously.

The doctor nodded his reply. ‘L4, L5,’ he said. ‘We’re going in here at L2.’ He showed Paul the spot on my back.

‘Is her blood pressure high enough to do an epidural?’ Paul came back again.

‘It’s a little low, but it should be fine.’

‘Are you sure?’ I said. I knew I was pushing him, but I was suspended on the tightrope of fear once again.

Perhaps the anaesthetist felt that my fear was challenging his professional judgement, because he responded swiftly. ‘Look,’ he said, ‘I’ve been doing this job for 35 years, since you were a baby; so let me get on with it, please.’

Stella shot him an exasperated glance and he shook his head in reply. All I could see from my position were their faces poised over me. I did not trust either of them. Inside I was screaming like a terrified animal in a cage. I knew my fear was irrational, but that did not make it go away. I was still reeling from the shock of my collapse two days earlier.

‘I’m sure you know what you’re doing,’ I said, ‘but…’ I continued before I could stop myself, ‘a little compassion would go a long way.’ Although I had said the words calmly, I was horrified at how smartly they seemed to ricochet round the walls of the labour room. Stella held her breath and the anaesthetist paused with the hypodermic syringe already in his hand.

‘My wife is nervous of having an epidural,’ Paul interjected, trying to smooth the atmosphere. Both of us were terrified by now – thanks to the close shave of two days before. Our fear was exacerbated by tiredness and the stress of the moment. ‘Come on,’ he said to me. ‘You can do it. You’re going to be fine. Soon you’ll be out of pain. We’re not going to let this fear get the better of us. It's just intimidation. Put your hands on my shoulders and look at me.'

Neither Stella nor the anaesthetist spoke as they sat me on the side of the bed to insert the needle into my spine. I fixed my eyes on Paul's and remembered the phrase 'stand firm then'.

'There we are. All over,' said the anaesthetist in an expressionless voice. 'That didn't hurt, did it?' I kept my mouth firmly shut this time. Paul darted from the room as soon as he could see I was all right. He sat with his head between his knees for some minutes to avert the overwhelming urge to faint.

It was nearly midnight. And then, quite suddenly, just when we needed them, Mike and Liz walked in. They were like reinforcements arriving in the heat of battle. Mike steadied Paul with a firm hug and Liz sat with her face level with mine and silently took my hand. 'We're here not just on our own behalf,' they said. 'We represent all the prayers and love of the church as a whole. We are all standing with you.'

Mike came close to the bed, his voice as gentle as it had always been since the day with the pineapple. 'I don't know what to say to you, Sarah,' he said. 'What do you say at a time like this? But I've brought you a gift.' He handed me an elastic band. 'I found it on the floor in the corridor as I walked towards the ward. Look at the band,' he said. 'Where does it start and where does it end?'

'Well, it doesn't,' I said, like a slow child, turning it round and round in my hands.

'Of course it doesn't. So God's grace has no beginning and no end; it goes on and on and it will never run out. It's available to you at every moment.'

I did not take that elastic band off my wrist for three months afterwards, not even to wash. We agreed to phone Mike's mobile when Cerian was born. They left us to find their hotel room for the night. The epidural was beginning to work by then, and the pain was abating.

19

Flight of the Skylark

I must have fallen asleep. It was one o'clock. Stella was standing next to me checking the epidural monitor.

'I don't know why I didn't have one of these things with both the other two,' I said to her as she took my blood pressure. 'I can't feel a thing.'

'They're great, aren't they? I had one with my son years ago.'

'How old is your boy now?' I asked.

'He's nearly 15. I can't call him a baby any more. He's at Crowborough Beacon School.'

'We used to play hockey against them.'

'Yeah, your mum was telling me you grew up round here.' She paused. 'It's a shame about your baby. You must be feeling pretty bad right now.' For the first time she smiled at me.

I wondered, if I had possessed Wren's lion-like confidence, whether I would have found some way of telling her about

God at this point. Instead I simply said, 'I'm grateful for the time I've had with her.' But in my heart I forgave Stella for her harshness earlier in the evening and under my breath I prayed God's blessing upon her.

'Your man's had it, I think,' she said. 'I told him to make himself at home. Things are quiet tonight and the delivery room's empty next door. He's crashed out on the bed.' I laughed. 'Your mum's fast asleep on the sofa. She's a nice woman, your mum is. Very kind of … gentle.' She filled in the blood pressure reading on the chart. 'Not many people want their mums with them these days.'

She was making her way towards the door when suddenly I wanted her to check Cerian's heartbeat. 'Please may I listen to the baby's heart?' It was the first time I had asked during the labour. We had requested that there be no monitoring.

'Are you sure you want to?' she said. I nodded. By now there was far less fluid and I could feel Cerian's form. There was no gallop this time. The sound was slow and faint. 'I think that's yours,' Stella said. Cerian was going, and I knew it.

Stella left me. I put my hands tight round Cerian's tiny body. I prayed for her, thanking God for the good things she had brought into my life, and I said goodbye.

It was at that moment that the presence of God came powerfully into the room. It was so tangible that everything inside me stilled instantly. I hardly dared breathe. The room was full of God. It was holy and I understood why the patriarchs of old took off their shoes in the presence of God. I knew with certainty that God the Father had come to take her home. There would be no painful bone-crushing for her, only the wonder of his enfolding.

It was later confirmed that Cerian had indeed died at this time of a placental abruption, a painless gentle death caused by the cutting off of the blood supply to her body.

After some moments I called out. Wren came straight in. 'What is it?' she said, briskly dispelling the sleep from her face.

'She's gone.' But Wren seemed not to hear me. The moment she stepped into the room she too was stilled, as I had been. 'God is here,' she whispered, kneeling down beside me. 'God is here.' We sat still for a long time. I wanted to call Paul, but neither of us moved. It was not a time for noise or words.

Things happened quite quickly then. Wren went to wake Paul. Stella fetched the doctor. I started to vomit and the pain became more intense again. The final stage was upon us. It was the worst of all. I tried to push, but my body would not respond. I had no will to push – who would want to give birth not to life but to death? There was nothing left to look forward to. I felt abandoned and desolate. God had come and taken Cerian home, but it felt as though he had left me behind. It was the worst hour of my life.

Finally, she came with a huge explosion of blood that hit the wall and covered the doctor's face and gown. Wren clapped her hand over her mouth to stifle a scream. The abruption had caused haemorrhaging behind the placenta. But I was barely aware of the staff flustering over my large loss of blood, removing the clot and stitching me back up. All I knew was that they had taken Cerian away. I thought I heard her cry, but I knew she was dead. Paul was with Cerian. The paediatrician was talking to him. I shouted, 'Is she alive?' but I knew she was dead. I could hear wailing. It was some time before I realised that the strange anguished howling was me. I still thought she might be alive when Paul brought her to me wrapped in the soft white fleece we had so carefully prepared. There was blood on the fleece. Paul's face told me she was dead, but still I hoped, even though I knew. I turned my head away. I could not hold her yet. I shook. Paul passed the baby to Wren and he held me. I wanted to cry, but I could only wail.

20

A Whole Lifetime Over

Eventually, they put Cerian in my arms. I was repulsed and yet compelled by her tiny form. She was still warm from my body. By this time she was dark purple all over and her colour shocked me profoundly. I had been warned, but still I was shocked. She had been dead for three hours. I kissed her forehead.

There were lots of things I wanted to say to her, many things I wanted to pray, but no words came out. I could not sustain a thought from one end to the other. When Mike came he took Cerian in his arms and he prayed all that I wanted to say. He gently put structure around what we could not articulate and he helped bring form to a time when our world had fallen apart.

Wren washed Cerian in a baby bath at the end of the bed. 'It's about all I'm going to be able to do for her as a grandma,' she said to Stella as she quietly extracted the poised flannel from her hand. Little did Wren realise how much she had already done. It was the first time I had seen Cerian's deformity. I did not want to look at her at first. I was frightened of her body. But Wren's loving attention gave dignity to her body in a way that I could not bring myself to do alone. Slowly I was able to follow Wren's lead.

It was strange that she was so very deformed, because all my thoughts of her had been filled with beauty. There was a shocking disjunction between the physical body that lay in front of me and the relationship that I had had with her spirit. I do not want to describe her body. I will keep this in my heart. But the comfort I gained from looking at her was this: she had a body which was suited for the purpose God had for her. It was not a body which could ever have walked, or run, or cuddled. It would have been nothing but a prison to her spirit. But for the purpose of being inside me, her body was perfect. I asked myself whether I could evaluate my body like this. God has given me the perfect body for all that he has destined me for. Can I accept this from him?

Wren dressed Cerian in a tiny embroidered cream silk dress which Paul had bought for her. She put the bonnet from Emma on her head and she wrapped her in the shawl. Finally, she put Hannah's slippers on her tiny feet.

Stella cut a lock of her copious dark hair and made a print of both her hand and her foot. We took as many photographs as we could. It was not a natural thing to take photographs; it jarred. But now I am so grateful for every one of them. Wren laid Cerian in a Moses basket and covered her with the quilt embroidered with her initials. She looked beautiful. I ached.

Paul took Cerian and set her beside him in the adjoining lounge while the staff washed and redressed me. I was still vomiting, even after they had sponged me down. 'That just about sums up the pregnancy, doesn't it?' I said, passing my very last bowl full of sick to Wren.

'I'm proud of you,' she said.

It was only later that I realised this was Paul's darkest hour. He sat in the gloom of the lounge with Cerian's body next to him. He had no energy left to support me any more. He was feeling his own pain and loss. For a man the moment of bonding is often the birth. It had been so for him with all our girls. Now she had come, he realised the full force of what he had lost. He held onto the image he had seen of her in his dream. It was the only time he had touched her alive except for the tiny fluttering through the wall of my stomach and the mass of grey and white on the computer screen. But he loved her a whole lifetime over.

Paul had called Mark at Wren's house shortly after Cerian was born. It was not long before he arrived at the hospital. I did not see him. It was Paul he had come for. When he walked through the door of the 'Home from Home' suite Paul left his dark chair in the corner and sobbed in Mark's embrace. In the privacy of their friendship there was no one Paul had to be strong for and he was able to let out the raw mixture of his own emotions that I could not have handled at that time. Mark was unperturbed as Paul moved from grief to anger to guilt and then back to grief again.

'I feel like it's somehow my fault. Her deformity makes me feel like I've failed as a man.' Mark understood the strange way in which manhood, even prowess, is linked almost primevally to the ability to produce healthy offspring. So many men are never able to voice this unconscious linkage and it can eat away at them over many years. Mark prayed with Paul, bringing the myriad of conflicting reactions into the open, and helped him find his strength in God again.

Mark left just before the staff took us back to the Hope Suite. He returned to Wren's house, where he and Janet spent most of the day playing with the girls and giving Emma much needed support.

Much to my surprise, the anaesthetist put his head round the door of the labour room just as the porters arrived in the corridor to wheel me away on a trolley. 'I'm just about to turn in,' he said. 'I'm sorry about your baby.' He looked bashful. 'I came to say – what you said to me last night about compassion was absolutely right and I want to apologise.'

I was stunned. I smiled at him. 'Thank you for coming to speak to me.'

Stella was also going off duty. She lingered in the room, clearing up various bits on the counter behind the bed. She seized a moment when no one else was in the room and came straight over to stand next to me. 'It's very sad, what happened.'

'Yes it is. Thanks for looking after me,' I said, trying to make it easy for her to leave. Her face contorted into what looked at first like an ugly grimace, until I realised that she was in fact dissolving into tears.

'You're a brave lady,' she spluttered. And then she fled at high speed from the room. I could hear her sobbing as she ran through the adjoining lounge. I do not know what became of Stella. We stayed in touch with Marilyn for over a year. Paul even helped her son get a job in the City in the end. What I do know is that Stella was not in charge that night. We all in our different ways had to make room for a much higher authority.

21

The Moses Basket

They took me back to the Hope Suite on the awaiting trolley. I had been in labour for 22 hours. Paul placed Cerian's Moses basket next to the pine bed and I sank into a troubled sleep.

I awoke to the sight of Cerian's purple face. Panic gripped me. I screamed. What had happened? I grabbed my stomach out of instinct. Paul was next to me. He tried to hold my hand.

'Find Mum!' I screamed. 'No, don't leave me.' I was terrified when he went to rouse Wren. 'Are the girls all right? Paul, I have to know if the girls are all right! I have to go to the girls. They may be hurt.' The trauma crashed over my brain. I tried to climb off the bed. My legs gave way and I caught sight of Cerian again. I thought she was breathing. I had not fed her. Had I killed her? Was I going mad? Her body frightened me. My body frightened me.

Wren came in. I was shaking all over and screaming from the shock. She and Paul took my hands and began to pray quietly. Paul took his battered Bible and above my broken cries he read:

> Though you have made me see troubles, many and bitter,
> you will restore my life again;
> from the depths of the earth you will again bring me up.
> You will increase my honour and comfort me once again.
> (Psalm 71:20)

When he reached the end he read the words again twice more, with an authority that began to calm me. I rallied my shattered mind to concentrate on the words. I was still again. In the distance I could hear the faint sound of the seagulls. All would be well, but I realised it would be a long slow climb through the grief and I needed to be very gentle with myself. I was terribly vulnerable. In my Bible I have etched the date in the margin by the psalm Paul read me that day – Saturday the 31st August, Cerian's birthday.

I did not panic like that again. As I look back on it, I realise how very normal it was after the trauma and shock of nearly dying myself, the protracted physical and mental strain of the labour, and the intensity of seeing and holding my dead baby. Once Cerian died the protective shell with which we had encased ourselves in order to survive the run-up to the delivery was stripped away and we were subject to the full force of the grief. But at the time, I thought it was insanity. I was not in control of my mind, and fear and panic overwhelmed me. Paul's wise response brought order without taking away the necessity of somehow allowing all that mixed emotion to come out.

When I had settled, Paul went to collect the children. I will never know what their faces looked like when Paul told them their sister was dead. Janet told me later how she had heard them cry from the next room. She walked down the garden at the sound and wept herself, holding her own bump and trying to ward off fear for her own little one.

When the children arrived at the hospital Emilia strode straight across the room to Wren, who was holding the baby. She held out her bunch of flowers as if she expected Cerian to take them. Hannah lingered at the threshold with Emma. She was very white. Wren took the flowers and showed Emilia the baby. Immediately, she wanted to touch the body as Wren had done, to hold her, and I do believe she would have undressed her like a doll if we had let her. Only the expression on her face displayed that she knew this was not a living child.

'Why is she so purple, Wren? She looks like a plum. Why is Cerian cold?'

Hannah suddenly threw herself onto the bed next to me. 'That's not Cerian!' she cried. 'That is *not* Cerian.' I took the crumpled card from her hand and tried to smooth it out. *I love you little sister*, it said. All I wanted to say was 'Sorry – I'm so sorry, I couldn't give you another sister.' Hannah's grief and distress were acute. I held her close to me for a long time and then abruptly she needed to talk. She wanted to know everything about the birth, when Cerian had died, and how I felt. She would not look at the body. She seemed to relax when I told her that I had not really wanted to hold Cerian at first.

The nurse stuck her head round the door. 'Are you all right? Have you got everything you need? I'm sorry about the noise!'

'Thanks, we're fine,' we told her. 'I can't hear any noise,' I added to Paul.

Meanwhile, Wren was having her work cut out to prize Emilia away from Cerian's body. 'Why is her nose all funny, Wren? Why are her eyes closed like that? Has she got any arms?' Cerian was completely covered when the girls saw her. Seeing her face was enough. They did not need to take on board the detail of the rest of her body. We were glad that we had done it like this.

Emma was still standing in the doorway. She looked awkward. I called her over to sit with Hannah and me on the bed. 'You look more exhausted than I do,' I said to her.

Emma was focused on Hannah. 'I'm not sure I could do what Emilia's doing right now, could you, Han?' she remarked to Hannah across the bed. 'Has she got your boots on, Han?'

For the first time Hannah looked over at the body. Wren put the baby in the basket and took Emilia out to the kitchen. Emma took Hannah's hand and they went over to have a look. They both stood a long way back and peered. Emma did not push her to go close. 'Can't see,' said Hannah. Emma went closer and bent over the basket, pulling back the shawl fractionally. Hannah followed her slowly. They both looked in. The boots were there. Emma gave Hannah a hug and they sat down on the sofa next to each other.

'Do you want to hold her?' Emma asked.

'Not sure,' said Hannah. 'Kind of yes, kind of no.'

'Same here,' said Emma. 'I will if you do.' For half an hour they sat there talking, and every so often Hannah returned to the question. 'Shall I hold her? I'm not sure.' Emma was careful not to push her.

'I'll hold her after you,' Emma said finally. Paul passed Cerian to Hannah. She held her and her tears fell on the white spidery shawl.

'I did it, Emma,' she said triumphantly. Emma held Cerian too and I thought about the bonnet she had given her.

When the girls had said goodbye to Cerian, Mark and Janet came briefly. Janet told me all about Wren's garden, the girls, the dogs and the woods. Mark held Cerian, as he has all our children. None of us expected Janet to hold her. But as Mark put Cerian back into the basket, Janet asked bravely if she could. The incongruity of her own tummy full of life pressed against Cerian's now very cold body was hard to see. 'She's like a little china doll.' To us, their holding Cerian, as Mike had done earlier that day, felt like the ultimate expression of love. It is not easy to hold a dead baby and their acceptance of her was a recognition of the depth of our feeling for her and an acknowledgement of her personhood.

'The drink can wait a bit, mate,' Mark said to Paul as they left. 'But don't think you're getting out of it that lightly. You're buying this time.'

Paul and I were alone, and we knew that the moment we had been dreading all day had come. We too had to say our final goodbyes. We said nothing to each other. What could we say? Paul took her in his arms. He held her away from his body and looked at her for a long time. Eventually he passed her to me. I touched her cold cheek. There was a knock at the door. The nurse had come to take the body away.

Seeing the basket containing our daughter disappear through the doorway was worse than the agony of searing physical pain. As the door closed there was nothing but the void where she should have been. Although I had anticipated her going so many times, prior to this moment I had been full of her. This was my first real taste of loss and although I knew she had left me to be with God, that did not insulate me from the deep heart-rending wave of human sorrow.

I crawled to the bed and curled up small. Paul said nothing. He knew I needed silence then. Quietly, almost imperceptibly, he cleared up the room. He straightened the sofa, he turned on the small lamps, he drew the curtains. He took the table on which her basket had been standing and he pulled it slightly away from the wall. He placed one yellow candle in the middle. Around the candle he placed the flowers Emilia had brought, Hannah's crumpled card and the bright yellow dress. When the nurse came back with Cerian's things, Paul silently placed the boots, the bonnet and the quilt on the table, along with the tiny pink wristband that she did not need any more. He draped the shawl across the back and he let his own cream silk gift fall over the front. His silent actions ministered to me far more than words could have done. Intuitively he had created a visual focus for us where the basket had been. It seemed to say, *She has gone, but not the memories*. We can treasure them for ever.

22

The Seagulls' Cry

'I *am* sorry about the noise,' said the nurse as she came in with a cup of tea the next morning. 'It's the only problem with this room.' Paul and I looked at each other, bemused. 'The doctor's expecting you, Paul, at 10 o'clock and the registrar of deaths should be free at 11.' While I wrote my journal Paul went to handle the paperwork. He returned an hour and a half later looking exhausted and clutching a stark certificate on which the word **Stillbirth** stood out in bold letters.

We began to prepare to leave. When Wren arrived to help us we asked the staff nurse if we could visit the Delivery Suite again. We needed to lay a few memories to rest. 'Sure, no problem,' she said. 'Take as long as you need.'

The bed had been remade with fresh sheets ready for the next delivery. I looked at the place where my yellow flowers had been and took a deep breath. It was hard to go back into the evocative atmosphere once more. The memories were acute and we recoiled from the touch.

I looked at the mat on the floor where Paul had lain down next to me. Wren ran her hand along the freshly scrubbed wall where my blood had been. Paul sat in the chair in the corner of the lounge. Each of us remembered in our separate ways, reassessing the good elements of the memories as well as the bad.

I lay back on the bed and recalled the horror of the longest hour of my life. 'I felt as though you left me then,' I whispered to God under my breath. 'Where were you?' Psalm 22 came flooding back into my memory. *Is there room in our understanding of God for his absence? Will we trust him still?*

Paul came over and stood next to me, where he had been during that hour. He looked down at me and said very quietly, 'I think God wants to say to you, "Well done, good and faithful servant. You were obedient even without the hope of a reward." '

'Thank you, Lord,' I said.

But my overriding memory, the one that I will carry from that room for the rest of my life, was of catching a glimpse of the glory of God. That memory caused all the other recollections to pale into insignificance. I stood at the foot of the bed where I believe he stood, and I worshipped. God the Almighty, King of the universe, had come to take a tiny deformed baby, who did not even have any legal rights, home to be with him. And he had come masterfully, like the urgent rider on the stallion, just in time to spare her a moment's pain. I was amazed to find as I stood there that at the heart of all the grief was the paradox of profound gratitude and joy. My dreams were in tatters around me, but Cerian had left me with an infinitely valuable gift.

We had washed the sheets of our minds. I was ready to go home now.

As we left, the ward sister came to say goodbye. 'I do hope the noise hasn't troubled you too badly,' she said. I had to find out what they were talking about.

'Do you mean the seagulls?' I said.

'The seagulls?' It was her turn to look bemused. 'What do you mean, the seagulls? There aren't any seagulls!' Strangely this had not occurred to me, even though we were 50 miles inland. 'It's the sound of babies crying on Ward 4.'

I looked down at the elastic band on my wrist. 'Father, you knew my limit. I could not have coped with babies crying, so you let me hear seagulls instead. Thank you…'

'Please,' I added, 'let me carry on hearing seagulls for a while!'

23

No Morning in Heaven

After Cerian's death the word 'paradox' took on a new and poignant meaning for me. Throughout her life I had seen that it was possible to experience two entirely different and apparently contradictory things at once: grief and hope, pain and joy, ugliness and beauty. I had rediscovered the paradox of death and resurrection, weakness and strength, at the heart of the Christian gospel. It amazed me that this experience of paradox did not end with her death, but deepened still further in the time of mourning that followed. The funeral itself embodied this paradox. I encountered it again as I returned to work and, most of all, I faced it in a stark and alarming way as I began to consider anew the culture of which I am a part.

'I keep calling it Cerian's wedding,' I remarked to Paul after I had mixed up funeral and wedding for the fifth time. 'My brain's scrambled.'

'Maybe it's not such a bad description. It is a celebration, after all,' he said pensively.

As I existed in an aching vacuum of shock and loss in the days following Cerian's death, Paul organised the funeral with energy and focus. He had a clear vision of what he wanted the day to be like and he carried us along with his determination. He gathered the music that had been special to us during the pregnancy. He asked Mark to lead the worship at the thanksgiving and Mike to conduct the service and the ceremony at the crematorium. Our neighbour Adrienne, whose baby I had held on that day of trouble in May, agreed to arrange the flowers for us. Paul selected Bible readings which had been our anchor points for the last nine months and he invited all the people who had carried us through the pregnancy. He had Hopkins' skylark poem printed on the order of service. He ordered lavish quantities of bright yellow sunshine flowers, the colour of those I had picked on the day Cerian was born and the colour of the dress Emilia had chosen for her. He planned a supper party for our family and closest friends at Sissel's house after the crematorium. He even had Cerian's name engraved on a tiny brass plaque and fixed to the top of her coffin. Every detail was expressive of the beauty of her life and our pride in her. It was only other people who saw any incongruity in the paradox of loss and celebration.

'Why have a banquet for a stillborn child anyway?' We sensed that the florist would have liked to ask this question directly as she snapped impatiently at us while we deliberated over which flowers to choose. At the department store the checkout lady asked me if the large quantity of bright yellow ribbons, candles and napkins were for a special occasion. She looked bemused when I said, 'Yes. They are. They're for my daughter's funeral.'

After this exchange I struggled to find my way back to the car through my tears. I had to pray I would hear the sound of the seagulls in my head again.

I touched the paradox the day before the funeral. Over and over I thought, *Tomorrow I bury my daughter. Tomorrow I bury my daughter*. I wandered around the house aimlessly. My arms were the biggest problem. They should have been holding something, but instead they hung like clumsy redundant objects at my side. They should have been pushing a buggy, but my hands were empty. I kept folding my arms across my chest and stuffing my hands inside my sleeves. In the end I had to resort to hugging a hot-water bottle and rocking myself on the sofa. No one had told me how physical the pain of losing a baby would be. 'I can't do this,' I murmured over and over in rhythm with my body. In the night I woke three times, thinking that surely it must be time to feed her now. When I finally got up on the morning of the 13th September I found a card on my dressing table with the words from 2 Corinthians 12:9–10 scrawled on it, along with a tiny bunch of flowers. Wren had had a restless night too. I sat down on the floor of the bedroom and searched my Bible for these words:

> My grace is sufficient for you, for my power is made perfect in weakness. Therefore I will boast all the more gladly about my weaknesses, so that Christ's power may rest on me … For when I am weak, then I am strong.

I had nothing to bring to the day, but I resolved that I would let God be my strength.

The service went as planned, but I had little sense of it. I was aware of faces all around me. There was sound and movement, but it all seemed a long way off. I felt suspended alone with Cerian. I wished there had been two coffins at the front of the church. I imagined a larger one for me nestling close to the miniature version, which looked forlorn, set on its own at a distance from the congregation. I thought of Hopkins' poem 'Heaven-Haven' as I took my seat on the front row and waited for my turn to take the microphone.

> I have desired to go
> Where springs not fail,
> To fields where flies no sharp and sided hail
> And a few lilies blow.
> And I have asked to be
> Where no storms come,
> Where the green swell is in the havens dumb,
> And out of the swing of the sea.

When I stood up to pay my tribute to Cerian I had no idea if words would come out of my mouth. I was dazed to see the vast array of faces turned gravely towards me. I looked at them for some time, wondering if they had any idea what abject pain I was feeling in my heart at that moment. They were close to me physically in terms of proximity and some of them were close to me through ties of family and deep friendship; but just then I felt as though I was looking at them all, even Paul, Hannah and Emilia, from another shore. I had known Cerian intimately. I had enveloped her in my own body and protected her as myself.

They had never known her in this way. At that moment I felt closer to her than I did to them and I wanted to be with her more than anything else. I felt as bleak as a rock pounded by the wind and the waves. But as I turned to one side to let my eyes rest on Cerian's coffin so that I could address her one last time, I realised that although I could not go on speaking *to* her, I could go on speaking *for* her. That thought fortified me. It broke through my silence and I read the words I had written some weeks earlier in the garden at Wren's house.

People normally write tributes to recollect the memorable things that loved ones have done *and to celebrate their achievements. You do not have any achievements for us to celebrate, Cerian. You spent your short life resting in a hidden place.*

But had you lived a long life crammed full of activity and accomplishment, I could not have been more grateful to God for you, nor could your life have had more value and significance to me. I am so grateful to you for taking me to a quiet place of intimacy with God – for giving me a glimpse of the nature of his love.

There was nothing you had to do to earn my love. I didn't require anything from you before I loved you, not even your physical normality. I loved you simply because you were mine.

You were not precious to me because of the things you did. Your worth was written into your being from the very first moment of your existence. The value of your person was not measured by your usefulness, nor was your identity composed of hard-won achievements or the gleanings of experience.

Thank you for helping me hear an echo of God's eternal love for us.

Thank you for giving me a message and a song.

You whispered them to me in the secret place, but I will shout them out. I'll shout them to a world afflicted by activity, obsessed with strength, afraid of weakness, outraged by deformity and intimidated by death.

You were precious, Cerian, because you were created and given as a gift. I am privileged to have carried you. As a mother, I honour you and all that your life has been.

There was silence when I sat back down. No one moved. It was some time before Paul's voice filled the auditorium.

Mike took the microphone from Paul as he sat back down next to me. He took my hand in his and put his arm round both the girls. The service ended with the hymn 'The King of Love my Shepherd is', and the congregation dispersed to eat the tea we had planned for them. Mike had to pull Paul and me away from our friends at the end of the service, sheltering as we were in their love and companionship. 'Guys, you will miss your slot at the crematorium if you don't leave now.'

The undertaker let us take the tiny coffin in Rocket so that Cerian could be with us on that last journey. As we pulled in to park by the Chapel of Rest, Emilia began to reflect back on what she had heard at the service. 'Why did Uncle Mike say there would be no mourning in heaven?' Out of the corner of my eye I could see Paul preparing an intense theological answer. But Emilia carried on. 'If there's no morning in heaven, when will Cerian wake up?'

Despite the extremity of the moment, we all began to laugh. The sun was shining and our sorrow was tinged with an odd sense of festivity. We were surrounded by those we loved the most. My oldest school friend was there. Others had travelled down from Birmingham and Northumberland and up from

Kent. Mark and Janet had brought the children with them. People's love was a warm and needed blanket. Later, when the curtain finally obscured Cerian's coffin from view, Emilia raised her hand and waved goodbye. The tears streamed down her face onto her bright pink dress. Hannah whispered 'Adieu' and crumpled onto my lap. Paul and I had no other language but tears, and they came like waves. We clung to one another. There was a strange relief in the tears after the days of numbness. I finally let the distance flood in between Cerian and me and I began to connect with others again.

I remember almost nothing about the rest of the day except the light, the golden flowers and the sense of love, family and belonging together. It had been a fitting end. The day, like Cerian's life, had been filled with that acute mixture of pain and beauty, bereavement and joy.

24

Married and Male

The colour of autumn leaves will for ever remind me of loss, for I spent that season grieving intensely for Cerian. Although it was a clean grief in which I felt no guilt or regret, it was still far more encompassing than physical illness. People told me the journey of grieving would take me through a spiral of many different stages, such as shock, denial, anger, even depression. But at that time I did not seem to move very far. I stayed revolving, fixed on one small spot; I missed her, from whichever way I looked at it. The loss continued to come in waves, such as the time I found a tiny pair of white baby tights stuffed at the back of Emilia's sock draw. She had put them there in February ready for the baby to share her bedroom. Then there was the time when I caught sight of the baby provision aisle at the supermarket and had to fight the desire to put nappies in my trolley. Between the waves, and sometimes during them, I poured my energy into making a large album of photographs, poems, quotes and verses, pictures the children had drawn and flowers I had collected, to preserve the memories of the pregnancy. I found a tiny mid-nineteenth-century elm chest in an antique shop in nearby Burford and I used it to keep safe the precious things we made for Cerian.

It was not until late autumn that a letter arrived to notify us of the arrangements for discussing the post-mortem. It was addressed to Ms Williams.

'There's no mention of me,' said Paul with a strangely plaintive tone as we sat at the breakfast table. 'They haven't even included my name in the letter. It's not as if they think you're unmarried.'

I suddenly remembered a poor joke I had read in a glossy magazine whilst waiting to have my hair cut: 'Motherhood is a fact, paternity merely a hypothesis.' For the first time I understood what was meant by the anger element of grief. I was angry, blindingly angry. Paul had arranged the postmortem, he had chivvied them along, he had watched over the organisation of it, taking care to ensure that the restrictions we had placed on the process were carried out, and they had not even included his name in the letter.

I grabbed the phone. 'Can you put me through to the secretary of the Prenatal Diagnosis Unit, please?'

There was a pause. Paul looked stunned. 'What are you doing?' he asked across the kitchen. I turned the other way so that I would not lose my nerve.

'Prenatal Diagnosis, can I help you?'

'Yes, hello. Am I speaking to –,' I read the name on the bottom of the letter, 'secretary to the Prenatal Diagnosis Unit?'

'Yes, how can I help?'

'I have just received a letter from you informing me of the date and time of a meeting with the consultant to discuss the results of our daughter's post-mortem examination.'

'Oh yes – Ms Williams, is it? What can I do to help?'

'I know this may seem a rather strange question, but would you mind telling me why you wrote "Ms Williams" at the top of the letter?' There was a pause at the other end of the line. 'You see,' I continued, 'I'm married.'

'Yes, Ms Williams, I know that.'

I paused this time. 'Then why didn't you address the letter to Mr and Mrs Williams?' I wondered fleetingly if I should say 'Mr and Dr Williams to be precise', but I knew that would only cloud the issue, and besides I have always been meticulous in confining my academic title to the professional arena.

'Oh, it's standard practice for us to write just to the mother.'

'Can you explain why that should be so?' I pressed.

'It's hospital policy.'

'I understand that, but can you explain why?' My voice was unduly calm, but inside I was raging.

'It's not my decision, Ms Williams. We're told to do it this way.'

'I do appreciate that, but I would be very grateful if you could explain why.'

'It's considered the best etiquette so as not to offend anyone. We don't wish to offend unmarried mothers.'

'I see. What about the offence caused to married women, to fathers and to married fathers?' I said. It was difficult to keep my voice under control. 'I do understand that this is not your decision individually but a matter of policy, but can I please ask you to rewrite your letter to us? I am not Ms Williams. I am

Mrs Williams, and I'm offended that I should be addressed in any other way in this context. My husband is also offended. It is as much his daughter we're coming to discuss. Can you please formally relay the fact that this hospital policy of exclusion is deeply offensive to us?'

Paul was squirming in his chair. 'Steady on,' I heard him say.

'I didn't raise my voice, did I?' I said in defence as I replaced the handset, shaking slightly.

'Well, no … but I think she got the message loud and clear all the same. Poor woman. I'm glad it wasn't me. It's not her fault.'

'Then whose fault is it? The system doesn't have a name or a face, otherwise I'd find out who it is and give it to them straight. That would be easier. But someone's got to say something. In one generation our culture has shifted so far that it's now politically incorrect to be married and male.'

'Making her rewrite the letter may have been a little steep.'

'But language is important. You can say it's only a form of words, but the language bullies us into conforming to a social standard that I don't want to be part of.'

'You get called Ms every day in bank and business letters. Why are you so angry about it now all of a sudden?'

'It's the spirit of that place that I can't stand and the Ms is just one symptom of it. It's hard to put it into words.'

'Well, try,' said Paul.

'Look at this.' I grabbed a copy of *The Times* and began to read. ' "Yet while a foetus is being saved in one operating theatre a termination for social reasons may well be taking place in the next theatre on a foetus at exactly the same stage of development."[6] Somehow in my mind that Unit seems to sit right between these two operating theatres, mediating the whole business of human quality control.' I remembered how we had sat in the car looking out across the two entrances of the Women's Centre just after our third scan with Cerian.

'But you can't blame the Prenatal Diagnosis Unit for that. They're only doing what individual people want them to do.'

'Demand and supply. That's such an economist's answer.'

'It's true! It's the demands of individuals which are creating the resources and the politically correct justification to develop all the spin-off technologies.' Paul lowered his voice again as we both looked across the kitchen table to the spot where the high chair should have been. I remembered the tattered quote stuck on the side of his filing cabinet: 'Evil prospers when good men are silent.'

'Paul, would you adopt a severely mentally and physically handicapped child? That's where the rubber really hits the road, isn't it?'

He looked at me and after some time he said, 'Would I adopt Cerian? Is that what you mean?' I knew from the look of love and sadness in his eyes that the answer was yes, a hundred times over, yes.

I left the table, shoved the washing into the machine and stomped around the house for the rest of the day feeling ineffectual against the great giant of culture.

Two days later a letter arrived addressed to Mr and Mrs Williams. It was hardly a slaying of Goliath, but I did smile when I opened it and I replied immediately, thanking them

[6] The Times, 4th July 2004.

specifically for the letter and for their help in organising the post-mortem.

My moment of confidence rapidly dissolved, however, when we walked through the entrance to the Prenatal Diagnosis Unit to attend the actual meeting. 'I think I'm going to faint,' I said, leaning heavily on Paul's arm. 'I can't go back in there.' Paul's steadiness led me forward to the reception desk. I hid behind him.

'We've come to see the consultant,' Paul said to the receptionist, his own voice betraying an undercurrent of trepidation.

'Your name, please.'

'Williams,' said Paul.

'No, *your* name, please,' said the receptionist, bypassing Paul with her gaze and looking directly at me.

'Williams,' said Paul again, keeping his arm firm so that I could hold myself up.

'I need to know *your* name, please.' The receptionist was staring straight at me resolutely.

'Mrs Williams,' I said finally. At which point she signed the form and picked up the phone to notify the consultant of our arrival.

'Unbelievable,' said Paul as we sat down in the waiting room. 'That wasn't just my imagination, was it? Am I right in thinking she didn't even look at me?'

'I think that must be hospital policy too,' I whispered. 'I think it's unwanted fathers they're worried about in here, not unwanted children.'

The meeting that followed was both civil and reassuring, despite the reception. 'Well, it has been good to meet you, Mr and Mrs Williams.' The consultant rose to shake our hands, having spent half an hour explaining the medical details to us. 'It's reassuring to know that there is no reason at all why this condition should recur. Technically you have a slightly higher statistical chance than you would have done if this had never happened at all, but there is still roughly only a 1 in 700,000 probability of recurrence. I hope we shall be seeing you here again very soon under better circumstances next time.'

'The trouble is,' I said as we made our way back to the car, 'you can never replace people.'

25

The Shaming of the Strong

I touched the paradox again when I returned to work at the university just after Christmas. Going back to work was the bleakest part of the grieving process. I opened the door of my study and looked at my bookshelves. I felt old, tired and empty. I revisited the toilet where I had first been sick. I was back in the same place, at the same time of year, with nothing to show for it except my fatigue. Everyone moved so fast and talked so loud. Life was crashing back in like the turning tide and I was raw with vulnerability.

'How are you?' beamed a visiting professor at lunch during my first week back. 'Last time I saw you…' She pointed at my tummy with a conspiratorial smile. 'How is your baby? It must be about four months old by now? Did you have a boy or a girl?'

'Dead,' I said. It was the only word I could get out of my mouth. The yoghurt I had been eating glazed over in front of me. I did not wait to observe her response. I simply fled.

A week later the same thing happened again. A new lecturer introduced himself as I sat down at High Table to consume a rapid lunch between tutorials. 'I haven't met you yet. I'm new here.' He shook my hand. 'I came in October. Were you away last term?'

'Yes,' I said. 'I was on leave.'

'Somewhere nice?' he said, digging into his casserole. Perhaps he should have heard the note of warning in my emphatic 'no', but perhaps that was asking too much. 'Oh, come on, you must have done something fun! Interesting research project? All you lucky people taking leave. I'm desperate for a break.'

I said, 'Maternity leave.' And before he could interject with yet another comment, I added, 'My daughter died.' I do not remember ever seeing that lecturer again. His skill in avoiding me from that day on was unrivalled.

But he was not the only one who avoided me. When I approached, people suddenly seemed to forget things and scuttle back into their offices. On one occasion I even saw the tip of a colleague's skirt disappear into the broom-cupboard when I turned into the main corridor. Those who could not escape me directly avoided eye contact and steered conversations on to safe and busy ground. I felt the isolation of ongoing grief. Even Paul seemed to have settled back into a rhythm of life and work, and I found it increasingly difficult to share the persistent sense of loss with him or with anyone else. Mike and Liz had warned me that grief is both a long and lonely journey, but still the experience caught me painfully off-balance.

I remained in this state of internal distance until one memorable day in early May. I had organised a lecture in college by a Catholic theologian named Heather Ward. Knowing that her topic, the gift of self, would be both highly contentious and explicitly Christian, I only invited those I thought would be sympathetic. As I was leaving the building to dash home and put the children to bed before the evening lecture, I met my feminist colleague. I had avoided walking to the car park with her since our conversation in late May. I now lingered in the lodge, hoping that our paths would not coincide. But she lingered too. I checked my mailbox, sorted my letters, resorted them, opened them, read them, reread them, buying time to let her leave before me.

Eventually, she asked me the inevitable question. 'How are you, Sarah?'

I hesitated and continued to fumble with my post. 'Oh, OK, thanks. Teaching is busy, as ever. I'm teaching a heavy Further Subject load this term, but I'm surviving.' *That was pathetic, Sarah*, I said to myself. *For goodness' sake, be real*. 'Actually, life is quite hard just now,' I muttered, still not looking up properly from my post. 'I'm still grieving, to be honest.'

'Have you got time for a drink on your way home?'

'I'm afraid not,' I said, relieved that I had a deadline to hit. 'I have to go home fast, turn the children round and get back here for an evening lecture.' As soon as I said the word 'lecture' I bit my tongue.

'Lecture? Here? I didn't know about that. What's it on?'

'The gift of self,' I muttered timidly.

'That sounds interesting. Who's it by?'

'Dr Heather Ward.'

'Who is she?' my colleague persisted. There was no way back now. I would have to explain.

'A Catholic theologian who's interested in how different historical periods have understood ideas of personhood.'

'Sounds really interesting. Why didn't you tell me it was on? What time is it?' I was making a rapid exit now.

'It's at 7.30 in the Charles Well Beloved Room,' I called as I sped off to the car park.

I was late back to college that evening. Emilia had had what she called 'a highly horrible day' and I sat on the end of her bed until she fell asleep. By the time I arrived the only vacant seats were at the back. I tried not to sound out of breath as I slipped into the back row and hid behind my officious pad of paper, busily writing the title and date at the top of the page.

'This evening,' Heather began, 'I want to ask a question. What is the self? What is it that constitutes human personhood? Our culture regards personality as the key to selfhood. We spend our time trying to expand our personalities, removing the blockages to our emotional and imaginative life and therefore to our social relationships. Existence is justified and defined in terms of abilities, talents and achievements. Each of us must earn our salvation by virtue of the gifts we possess.'

My note-taking ceased and I began to listen spellbound to the lecture, my mind working in many directions at once. *What happens if you have no abilities*, I thought, *if you are born with no talents? Are you a pre-person before you achieve anything? And if you cannot even achieve the proper formation of the body in the womb, does this mean you are not a person?*

'This is not how the early church Fathers understood the self. St Irenaeus of Lyon, for example, like St Paul of the Bible, placed the emphasis on the spirit. In their definition the spirit is placed at the centre of personhood rather than body or personality. The self is seen as a capacity for God. Rather than equating my selfhood with my ever-changing physical substance, which will in the end let me down in death and decay, Christianity defines self as a spirit whose substance and meaning is derived from relationship with the eternal God.'

I sat back in my chair and allowed my mind to probe this thought further. *If the self is defined as a capacity for God, then it allows us to confer the intrinsic value of personhood on beings with spirits whose bodies are unusable and whose personalities cannot develop – like Cerian, for instance. She could not justify her existence in terms of abilities, talents and achievements. But I had no doubt she had a capacity to respond to God. Her worth was related to her being, not her functional utility.*

We were ten minutes into the talk. Then, to my horror, my feminist colleague walked in. The only seat left was next to me. I smiled politely and then prayed, 'Oh God, please don't let anything be said that will offend her. I'm so scared of her.'

'If the self is a capacity for God, then it follows that for the self to grow it is not a matter of increased size or number of quality attributes or accolades, but rather it is about our responsiveness to God as a person and our increased receptivity to his spirit.'

I glanced at my colleague. This was heavy stuff. Heather continued, 'The ego is the enemy to the development of our potential. For the self to become what it was made to be and to realise its fullness as a capacity for God, there must be a growing freedom from ego and a thoroughgoing reorientation of our beings towards God.' To my amazement my colleague was taking notes. I did not dare look. 'It follows, therefore, that in order to reach my self – my capacity for God – there must be a deep, often painful, lifelong experience of dying to ego. Since man in his state of estrangement from God regards his ego as himself, the experience of ego-denial, of removing the desires, needs and illusions of the ego from the centre stage, is perceived as an act of undoing, of disintegration, of loss of all that we call ourselves and our lives.'

I could not help thinking about my loss of Cerian. I had decided to carry her to term in spite of the screaming of my ego. This decision had felt like the ultimate destruction of my ego, my plans, my dreams and desires; and yet from the point of view of my spiritual life – of my self – it had been the most constructive and life-giving thing I had ever done. By allowing God to gently break what I once thought of as strength, he had brought me increasingly through weakness into the life of God. The clamour of my ego had made me like a closed system centred on my needs, flaws and attributes through which I had set out to win and deserve my existence and acceptance. I thought about my Oxford First, my hard-won job, all my well-crafted plans. My life and even my religion had for so long revolved around servicing these things. I had busied myself with perfect home, perfect children, perfect garden, perfect body (at least – I wished!) and all the time God was trying to draw my heart into a wild and free adventure with him. I had become joyless, controlled and predictable. I had no passion and even less compassion. My eyes did not, as one writer has put it, 'search for other people's souls'. I was too busy to care. I knew I had lost something deep and precious, but I did not know what it was. And the more I felt the lack of it, the harder I tried to find it through effort. I thought having children, or moving house, or being part of a new community would fill the void. And then God had given me Cerian.

She was an unexpected treasure. She appeared at first to be the loss of hope and the disruption of all my plans, but through her, God came close to me again, wild and beautiful, good and gracious, strangely familiar but infinitely exciting. I touched his presence as I carried Cerian. I remembered the unspeakable joy of life in communion with him and I realised that underneath all my other longings and my attempts at my own redemption lay an aching desire for God himself. Cerian shamed my strength and in her weakness and vulnerability she showed me a way to intimacy with Jesus. As I died to my own strength in carrying her, it had felt as though my identity was being negated and yet I was in fact finding my identity as a gift given by God himself. It says in 1 Corinthians 1:27–29:

> God chose the foolish things of the world to shame the wise; God chose the weak things of the world to shame the strong. He chose the lowly things of this world and the despised things – and the things that are not – to nullify the things that are, so that no-one may boast before him.

Cerian was, by the world's definition, a weak thing, but the beauty and completeness of her personhood had nullified the value system to which I had subscribed for so long.

I could not believe Heather had been speaking for over an hour when we reached the end. After a short pause, hands flew up all over the room to ask questions. With quiet dignity Heather responded to question after question.

'What role does reason have in this definition of selfhood?' asked one student with curly ginger hair in the front row.

'Can God be considered a person by this definition?' asked another.

Then my colleague's hand went up. I swallowed hard. 'How do cultural constructions of gender mediate the way in which the self is understood?' I was glad I did not have to answer that question. To my amazement she listened to Heather's answer with rapt attention. After an hour of questions Heather drew the session to a close and a queue as long as the aisle developed for further informal questions. We would be there for some time.

My colleague did not move. She sat with her eyes fixed straight ahead. As I sat next to her in silence I could feel her pain. It was palpable. I felt a nudge in my heart and with trepidation I turned to her and looked her straight in the eye and said the words I felt God was impressing on my heart. 'God does not rape, you know.' After a moment when I wondered if she would ever speak to me again, tears slowly welled up in her hard eyes and she whispered, 'But people do.' And there was the key to her heart. I did not need to say anything else. I simply put my hand on her arm and we sat there in silence. In the absence of words I imagined myself taking her by the hand and bringing her right into the throne room of God.

The next day she e-mailed these words to me: 'Thank you for inviting me last night. I found the lecture very moving. On your way back to the car park, look round the back of the courtyard by the kitchen. The wisteria is in bloom. Right now that is all that is keeping me going.' I put my head on my arms and leant down on my desk and wept. There was the paradox again. God is the God of the wisteria bloom in the unseen places of the heart. Somehow in my pain I had been able to meet my colleague in hers. For a woman like her to notice a flower and to give a colleague a glimpse of her vulnerability bears the unmistakable finger-prints of the living God. Few weeks pass now when we do not talk to one another. We talk of many things. Most of all we talk of life, friendship, pain and faith.

My colleague allowed me to see a precious thing at a time when I was becoming locked in my own sorrow. Everyone hurts. At some stage most people find that life does not deliver what we expect it would or should, and sometimes, worse still, life damages us directly. Although we may try to use our strength to control what happens to us, often we have little power to prevent difficult things happening. What we do have, however, is the power to choose how we respond. Everyone can choose to turn towards God and to love him in spite of difficulty and injustice, even in the midst of a situation. This is ultimately the freedom that Jesus won for us by being willing to walk right through the middle of pain, even to his death, without turning his heart away from the Father. Without his sacrifice we would all be subject to the corrupting, distorting and dehumanising effects of loss. All we would have without him is the illusory freedom of our own strength to protect ourselves and our autonomy to isolate ourselves. Behind my colleague's strength, which had so impressed and intimidated me, there was in fact profound weakness.

After that my eyes began to search for people's souls. I began to be aware of other people's pain in an unprecedented way. And to my amazement I discovered that behind all my weakness God had actually begun to weave his strength into me. I discovered a new confidence. I began to be sure of who I am as I realised that I am no less deformed than Cerian by my sin, but the God who came to take her home also knows and loves me unconditionally. I found myself no longer afraid of situations and people I had been afraid of before. My need to control and order everything around me started to evaporate and the peace I had discovered when I carried Cerian became earthed in the pattern of my everyday life.

26

The Bird Tree

The girls too were changed. Emilia, despite her ongoing struggle with chronic illness, developed an antenna for pain. At the end of the church service each Sunday she would disappear to give someone a hug or simply to say hello to outsiders on the edges who were reading news sheets awkwardly while everyone else chatted in their comfortable friendship groups over their cups of coffee. She even went up to a little boy on the bus one day. The boy was crying uncontrollably and she wiped his face with her hand and said, 'Don't cry.' He was so amazed that he stopped crying instantly and his mother noticed her son for the first time and began to talk to him.

Hannah's depth of spirit increased and she developed her own quiet passion for God. In the morning, when I went downstairs to make a cup of tea, the light in her room would be on and she would be reading her Bible. In one of the worst stretches of grieving a letter arrived on our doorstep addressed to Mr and

Mrs Williams. The familiarity of the writing disorientated us. Inside we found this:

Dear Mummy and Daddy,

I wrote this poem in spare time at school. I hope you like it.

A Journey
hard stormy journey,
the wind roaring,
clouds moving,
times you feel like giving up.
you remember the warm end,
you can rest.
remember when you did so nearly give up.
now that you have done it, it's all over,
you know that you can rest.

Love from Hannah XXXX

The poem accurately depicted the sense of journeying in grief and the longing for rest from the unrelenting fatigue of sorrow. We marvelled at the depth God had planted in our daughter through her own loss.

Cerian was not only expanding our humanity, but the grief of losing her was also paradoxically heightening our joy. The strange thing is, bereavement enhances our capacity for life. Not only does the fleeting nature of existence force a recognition of mortality and thus the imperative of making the most of every opportunity to love and receive love, but it also makes us cherish one another more and recognise the value of good gifts. The birth of Mark and Janet's son was just such an occasion for Paul and me.

Janet was on the seventh floor of the John Radcliffe Hospital. I had not been there since the day I visited Adrienne. I felt sick as I entered the lift. Daniel was 12 hours old. I was terrified of seeing him. I had not held a baby since Cerian. But the moment we opened the door and saw his tiny scrunched-up little body, there was an explosion of joy. We loved him. I had to wrench Daniel away from Paul in order to hold him myself.

'Is it all right?' Janet asked tentatively.

'What do you mean?' I said, not immediately registering what she was saying. I smiled when I realised. 'Oh yes,' I said. 'It's all right.'

Sometimes when I see Daniel, I imagine Cerian playing with him. Janet seems to know when I am thinking this and she always talks about Cerian every time our families meet. The thing about losing a child is that you do not just lose them once, but you go on experiencing the loss of what they would have been.

Mark and Paul had their drink together at last and again there was celebration. God gives and God takes away. It is possible for both to solicit from us the response, 'Blessed be the name of the Lord' (Job 1:21).

We spent the first anniversary of Cerian's death at Wren's house. Emma came with us, having just finished a year of study at Bible college, which she fitted alongside continuing to work for us. Soon after breakfast Paul and Wren disappeared to the garden centre together. They returned an hour or so later with a small tree cut beautifully at the top into the shape of a bird in flight.

'The skylark!' I exclaimed when I saw them heaving it from the car into a wheelbarrow.

'Wait and see,' they said conspiratorially, disappearing through the wood to the bottom of the garden. Eventually we were allowed to take a look at their creation. The bird tree stood overlooking the field and below its outstretched wings Paul and Wren had gathered rocks around a tiny plaque engraved with the words:

> Cerian Williams
> Loved One – Consecrated to God

We all stood around the bird tree and from there I looked out over the open countryside to the sky beyond.

Some months later Wren phoned us, ecstatic. 'You'll never guess what has happened!'

I could not guess. But I had to admit that her voice sounded unusually alive. She had grieved intensely for Cerian and it had taken her many months of anguish to get over the shock of nearly losing her own daughter. 'Is it a miracle?' I asked, waiting to be told.

'Yes it is! It's the bird tree!'

'Has it come alive?' I laughed.

'Yes it has!' she said. I was beginning to worry about her. 'A pair of wrens have built a nest inside the breast of the bird tree. And this morning I saw an entire family of wrens hatching. Isn't that a beautiful thing?'

It was indeed, although I could not trust my voice not to wobble with tears, so I mumbled my agreement.

'I am going to take this as a reminder from God of his character,' Wren said. 'He is able to bring life out of death and hope out of grief.'